SUCCESSFUL WRITING

FOURTH EDITION

D1106820

SUCCESSFUL WRITING

FOURTH EDITION

MAXINE C. HAIRSTON

The University of Texas at Austin

W. W. NORTON & COMPANY

NEW YORK • LONDON

Copyright © 1998, 1992, 1986, 1981 by Maxine C. Hairston

All rights reserved.
Printed in the United States of America.

*The text of this book is composed in Sabon
with the display set in Frutiger Roman.
Desktop composition by Gina Webster.
Manufacturing by Courier Companies, Inc.
Book design by Joan Greenfield*

The image of Rosa Parks on page 206 is reprinted by permission of UPI/Corbis Bettmann.

Library of Congress Cataloging-in-Publication Data

Hairston, Maxine.
Successful writing / Maxine C. Hairston.—4th ed.
p.   cm.
includes index

ISBN 0-393-97196-1 (pbk.)

1. English language—Rhetoric. 2. Report writing. I. Title.
PE1408.H297   1997
808'.042—dc21   97–14163
                    CIP

W. W. Norton & Company, Inc., 500 Fifth Avenue, New York, N.Y. 10110
http://www.wwnorton.com

W. W. Norton & Company Ltd., 10 Coptic Street, London WC1A 1PU

2 3 4 5 6 7 8 9 0

CONTENTS

PREFACE

This Fourth Edition of *Successful Writing* maintains the focus of the previous editions in offering practical and straightforward advice to writers who have mastered the basic elements of writing and now want to strengthen their skills and polish their prose. But this new edition also introduces writers to some of the new electronic dimensions of their craft: using the Internet for research and exploration and applying some of the principles of document design and desktop publishing to their work. Most of the chapters of this edition incorporate suggestions about ways to make writing more readable by using the capacities that computers offer for creating graphics and producing several varieties of type, and the book itself has been designed to make it easier to use and to demonstrate the principles of visual appeal.

This edition of *Successful Writing* retains features that have distinguished it from the beginning. These include

- Emphasis on the writing process

- Stress on the crucial role of audience and purpose in every writing situation

- Stress on revision as essential to the creative process

- Pragmatic advice about editing and rewriting

- Emphasis on and guidelines for writers working in groups

In addition, almost all examples have been replaced with material from contemporary sources, and a quotation about writing now introduces each chapter. Overall, I have tried to make the text more concise by tightening discussions and, wherever possible, condensing material into boxes and lists. Special tips for writers appear in boxes throughout the book. In each chapter, I have made a number of changes, listed below.

- Chapter 1, "Writing in College," has been condensed and some of the information rearranged in more visually accessible boxes and lists. A new section has been added on avoiding common pitfalls in choosing topics.

- Chapter 2, "What Is Good Writing?" no longer contains negative models of bad writing; the criteria for good writing have been expanded to include visual appeal and good design.

- Chapter 3, "What Happens When People Write?" streamlines the discussion of explanatory and exploratory writing, makes those concepts more accessible with lists and boxed summaries, and adds tips about using the Internet for invention. Preliminary discussion for a new model paper on the need for heroines in children's literature begins in this chapter.

- Chapter 4, "What Is Your Writing Situation?" has been condensed somewhat from the third edition and now contains analyses of the audience, purpose, persona, and message for the new model paper.

- Chapter 5, "Drafting Your Paper," includes a revised section on patterns of organization, substituting "assertion and support" for "claims and warrant" and adding a discussion of "classification." This chapter now offers material on civil discourse and a section on how a writer can tell when he or she has written an adequate draft.

- Chapter 6, "Revising," has been made more accessible through headings, lists, and special guidelines for helping students evaluate and revise their own papers and those of their peers, especially when they are working in collaborative writing situations.

- Chapter 7, "Holding Your Reader," opens with a new section on presenting writing in a form that is visually appealing to readers. The chapter has been condensed somewhat by moving much of the Third Edition's discussion on opening paragraphs to Chapter 9, "Crafting Paragraphs."

- Chapter 8, "Writing Clearly," expands the section on sexist language to include guidelines for avoiding other kinds of biased language and adds a section on civil discourse.

- Chapter 9, "Crafting Paragraphs," includes new material on adapting opening paragraphs to a writer's audience and purpose.

- Chapter 10, "Editing," has been streamlined and rearranged for easier access and now includes material on editing to improve a paper's visual appeal. Once more it offers advice about usage and writing conventions based on actual surveys of how readers respond to lapses in usage and mechanics.

- Chapter 11, "Writing Research Papers," has been substantially revised to add material on using electronic sources and the conventions for citing such sources. It includes suggestions—and cautions—for doing research on the Internet and the World Wide Web.

- Chapter 12, "Document Design," is new to the Fourth Edition. It incorporates much of the material from the "Writing on the Job" chapter of the Third Edition but is essentially an introduction to the basic elements of document design and to desktop publishing. This new chapter includes advice about planning documents, choosing type, arranging layouts, and integrating graphics and illustrations into documents. It begins with suggestions for enhancing academic papers and class presentations with visual elements, but also includes help with job-related projects such as brochures, agendas, proposals, and résumés. The second part of the chapter offers sixteen model documents along with comments and checklists for designing each kind.

The underlying principles of this Fourth Edition of *Successful Writing* remain unchanged from previous editions:

- Writing is a dynamic social process that can be taught and learned.

- People grow as writers by learning to draft, revise, and polish their writing through stages.

- Every writing project must be considered in the context of its audience and purpose.

- Learning to interact and work with other writers is an important part of every writer's development.

I believe in these principles as strongly as I did sixteen years ago when the First Edition of *Successful Writing* appeared.

MAXINE HAIRSTON

ACKNOWLEDGMENTS

I received encouragement, support, and valuable advice on this book from a number of colleagues and friends, but I want to express my special appreciation to Professor Michael Keene of the University of Tennessee. I owe him a great deal. I also wish to thank Mary Trachsel for her assistance in revising the chapter on research papers.

I also want to express my thanks to the following people, whose reviews of the Third Edition helped me plan the Fourth: P. Michael Brotherton, Labethe Community College; Gary Sue Goodman, University of California, Davis; Betty L. Hart, University of Southern Indiana; JoAnn Harrill, Virginia Polytechnic Institute and State University; Phillip A. Snyder, Brigham Young University.

1

WRITING IN COLLEGE

> People who write well are more likely to get what they want than people who write badly.

WRITING AS A WAY OF LEARNING

If you are like most college students, you write a great many papers, not only for your English and history classes but in courses such as accounting, geology, or engineering, areas that you may not have thought would require writing. Professors in those courses are having you write not only because you must report what you're learning but because writing is a powerful tool for learning. They know that all of us benefit from writing in important ways:

- We understand material better and retain it longer when we write about it.

- We generate new ideas when we write because the act of writing helps us make connections and see relationships.

- We think more critically when we write. When we get ideas down on paper, we're more likely to be able to clarify and evaluate them.

- We solve problems more easily when we write because we understand the dimensions of a problem better after we write out its components.

■ We gain confidence and more sense of control over our lives as we become better writers.

STRATEGIES FOR WRITING PAPERS IN COLLEGE COURSES

Some kinds of college writing assignments are so specialized that you may need to take a course in scientific or technical writing to do well in them, but in most cases, you can produce good papers if you follow some general rules for planning and drafting your papers. This chapter will give you general guidelines; you can consult other chapters to get more information about developing and polishing your papers.

Analyze Your Writing Situation

Before you start to write, take time to analyze your writing situation. Ask yourself the following questions:

■ What is my purpose?
What is my main idea? What impact do I want to make?

■ Who is my audience?
What assumptions can I make about my readers? What questions will they have?

■ What constraints am I working under?
How much time do I have? What resources—library sources, computer facilities, experts—are available to me? How long should the paper be?

It's a good idea to write out preliminary answers to these questions before you begin your first draft. Doing so will serve two purposes.

First, it will create a frame for your paper and help you focus on what you want to do. It will also remind you of your limitations—if you have only a week to turn in a first draft, you had better not take on a project that will require substantial research.

Second, writing out the answers will get you started on your paper because the very act of writing about a subject stimulates thinking and helps you generate ideas.

Here's an example of how one might go about analyzing the writing situation for a four- to six-page paper.

WRITING SITUATION ANALYSIS

Working title: Love That Truck! Americans and Their Minivans

Purpose: To show that Americans' love affair with cars like Suburbans, Cherokees, and Quests has increased gas prices and offset the fuel efficiency gains of the 1980s.

Audience: Readers of a general magazine like *Parade, Readers' Digest,* or *Newsweek.* Can assume they're interested in cars and driving habits and also interested in economic trends. They'll want to know who's driving such cars and why.

Constraints: A week to write a first draft—should be plenty of time. Can do library search for material in newspapers, auto magazines, and business journals.

Work to Limit Your Paper Topic

Some of the worst problems with college papers occur because writers— graduate students writing dissertations as well as first-year writers doing short papers—choose topics that are too broad. If you are asked to write a four- to six-page paper but choose a topic that could easily generate enough material for a long magazine article, you will almost certainly wind up with a paper full of generalities and few interesting specifics. Broad topics, such as "Combating Illiteracy" or "Controlling Traffic on the Information Superhighway," call for extensive and thoughtful analysis in order to do them justice; a short paper on such a topic couldn't give the details and information necessary to hold readers' interest. So it's important to limit your scope and write more about less.

Deciding how broad a topic you can treat responsibly in a paper of a specific length is tricky, even for experienced writers, but these rough guidelines may help.

Four- to six-page paper (1,000–1,500 words): A short paper, probably one of several for the course. Construct a narrow thesis that makes two or three key points and plan to expand on those points with specific details. Here are some topics that might be developed in such a paper:

- Understanding and managing the RAM memory on your computer

- The significance of the green light at the end of the dock in *The Great Gatsby*

- A profile of Emily Malcolm, founder of Emily's List, a women's political action committee

Ten- to twelve-page paper (2,500–3,000 words): A paper in which you can treat a substantial topic in some detail, giving background information and citing examples. You wouldn't want to tackle a large field such as impressionist art, but you might write on some subtopic within such a topic. Here are some possibilities:

- Van Gogh's last year in Arles

- Why illiteracy is a major issue for the women's movement

- How the discovery of the Chauvet Caves in southern France is changing theories of prehistoric art

Eighteen- to twenty-page paper (4,500–5,000 words): A paper that gives you room to go into substantial detail about a limited but complex topic. Usually this kind of paper requires research, and the professor who assigns it will want you to evaluate your material and draw conclusions. You still need to be careful not to pick a topic so broad it would take a master's thesis to do it credit. Here are some topics that could work well for a paper of this length:

- How the women's suffrage movement started in the United States

- Who supports legalized gambling in the United States and why

- From Hans Christian Andersen to Disney: fairy tales and modern media

---

POTENTIAL PITFALLS IN CHOOSING TOPICS

Topic	*Pitfall*
Popular "hot" issues, such as abortion rights, capital punishment, gun control	Readers often are not open to persuasion; so much has been written, it's hard to say anything fresh.
Very current issues, such as a new product, controversy, or current event	It's difficult to find material in the library; the Internet may have too much unrefereed material that is hard to evaluate.
Religious topics on which people have strong convictions	It's hard to have open, useful discussions of such papers, and it's difficult for professors to evaluate them.

GENERAL CRITERIA FOR ACADEMIC WRITING

"Academic writing" is hardly a precise term. Students write papers in many different disciplines, and the conventions for style, documentation, and presenting evidence vary considerably from one field to another. So I can't give clear-cut guidelines for writing college papers. It's not that simple.

Nevertheless, as I point out in the next chapter, it's possible to define good writing, and I believe it's also possible to lay down some useful ground rules for writing effective papers in college. Instructors do expect and tend to reward certain characteristics in student papers. We can divide those characteristics into matters of content and matters of form.

Matters of Content

- *If you can choose your topic, write on something that's fresh and interesting to you.* When you do, you're likely to write a better paper and put more effort into it. Moreover, professors are likely to value the student who comes up with a new idea or interpretation.

- *Don't overstate your case.* The writer who makes sweeping claims undermines her credibility almost immediately and invites challenge. If you can, avoid using absolute words like "everyone," "nobody," "always," and "never." Instead, practice using phrases such as "It may be . . . ," "This suggests . . . ," and "Almost certainly . . ."

- *Support your claims.* Professors are skeptical readers who expect authors to back their claims with evidence and rational arguments. As you draft your papers, try to anticipate at what points your readers might ask "How do you know?" or "What evidence do you have for that statement?"

- *Argue logically and avoid highly emotional language.* For most of the papers you write in college, depend on the weight of facts and reasoning to carry your argument. Most instructors prefer papers that maintain an objective tone and avoid sarcasm or invective.

Matters of Form

- *Choose an accurate title that reflects the content of your paper.* Your title introduces you and your paper, so make sure that it's clear and lets the reader know what to expect.

■ *Organize your paper so it's easy to follow.* Because professors read a great many papers, and they must read them quickly, they welcome the paper with a clear introduction that forecasts the argument, then leads them through it. If your paper runs more than a few pages, use subheadings to break it up and point the way. When you can, use lists, boxes, and diagrams to present information. (See Chapter 12 on document design for more information.)

■ *Document your sources.* You may not need formal footnotes, but let your readers know where you got your information. When your instructor does want formal documentation, invest in the documentation guide appropriate to your discipline—it will save you time. (See p. 187 for suggestions.)

■ *Turn in a double-spaced, carefully proofread paper that is typed or printed on quality paper.* If you use a computer, run your spellchecker (but don't rely on it—it's highly fallible). Do everything you can to make your paper look good. (See Chapter 12 on document design.)

2

WHAT IS GOOD WRITING?

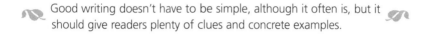 Good writing doesn't have to be simple, although it often is, but it should give readers plenty of clues and concrete examples.

Good writing has three characteristics:

- **It says something significant**

- **to a specific audience**

- **for some purpose.**

While good writing must also have other characteristics, these three form its foundation.

Under such a definition, we have to recognize many kinds of good writing. It can be formal or casual, elegant or plain, straightforward or subtle. One can encounter good writing in *Car and Driver* or *Rolling Stone* as well as in the *New York Times* or *Harper's* magazine; one can also find good writing in a lucid set of directions or an effective brochure. Its central quality, whether its purpose is to inform, persuade, or entertain, is this: *It communicates the writer's ideas effectively to the audience for whom it is intended.*

The qualifier "for whom it is intended" is particularly important because good writers don't work in a vacuum. They know that writing is an interactive process in which both the writer and the reader participate, and they realize that what works well with one group of readers may not work at all with a different audience.

SPECIFIC ELEMENTS OF EFFECTIVE WRITING

In spite of the changes in tone and style that writers make to adjust to different audiences, it's still possible to identify the elements found in effective expository writing—that is, nonfiction, factual writing. It must be

- Significant

- Clear

- Unified

- Economical

- In standard English

When your finished product meets these standards, it may not be graceful or dazzling, but you can be confident your readers will understand it.

If you want to become an excellent writer, of course, you'll have to stretch beyond these basics and work at developing two additional attributes in your writing:

- Vigor

- Authentic voice

I'll say more about all of these characteristics in the pages to come.

Unfortunately, some of the writing that one encounters in business, the professions, and in college is not very readable, usually because the writers haven't given much thought to their audience. Or sometimes writers seem to feel they can demonstrate their expertise and impress their readers by writing over those readers' heads. Whatever the reasons, readers can be intimidated by articles or critical analyses that are full of long sentences and unfamiliar vocabulary. They may assume that such writing reflects a brilliant mind. Not necessarily. I believe that if intelligent readers who have adequate background information about a topic have trouble reading a nontechnical piece of writing about that topic, the piece is probably badly written.

GOOD WRITING HAS SIGNIFICANT CONTENT

Good writing says something worthwhile to some readers. For writing to be effective, the readers for whom it is intended should find something in it they want and need to know—something interesting, informative, or even surprising. Thus writing that is no more than an accumulation of generalities or a rehash of familiar arguments isn't good writing, no matter how smoothly written or grammatically correct it may be.

Your response to such a definition of good writing might be that it's pertinent for job-related writing, perhaps a report or a proposal or a newsletter, but less helpful when it comes to writing a paper for a professor. How are you supposed to know what a professor wants or needs to know or even what he or she might find surprising? The answer is that you don't always know, but you should be able to make some good guesses.

For instance, if you write an argument that you construct off the top of your head without doing additional reading or consulting new sources, you're not likely to produce a paper your professor wants to read because you're probably repeating points already familiar to almost everybody. Similarly, if you make a report that consists largely of general assertions unsupported with details or examples, it won't be significant because you're not giving enough specifics to let your reader see what you mean.

Test for significant content in anything you write by asking yourself these questions:

- Does my paper have solid information and specific details?

- Have I given examples to illustrate points?

- Have I added something new to the conversation on this subject?

- Have I gone beyond what I already knew in writing this paper?

If you can answer yes to these questions, you're probably doing significant writing, whether it's for a professor or for another audience.

GOOD WRITING IS CLEAR

Expository writing is clear when the readers for whom it is intended can understand it if they read carefully. The phrase "for whom it is intended" makes a difference, of course. Most readers will have trouble understanding material outside their field or area of experience when they lack the context and vocabulary necessary to follow the discussion. I, for instance, would have trouble understanding my daughter's medical journals; she would have trouble understanding some of the books on rhetorical theory I have on my shelves.

Experienced writers whose success depends on being able to write clearly for a broad audience—and that includes a large and varied group of authors—employ dozens of strategies to get their meaning across. Their strategies, which range from telling stories to presenting information in lists, are techniques that less experienced writers can learn and quickly begin to put into practice. Several sections in the later chapters of this book will describe such strategies and give specific guidelines for writing clearly.

In the past few years, writers have acquired new tools for making their writing clear and accessible. Those tools come from document design theory and from the new capabilities that writers now have through computers and word processing programs. With such tools, writers can now lay out their writing to make it more visually attractive, use different type sizes and faces, set off elements by borders or boxes, and add graphs and charts to their papers. Chapter 12 explains the principles of document design and shows how they can be applied to different kinds of documents.

Let me add an important caution, however. Good document design won't improve a poorly written or badly organized paper; in fact, it will only highlight the paper's defects. Thus you should be sure that you've written a strong, clear paper before you enhance it with charts or other graphic devices.

GOOD WRITING IS UNIFIED

In all good writing one can sense a controlling pattern, a kind of master plan that holds the parts together. The reader can move from one idea to another easily because the writer lays down a path, points readers in the right direction, and guides them along so smoothly that they won't go off on a detour or find themselves distracted by irrelevant details. The controlling pattern might be one of the common patterns of organization described in Chapter 5: definition, cause and effect, comparison, assertion and examples, narration, or process.

Here is a tightly unified paragraph from a well-regarded professional writer, David Halberstam. He develops the paragraph using the pattern of an assertion supported by examples.

> There was nothing conventional about [Margaret] Sanger's life. As a mother she was, at best, erratic and distant—when her son Grant was ten he wrote from boarding school, asking what to do about Thanksgiving, since all the other boys were going home. He should, she answered, come home to Greenwich Village and Daisy, the maid, would cook him a fine dinner. She had little time for such intrusions as children and holiday dinners. She was an American Samurai and she had spent her life on a wartime footing. Her principal enemies were the Catholic

Church and clergy, because in her struggle to inform women about birth control, they did much to prevent her from reaching the urban poor, who were often Catholic.

—David Halberstam, *The Fifties* (New York: Villard Books, 1993) 283

Here is another example from a professional writer, a paragraph unified through a pattern of definition:

Ebola virus is named for the Ebola River, which is the headstream of the Mongala River, a tributary of the Congo, or Zaire, River. The Ebola River empties tracts of rain forest, winding past scattered villages. The first known emergence of Ebola Zaire—the hottest type of Ebola virus—occurred in September, 1976, when it erupted simultaneously in fifty-five villages near the headwaters of the Ebola River. It seemed to come out of nowhere, and killed nine out of ten people it infected. Ebola Zaire is the most feared agent at the Institute. The general feeling around USAMRID has always been "Those who work with Ebola are crazy." To mess around with Ebola is an easy way to die. Better to work with something safer, such as anthrax.

—Richard Preston, *The Hot Zone* (New York: Random House, 1994) 44

The careful writer reinforces the controlling pattern with a sequence of signals that nudge the reader along the way, signals like *first, second, finally, then,* and *consequently.* A writer may use other signals to tell readers when to stop for a qualification; those signals are words like *however, nevertheless, in spite of,* and so on. He or she may also regularly repeat keywords to reassure readers that they're on the right track.

GOOD WRITING IS ECONOMICAL

Good writers don't want to waste their reader's time, so they try to cut all excess words from their writing, get rid of what William Zinsser, author of *On Writing Well,* calls "clutter." As he points out,

The reader is someone with an attention span of about 30 seconds—a person assailed by other forces competing for attention. At one time these forces weren't so numerous: newspapers, radio, spouse, home, children. Today they also include a "home entertainment center" (TV, VCR, tapes, CDs), pets, a fitness program, a yard and all the gadgets that have been bought to keep it spruce, and that most potent of competitors, sleep. The person snoozing in a chair with a magazine or a book is a person who was being given too much unnecessary trouble by the writer.

> —William Zinsser, *On Writing Well*, 5th ed.
> (New York: HarperCollins, 1994) 9

If you want to hold that reader's attention, you have to work constantly at keeping your writing terse and streamlined. That doesn't mean leaving out interesting details—notice that Zinsser enlivens his claim by giving concrete examples of the forces that compete for a reader's attention—but it does mean trimming out many adjectives, eliminating repetitious phrases, and generally trying to do away with words that do not enhance meaning or advance your idea. You need to be particularly careful to squeeze excess words out of your writing when your main purpose is to inform, but you probably need fewer words than you think even when one of your purposes is to entertain.

Here is an economical yet highly descriptive paragraph from a young contributor to a collection of essays about living in the nineties:

> I am a twenty-six-year-old man, half black and half Jewish, who founded and edits a conservative magazine that deals with race relations and culture. Such a statement would have been extraordinary thirty years ago; today we treat it with mild interest and move along. No one would argue that my life has been typical—typical of the "black experience," of the "Jewish experience," or of any other dubious paradigm associated with a particular race or ethnicity. I have not overcome racism or poverty, and people become visibly disappointed when I tell them my mixed background has not been a cause of distress, or any other difficulty for that matter.

> —David Bernstein, "Mixed Like Me," *NEXT: Young American Writers on the New Generation*,
> ed. Eric Liu (New York: Norton, 1994) 59

It may help to remind yourself that most of the terse, uncluttered writing you find in the work of authors like Russell Baker, Ellen Goodman, or Jane Brody didn't start out that way; almost certainly those authors had to work at revising sentences and cutting out extra words. In several places in this book you will find guidelines for ways to keep your writing streamlined.

GOOD WRITING IS GRAMMATICALLY ACCEPTABLE

For our purposes, I am defining "grammatically acceptable English" as the kind of English most educated people in our society use and expect other educated people to use. Standard English is the kind of language you encounter in books, newspapers, and business documents or hear people use in serious programs on radio and television or in public speeches. Most of the time, such usage conforms to those grammar rules you learned in elementary or high school.

But only most of the time. Anyone who pays attention knows that many successful and well-educated people do not always speak or write absolutely "correct" English. Perhaps they confuse *lie* and *lay* or forget to use *whom* when they need it, or they might forget that one isn't supposed to use modifiers with words like *unique* and *perfect*. But such mistakes are minor, so common among well-educated people that others rarely notice them. Such grammatical lapses are *acceptable*—they don't trigger immediate judgments in a listener and so do little damage.

Other kinds of grammatical mistakes, however, are unacceptable in public writing. Errors like "He don't qualify for the job" or "Me and her went to school together" jar readers' sensibilities, distracting them from *what* the writing is saying to *how* the writer is saying it. Such conspicuous lapses can seriously damage a writer's credibility, and writers who cause such reactions in their readers damage their case before they even get through presenting it.

But how can you know which mistakes are relatively minor and which do real damage? Well, you can't always know for sure, of course—mistakes that don't bother some readers can offend others who are more particular. Nevertheless, a survey I did in 1979 and a follow-up survey I did with a colleague in 1987 have shown quite clearly that there is a hierarchy of errors, and one can determine which are the most damaging and which are comparatively minor. You will find a ranking constructed from those surveys and a discussion of the results in Chapter 10.

SPELLING

Writers also need to pay close attention to their spelling and realize that some spelling errors are more costly than others. Only a few readers will notice if you misspell *personnel* or *harassment*, but many readers will be outraged if you write *thare* for *their* or *no* for *know*. A surprising number of people get irrationally irritated by bad spelling, making quick judgments that the poor speller is incompetent or ignorant. Of course, that's not a fair judgment. Many educated, published writers are not good spellers, at least not when they're writing drafts. Professional writers, however, finds ways to correct their spelling. They also have editors and proofreaders to save them from disaster.

If you know you are a chronically bad speller and are likely to make noticeable blunders like writing *bare* for *bear* or *affect* for *effect*, you need to take whatever steps you must to correct your spelling before you release any piece of writing for public consumption. It's worth the extra care; poor spelling can cost you too much. In Chapter 10 I give several suggestions about ways to check and improve your spelling.

THE ADDITIONAL ATTRIBUTES OF EXCELLENT WRITING

Vigor

You sometimes hear an author's writing described as "strong" or "vigorous," and in a tone that makes it obvious that those terms are complimentary. These are terms that are easier to illustrate than to define, but in general they mean that a writer shows the readers what is happening through active verbs and clear images, that he or she uses specific examples and striking metaphors to get ideas across, that the writing is concrete, direct, and efficient. It moves along like a person walking vigorously and confidently toward a goal.

Vigor is a quality that you can almost count on finding in the writing of first-rate journalists and essayists like Garry Wills, Thomas Friedman, Ellen Goodman, or Anna Quindlen, and in books by essayists like Nikki Giovanni and Jacob Epstein.

Here is an example from Nikki Giovanni:

> . . . I am a sixties person. It's true that I didn't do tie-dyed T-shirts or drugs, and I never went to jail. I argued a lot in the coffeehouses and tried at one point to be a social drinker. It didn't work. I can't hold liquor at all. But I was nonetheless a sixties person and continue to be today because I actually believe in the people. That was never just rhetoric to me, although it has often been my undoing. Believing in the people is dangerous, because the people will break your heart. Just when you know in your heart that white people are not worth a tinker's damn and the future depends on us, some Black person will come along with some nihilistic crap that makes you rethink the whole thing.

—Nikki Giovanni, *Racism 101* (New York: Morrow, 1994) 50

The passage vibrates with simplicity and strength; its rhythms are quick and its images and personal references bring the writer right into the reader's presence.

Authentic Voice

In good writing the reader can sense the *presence* of the writer behind what he or she is reading. The writer's character comes through the writing and makes the reader feel that a confident person is trying to communicate ideas and information and is being careful to avoid formulas or clichés. Writing that has an authentic voice gives you the feeling that only that particular writer could have written that particular piece—it is stamped with his or her personality. The reader feels drawn into that writer's mind and stimulated to interact with it.

Here is an example from a distinguished American historian and social commentator that projects an authentic voice:

> Lincoln is here [at Gettysburg] not only to sweeten the air of Gettysburg, but to clean the infected atmosphere of American history itself, tainted with official sins and inherited guilt. He would cleanse the Constitution—not, as William Lloyd Garrison had, by burning an instrument that countenanced slavery. He altered the document from within, by appeal from its letter to the spirit, subtly changing the recalcitrant stuff of that legal compromise, bringing it to its own indictment. By implicitly doing this, he performed one of the most daring acts of open-air sleight-of-hand ever witnessed by the unsuspecting. Everyone in that vast throng of thousands was having his or her intellectual pocket picked. The crowd departed with a new thing in its ideological luggage, that new constitution Lincoln had substituted for the one they brought there with them. They walked off, from those curving graves on the hillside, under a changed sky, into a different America. Lincoln had revolutionized the Revolution, giving people a new past to live with that would change their future indefinitely.

> —Garry Wills, *Lincoln at Gettysburg* (New York: Simon & Schuster, 1992) 38

Writers are more likely to project an authentic voice in their writing when they care about their topic, as Wills obviously does about his, but you don't have to be immersed in a subject to sound authentic. You can communicate your own voice by referring to your personal experience and special expertise, by using specific examples to support your generalizations, and by trying to make your writing concrete, straightforward, and personal rather than abstract and impersonal.

EXERCISES

Passages for response:

1. Read carefully the following three passages from professional writers. Then

either working in a group with two or three others in your class or writing on your own, respond to each of the passages. What qualities of good writing do you find in each of them? What specific phrases or sentences do you find especially effective? How would you characterize each paragraph in just a few words?

A. The "work" the [chain] gangs do is valueless. The rock breaking is pure photo opportunity. The highway crews allegedly clear weeds and debris, but this is impossible to do on any useful scale with five men chained eight feet apart, each stumbling when the next one does. The real reason for stretching legions of chained, white-suited men for a mile or so along the highway is to let motorists gorge on a visible symbol of punishment and humiliation. Hanging, too, was once a public entertainment. No one would be surprised if some ambitious politician suggests making it so again.

—Brent Staples, "The Chain Gang Show," *New York
Times Magazine*, 17 Sept. 1995: 62

B. The problem, clearly, was the cold. The old lodge on the Beaverkill in which we planned to spend the winter was built in the 1920s, before the rising cost of oil created the need for three-paned glass and modern insulation. By today's standards, the once four-season lodge was now at best a summer home. There was a furnace of sorts, built for coal and later converted to burn oil at less than 40 percent efficiency. And the fireplace, a great stone maw that devoured all the fire's heat and a good deal more besides, was an even greater liability. When the wind drew across the chimney's mouth, it was like a giant pulling on a corncob pipe, and unless the flue was tightly shut, the pages of your book would flutter in the draw.

—Andrew Todhunter, "The Taming of the Saw,"
Atlantic Monthly, Jan. 1995: 16

C. How do we tell the truth in a small town? Is it possible to write it? Certainly, great literature might come out of the lives of ordinary people on the farms and ranches and little towns of the Plains, but are the people who farm, the people who work in these towns, writing it? The truth, the whole truth, tends to be complex, its contentments and joys wrestled out of doubt, pain, change. How to tell the truth in a small town, where, if a discouraging word is heard, it is not for public consumption?

—Kathleen Norris, "Can You Tell the Truth in a
Small Town?" *Dakota: A Spiritual Geography*
(New York: Ticknor & Fields, 1993) 79

2. How comparatively readable are these two examples from advanced writing

students' papers? What specific comments or suggestions might you make to their authors?

A. Today in the world there are more than 200 breeds of dogs and these can further be divided into six groups. Dogs perform a variety of services to the community. They have the intelligence and also the ability to bond with humans. It enables them to help us in different tasks. One such group is the "working dogs," which do many of these tasks. Dogs are helpful to many individuals in our society and are becoming more than just a household pet.

B. In bicycle racing, it takes much more than physical exertion to place well consistently. At the pro level, all racers have excellent fitness. Those who most often succeed go beyond that level. They must know when to exert themselves. They must know when not to. They must know how to cruise to minimize effort. And they must know how to relax during times of less than full effort. The whole game revolves around who has been best able to conserve his energy, using it only in controlled bursts to keep in contention or take advantage of a competitor's weakness.

3. Reread the two student paragraphs above. How strong a voice do you think each writer projects? Do you find the voice authentic? Does the writer seem to be talking about something he or she knows and cares about? If so, how is that impression conveyed? If not, what goes wrong?

SUGGESTED WRITING ASSIGNMENT

Write an informative and/or persuasive essay in one focused area of some topic that you find interesting and on which you have already done some reading or which you have already discussed with someone—perhaps an issue you are studying in another class, such as censorship in art, the high cost of television campaigns, or obesity in children. Approximate length should be four to six double-spaced pages (1,000 to 1,500 words). Select a publication in which you might get such an essay published and write its name under the title of your essay. Some possibilities could be *Parade* magazine, *Newsweek,* or *Health Today.* Here are some possible topics:

1. Discuss the issues that are raised in censorship battles of the kind that occur in a small town when a group of parents tries to have a book banned. A typical instance in recent years involved Maya Angelou's book *I Know Why the Caged Bird Sings.* A group of parents wanted the book removed from the high school library because they felt the author's account of being raped

when she was eight was unsuitable for adolescent readers. Other parents contended that the book was well-written and presented aspects of life that adolescents should be aware of. Remember, you are to write about the issues involved, not take sides in the argument.

2. Using your own high school experience as a source, identify two characteristics of a high school that you think help students to learn and to mature. As an alternative, identify two characteristics of a high school that work against student learning. Describe the characteristics and give specific examples. Some possible places to publish: *Reader's Digest* or *Change* (a magazine for educators).

3. Among the United States' most popular and profitable exports are Hollywood films. Identify an American-made movie or a popular television show you have seen recently and analyze and discuss how it portrays a segment of American society. What impact do you think the movie or TV show is likely to have on people who see it in France or Japan or India? What are the implications for our image abroad? Possible places to publish: *Premiere*, a magazine about the movie business, or the media section of *Time* or *Rolling Stone*.

3

WHAT HAPPENS WHEN PEOPLE WRITE?

 By the act of writing, a writer coaxes to life thoughts that didn't exist before.

People for whom writing is difficult may believe that writing is a mysterious process that the average person can't master. They assume good writers are naturally gifted—the rest of us just drudge along doing uninspired work. This "either you have it or you don't" belief can discourage would-be writers before they start.

Like most myths, this one has a grain of truth in it, but only a grain. The best writers, like the top people in any field, are likely to be especially gifted, but most successful writers have no special verbal abilities. Usually they are well read, to be sure, but they write well because they work at their craft and because they have developed a set of practices they know will help them consistently turn out good work.

AN OVERVIEW OF THE WRITING PROCESS

How Professional Writers Work

- Professional writers don't wait for inspiration. They write whether they feel like it or not, and they write on a regular schedule.

■ As a rule, professional writers consistently work in the same setting with the same tools.

■ Even successful writers often have trouble getting started; they expect such delays and don't panic.

■ Successful writers work constantly at gathering material. They keep a file of clippings, and they observe and take notes.

■ Successful writers do best when they have deadlines, and they set deadlines for themselves if necessary.

■ Successful writers seldom know exactly what they will write; they plan on discovering new ideas and angles as they write.

■ Successful writers plan before they write, but they keep plans flexible, subject to revision as they work.

■ Successful writers usually work with an audience in mind.

■ Most successful writers work slowly; four to six double-spaced pages is considered a good day's work.

■ Successful writers revise as they write and expect to do two or three drafts of anything they write.

■ Successful writers often procrastinate; unlike less experienced writers, however, they usually have a good sense of how long they can procrastinate and still avoid disaster.

Explanatory and Exploratory Writing

Several variables affect how writers work, but probably their process is most affected by the type of writing they're doing. I divide those types into two categories: *explanatory* writing and *exploratory* writing. Explanatory writing *tends* to be about information; exploratory writing *tends* to be about ideas.

Writers usually make plans when they are doing explanatory writing, plans that can range from a page of notes to a full outline. Such plans help them organize their material and keep track of it as they write. Writers working on explanatory projects find that traditional methods of development work well: assertion/support, cause and effect, process, compare/contrast, and so on. Much of the writing that students do in college is explanatory, as is most business writing.

Explanatory writing isn't necessarily easy to do. It takes care and skill to write an accurate and interesting story about North American bats or an informative report on how the movie *Congo* was made. But the process is manageable though sometimes slow. Much of the work lies in arranging the order of presentation, finding supporting material, and polishing the style to engage the readers.

EXPLANATORY WRITING

Purpose: To present, analyze, and evaluate information.

Typical examples: Book review, biography, environmental report, technical review, newspaper story, factual magazine article, historical analysis.

Task: Discover already existing material, organize it, and present it clearly to a targeted audience.

Because writers don't know ahead of time exactly what they are going to say in exploratory writing, it's hard to make a detailed plan or outline. They can, however, make copious notes and work out a tentative thesis sentence. For a piece on escalating violence among teenage gangs, such a thesis might read like this:

> In many inner-city areas, young gang members are killing each other because of Mafia-like codes that mandate death before dishonor; unfortunately, dishonor can mean something as trivial as not wearing the right kind of jacket or being offended by a slighting remark or an insolent look.

Such a sentence could serve as an anchor for a first draft, but it could change or even disappear as the paper developed.

EXPLORATORY WRITING

Purpose: To explore a topic, to develop a theory, to speculate about an event, or to follow a hunch.

Typical examples: Reflective political essay, exploratory essay about the causes of teenage suicide, a profile piece about a family who won the lottery, an investigative piece about the militia movement of the 1990s.

Task: Choose a promising topic, follow sources to get ideas, develop material by writing, choose an audience, and organize and shape material into a coherent piece for that audience.

Exploratory writing isn't necessarily harder to do than explanatory writing, but it is harder to plan because it resists a systematic approach. Often it takes longer and requires more drafts. Nevertheless, it appeals to many writers who like the freedom of being able to discover ideas through the act of writing, even though they then face the sometimes difficult task of shaping those ideas into readable form. Many academic papers are exploratory, particularly in the liberal arts; so are many magazine articles and personal essays.

Combining Explanatory and Exploratory Writing

Of course, not all writing can be easily classified as explanatory or exploratory. Sometimes you'll be presenting information and exploring ideas in the same paper and move from giving facts to reflecting about their implications. For example, in an essay about "downsizing" in many American companies in the 1990s, you could document the cuts in the work force in a particular factory, then reflect on the impact those cuts had on the families who had worked in that factory for decades.

In general, readers respond best to writing that thoughtfully connects facts to reflection. Many people want to see speculation and theorizing tied to solid evidence; otherwise, they're apt to say, "Well, this is just a lot of speculation—I'm not impressed." So don't hesitate to mix the two kinds of writing if it makes your paper stronger.

Why should you even bother to think about what kind of writing you're doing? For at least two reasons.

First, it's helpful to realize there isn't just one writing process. There are different writing processes, and some work better than others for different situations. Second, you'll become a more proficient writer if you develop the habit of analyzing your writing situation ahead of time. Then you can consciously choose the process that is most likely to work for a particular task.

I caution you, however, to resist the idea that one kind of writing is better than another. It's not. The imaginative, thoughtful writing about theories and opinions that I am labeling *exploratory* is important because through it writers generate and communicate original ideas. Writers who excel at it contribute significantly to our culture.

The informative, factual writing that I am labeling *explanatory* is important because we depend on it to find out what is going on in the world. It keeps the machinery of society going, and those writers who are good at it are invaluable. But anyone who hopes to be a confident and effective writer in a variety of situations should develop habits that will enable him or her to master both kinds of writing and to combine them when necessary.

EXPLANATORY WRITING

Case studies, research reports, news stories, and so on.

1. Narrow your topic.
2. Rough out an outline, listing main points.
3. Research the topic, gather data, find examples.
4. Review patterns that might work: cause and effect, process, assertion/support.
5. Draft your paper.
6. Revise and polish.

EXPLORATORY WRITING

Literary criticism, political analysis, essays of opinion, and so on.

1. Choose your topic.
2. Read in the area, browse the Internet, talk to friends.
3. Compile extensive notes.
4 Narrow your topic and draft a tentative thesis.
5. Write a discovery draft.
6. Review the draft to find your main idea.
7. Rough out an outline to develop that idea.
8. Write a second draft and perhaps a third.
9. Revise and polish.

THE STAGES OF WRITING

When professional writers write, they seem to go through the same stages that creative people in other fields do: preparation, planning, execution, incubation, and revision or verification. In writing, those stages look like this.

STAGES OF WRITING

Prepare: Identify a topic, read and do research, talk to others to generate ideas.

Plan: Take notes, develop examples, consider ways to organize, and rough out an outline.

Draft: Write a serious first draft or write a tentative discovery draft.

Incubate: Relax and turn your attention to something else.

Revise: Reread your draft, get feedback, and rewrite, perhaps two or three times.

Edit and proofread: Edit for style and diction. Correct grammatical errors. Proofread for typographical errors.

Such a summary makes writing look like a neater, more linear process than it really is. In practice, the writing process is often messy, inexact, and unpredictable as writers move back and forth between stages, replanning and revising as they go. Nevertheless, roughly speaking writers do work in stages, and it's enlightening to consider what typically goes on in each stage.

PREPARATION

Preparation for writing divides into two parts: *preliminary* and *immediate*. The preliminary part includes all the writer's experiences, interests, and activities that make up the bank of resources available to him or her. In the immediate part of preparation, the writer employs a set of strategies to access those resources.

Stocking the Bank

People who expect to be doing a good deal of writing—either in school, on the job, or with the hope of publishing—can work at stocking their resource bank in a number of ways:

- Keep a notebook with you and jot down ideas and insights.

- Read a major newspaper and some general magazines—don't depend on TV for your news. Look especially for in-depth stories on current issues.

■ Keep a file of newspaper and magazine clippings about a variety of topics that interest you—organize them by topic.

■ Watch for announcements of lectures and public appearances by figures of current interest—politicians, educators, writers, and prominent individuals. Attend when you can.

■ When you're with groups, ask questions. Draw people out about what they do and what they're interested in.

■ When you have time, cruise the Internet to find out more about a topic that interests you. Type your key words—for example, Western photography—into the search frame for Yahoo or Excite and see where the quest takes you. Be prepared to invest some time, however.

■ Read book reviews regularly to keep up with current hot topics and keep a list of books that interest you. If you can afford it, buy them for your library even if you don't read them immediately.

In other words, develop an intellectual radar that sweeps your environment constantly and picks up signals from everywhere. Remember that a well-furnished mind is a writer's greatest resource.

Immediate Preparation

Part 1

Tentatively identify your topic.
Apply discovery techniques:
      Brainstorm.
      Narrow the topic by subdividing.
      Freewrite.
      Ask the journalist's questions.
      Talk to people about the topic.
      Browse in the library or through your computer. Count on
        serendipity.

Part 2

Focus your topic.

Tentatively identify your audience and purpose.

Collect material through research and interviews.

Choose a preliminary method of organization. Make a scratch outline
or list, giving your main points.

Choose a tentative title.

Write a tentative thesis sentence.

Model Topic: Preparation

Part 1

Tentative topic: Need for better role models for girls in books for children.
Brainstorm: Write down everything you can think of on your topic even if
you're not sure it's relevant or even accurate. You can write by hand, on a
typewriter, or on your computer. For example:

BRAINSTORMING—GIRLS' BOOKS PAPER

Typical children's classics have mostly male heroes: *Huckleberry Finn,
Treasure Island, King of the Wind,* Aladdin. Greek myths: Theseus,
Hercules, Odysseus, etc. King Arthur legends, Norse legends. *Jungle
Books.* Books about heroes—Siegfried, Sir Gawain, Beowulf.

Women are seen as waiting to be rescued—Sleeping Beauty, Cinderella,
princesses in castles.

Strong women are often the witches or evil queens.

Can't think of any traditional books except Nancy Drew series in
which women show courage and daring.

A few more modern books—*The Island of the Blue Dolphins* and *Julie
of the Wolves*—show girl heroines. Current Baby Sitter series also
good for showing girls taking responsibility.

Some nonfiction books about women like Florence Nightingale and
Joan of Arc but no engrossing novels.

Argument against books for and about girls is that girls will read boys'
books, but boys won't read girls' books.

It's harder to get boys interested in reading, so teachers cater to their
tastes.

Becomes a self-fulfilling prophecy—few girls' books written because publishers think they won't sell. Yet *Island of the Blue Dolphins* was an international best-seller.

Stereotyped female characters reinforced by most movies children see.

Narrow topic by subdividing from brainstorming list:

Books of myths and legends	*Standard classics*
Heroes are all males doing great deeds	Glorify adventures open only to boys
Hercules, Perseus, Bellerophon, Theseus, Jason, Odysseus, Siegfried	Huck Finn, Robinson Crusoe, *Swiss Family Robinson*
Greek-Roman myths also glorify men: Zeus, Neptune, Mercury, Ares, Apollo, Orpheus, Prometheus—	*Jungle Book, Tarzan, King of the Wind, Ivanhoe*

Women either not there or in the role of servants or victims. Exceptions: Diana, Athena. Pandora made to look like a fool.

Current versions of these tales also tend to have illustrations of blond, blue-eyed heroes . . . hard to use in many schools where black, Hispanic, and Asian youngsters are in the majority.

Ample examples of women heroes in history to write about . . . Joan of Arc, Queen Boudicca, Zenobia of Persia, Semiramis, Vietnamese sisters who led a rebellion, Rani of Jhansi, 19th-century Indian queen . . . Judith and Esther in the Bible.

Ask the journalist's questions:

Who: Focus is on girl readers who need role models of courageous and daring women leaders.

What: Argument to publishers and educators to seek out and publish more books about women leaders similar to the heroes of myth and legend.

Why: Girls need role models that will reinforce their ambition and counteract the messages they get from many traditional books.

When: Present time. Families and educators who are trying to convince girls they can do anything they want to need role models for reinforcement.

Where: Argument could appear in an educational journal about children's literature, in a trade journal for publishers, or in a magazine like *Parenting*.

How: Convince educators of the need to bring such books into classrooms and libraries to promote equity, and convince publishers that publishing such books would be profitable.

Talk to people to get ideas:

Parents of girls

Librarians in children's section of public library

School librarians

Primary- and middle-school teachers

Professors of children's literature; ask for leads on professional literature on the topic

People who work in children's bookstores

Browse in the library and through a computer: Go to the children's sections of the library and browse through books about leaders and heroes. Check educational journals on the topic. Use the on-line catalog in your library to look for articles on the topic. If you have access to the Internet, look for user's groups on the topic.

Cultivate serendipity: In the long run, your most productive discovery strategy may be serendipity, the faculty of finding good things, apparently by accident. Serendipity is more than luck. It is the ability to keep out antennae for the unexpected. It is the habit of ferreting out interesting people and asking questions. The more curious you are and the more interests you have, the more likely you are to be intellectually lucky.

Part 2

Focus your topic: Through brainstorming and subdividing, I have generated considerable material for this model paper, more than I can do justice to in the 1,500-word article that I would like to submit to a magazine or educational journal. Looking over the material, I decide to focus on the lack of women in legends about heroes for these reasons:

1.   I think it's narrow enough to cover adequately in the allotted space.

2.   Since I recently read a book of legends to a third-grade class in a predominantly minority school, I have first-hand knowledge about the topic.

3. As a member of the American Association of University Women and of Emily's List, an organization dedicated to electing women to Congress, I am especially concerned about the lack of leadership role models for girls.

4. In research to find women leaders in history who might be used as models in stories for girls, I have found several good subjects so I already have specific examples I can use.

Notice that I'm choosing a topic in which I'm very interested and on which I already have substantial information. With such a topic I already have a good start.

Tentatively identify an audience and a purpose:

   Audience: Elementary teachers, librarians, and principals who want all their students to read books that provide strong, nonsexist role models. Possibly publishers and parents of girls.

   Purpose: To convince readers that it's crucial for all students, but especially girls, to read literature that shows diverse role models for courage and leadership

Collect material through research and interviews. For this project, I interviewed these people:

Elementary school librarian

Owner of a children's bookstore

Two mothers of young girls

Second-grade teacher

Two faculty specialists in children's literature

Librarian in children's section at public library

I also browsed in the children's section of the public library and through books in the children's bookstore. I did on-line research in the University of Texas library with discouraging results. A key word search with *Sexism and Children's Literature* yielded one article, but a good one; a key word search with *Women and Heroes* yielded three potentially usable articles. A key word search with *Girls and Literature* yielded no usable articles.

It looks as if my best source will be a book I own, Antonia Fraser's *The Warrior Queens.*

Choose a preliminary method of organization; make a scratch outline giving main points: I'll probably develop this essay by the assertion/support method of organization and also use reasoning from evidence. A scratch outline might look like this:

I. The traditional legends that have been handed down in our culture are highly male oriented.
    A. Early heroes
        Siegfried, Hercules, Jason, Odysseus, Prometheus, etc.
    B. King Arthur's round table
    C. El Cid, Song of Roland, Horatio, little Dutch boy

II. Women tend to be helpers (Ariadne), victims waiting to be rescued (Cinderella and Sleeping Beauty), or witches or grotesques (Medea, Medusa)
    A. Some exceptions—e.g., Hippolyta, Athena, Diana
    B. Princesses in towers
    C. Foolish girls—Pandora, Eurydice

III. As part of our Western heritage, this body of literature lacks important role models for girls if they are to aspire to becoming leaders.
    A. No examples of women taking charge and vanquishing evil.
    B. Comments of elementary school girls to whom these legends were read suggest that they feel left out.
    C. Also important for boys to read and hear literature that promotes respect for women and their abilities.
    D. Illustrated collections of these legends portray most of the heroes as blue-eyed blonds—thus black, Hispanic, and Asian youngsters are also left out, the girls from these groups doubly excluded.

IV. Parents, educators, and publishers need to work together to find tales of women's heroism and courage or to have them written.
    A. Plenty of heroines in history who would make good subjects for tales—Boudicca, a Celtic queen; Zenobia of Persia; Vietnamese sisters who led a rebellion in the 11th century; Maxine Hong Kingston's woman warrior; Rani of Jhansi; and Esther and Judith from the Bible.
    B. Conventional reasons for de-emphasizing books about girls must be counteracted.
        1. Theory that girls will read boys' books but boys won't read girls' books becomes a self-fulfilling prophecy.
            a. No books available with strong women having adventures.
            b. If boys are exposed to exciting girls' books in the early grades, will help to overcome biases.
        2. Two books about girls—*Wizard of Oz* and *Island of the Blue Dolphins*—very popular.

V. Educational and cultural climate is right for new efforts to break out of sexist constraints.
  A. Don't suggest that we give up reading the traditional legends to children, but they need to be interpreted and explained in context.
  B. Begin to practice a kind of literary affirmative action for books about women heroes.

Comment: Some writers love outlines, others hate them. The well-regarded writer for the *New Yorker*, John McPhee, makes elaborate detailed outlines before he writes and says that as he does so, the ghost of his high school English teacher smiles down on him. Jacques Barzun, another highly regarded writer and scholar, says in his book *On Writing, Editing, and Publishing*, "For my taste, outlines are useless, fettering, imbecile." Both writers do what works for them, and so should you. An outline helps me generate material and draft some pattern of organization, but I don't necessarily stick with it when I write.

Choose a tentative title: "Missing from the Action: Women Heroes in Children's Books."

Write a tentative thesis sentence: "Because strong role models are so important for a child's development, parents, educators, and publishers need to make special efforts to locate and promote books with female heroes and leaders in order to overcome the negative message children now get about women's roles from much traditional children's literature."

DRAFTING

Create a Writing Environment

As a college student you already write regularly; when you're in a profession, you'll probably write even more, especially if you go into law, public relations, college teaching, or even accounting or engineering. With that fact in mind, you'll do yourself a favor if you establish writing habits that will make writing easier. Professional writers all have such routines—mainly they involve being consistent and organized.

- Choose a writing place that's comfortable and relatively quiet and do your writing there whenever you can. It doesn't have to be perfect or even conventional. I wrote my master's thesis sitting in a parked car with a portable typewriter on my lap in order to get away from family distractions. You may have to write at the dining room table or at a computer terminal on campus. The important thing is to get used to writing in a specific place so when you get there, your subconscious gives you the signal to write.

- Choose a time that suits your personal rhythms and gives you some uninterrupted chunks of time. Make it a time when your energy level is high and your mind is running in high gear. Like many other writers, I work best in the morning. Other writers do their best work at night, however, and you should do what works best for you. Also indulge yourself with whatever little trimmings you need—background music, chewing gum, Sprite or Coca-Cola (not near the computer, though).

- Find a favorite set of tools and stick with them. Most writers I know now use a word processor and would fight anyone who tried to take it away from them. Unquestionably, a word processor makes writing infinitely easier, and I strongly recommend that you learn to use one, particularly since anyone who doesn't have minimal keyboard skills these days is almost as handicapped in this culture as someone who can't drive. Still, some few writers still prefer drafting with a yellow pad and pencil or on their old typewriters—if that works best for you, OK. But you really should learn to type.

Having said all that, I will add a caution. Even though you may work your best at certain times and under certain circumstances, sometimes you can't afford the luxury of having everything exactly right. Occasionally every writer has to work under unfavorable circumstances to get a job done. I have written speeches on an airplane with a pencil and legal pad, and I have gone back to my desk at night to meet a deadline. So if you have to take a child to the doctor or help your sister, you'll have to throw your routines aside and do the best you can. Rituals and routines are enormously helpful, but there's always the risk of allowing their absence to become an excuse for not writing.

Overcome Writing Blocks

Beginnings are hard—no question about it. Even experienced professional writers acknowledge that. For some interesting reasons, such blocks are not surprising.

One reason is that writing is a powerfully recursive activity in which writers continually read back through what they've already written for prompts that keep them moving along. That rereading helps them generate ideas and solidify their goals. But when you're just starting, you have nothing to go back to for stimulus; that's why freewriting and outlining can be so important in helping you to start.

Second, most of us sense that beginnings are very important; thus we tend to take them too seriously, feeling that they must be good or we're in trouble. Well, yes, they *are* important, but you're only writing a draft. Whatever you put down now can be revised later when you have a clearer idea of your thesis. So when you're drafting, if you can't think of anything good, lower your standards. Just get something down that will let you push off and start writing.

What you should *not* do is wait for inspiration to strike. If you wait until you feel like writing, you may never start. As the noted economist and author John Kenneth Galbraith has put it,

> All writers know that on some golden mornings they are touched by the wand—are on intimate terms with poetry and cosmic truth. I have experienced those moments myself. Their lesson is simple: It's a total illusion. And the danger in the illusion is that you will wait for those moments. Such is the horror of having to face the typewriter that you will spend all your time waiting. I am persuaded that most writers, like most shoemakers, are about as good one day as the next . . . , hangovers aside. The difference is the result of euphoria, alcohol, or imagination. The meaning is that one had better go to his or her typewriter every morning and stay there regardless of the seeming result. It will be much the same.
>
> —John Kenneth Galbraith, "Writing, Typing, and Economics," *Atlantic Monthly*, Mar. 1978: 104

If you are working on a paper over a period of days, temporary paralysis may set in every time you have to start over after an interruption. And the longer you are away from your writing, the harder it will be to get started again. When that happens, try going back to reread what you've written or even rewrite your last page. Usually that kind of backtracking will get the creative juices flowing again.

Find Your Pace: Sprinters, Plodders, and Bleeders

Writers work at different paces, and you need to find the rhythms that suit you best. Some compose their first draft rapidly, in a rush to get thoughts down as rapidly as they come. They don't stop for long periods to think or hesitate about word choice. I call these writers *sprinters*. Most sprinters think of their first draft as a discovery draft, and they plan to revise heavily on the next draft.

Other writers write first drafts much more slowly, stopping frequently to reread what they've written and to think. They change words, delete, and move sentences around, and they spend considerable time staring at their typewriter or screen. They also pace, snack, do little chores, and worry. I call these writers *plodders*. While the plodder doesn't usually regard the first draft as final, he or she knows that when it is done the hardest part of the job is probably over.

A third kind of writer is the perfectionist. These writers have to get everything right the first time—think out each sentence as they write it and change words as they work. They cannot go on with a paragraph until they are completely satisfied with the one they're just written. I call these writers *bleeders*. They suffer more than other writers, and it takes them forever to produce a piece of writing.

I recommend that you try to start out as a sprinter. Sprinting gets you started, you get a sense of accomplishment from producing something, and you create a text you can start working on. But if you're not the sprinter type, don't worry about it. Many productive writers are plodders, and some of us just have to work out our ideas as we go. In the long run, plodders may not take any more time turning out a good finished product.

But don't allow yourself to be a bleeder. Bleeders are the ones most likely to develop writer's block and to miss their deadlines. And at the distance of a day or two, that perfect document that you agonized over may seem less perfect. Then you'll regret the original agony.

Postpone Corrections

Whether you are a sprinter or a plodder, put off making corrections in spelling and mechanics until you're ready to turn out your final copy. When you are actually writing, you shouldn't be fretting about where to put commas and whether *harass* has one or two *r*'s. You can fix such details later. Writers who worry about mechanics too soon stifle their creative energies and divert energy from developing their ideas. Better to write first and edit later.

Maintain the Creative Tension

When you are engaged in serious writing and want to do the best job you can, it's important that you try to maintain a *creative tension* as you work. Try to be simultaneously a writer and a reader of your own work. One writer and teacher puts it this way:

The act of writing might be described as a conversation between workmen muttering to each other at the workbench. The self speaks, the other self listens and responds. The self proposes, the other self considers. The self makes, the other self evaluates. The two selves collaborate: a problem is spotted, discussed, defined; solutions are proposed, rejected, suggested, attempted, tested, discarded, accepted.

—Donald Murray, "Teaching the Other Self,"
*College Composition and
Communication,* May 1982

Both selves are important in the process; the self that is producing writing has to learn to distance itself from what he or she has done and listen as the other self critiques it.

When you've finished the first draft, put it aside—overnight if you can—to allow your mind to clear and give you a fresh outlook on what you've written. This is the time for incubation, a period to let your unconscious mull over what you've done before you start to revise.

INCUBATION

People who study the creative process believe that when scientists, architects, composers, writers, and other kinds of creative problem solvers stop working for periods of time, they aren't idle at all. Rather they are giving their minds and imaginations the necessary interval for renewal that the subconscious mind must have in order to absorb, sift, and process material and select what it needs.

We don't really know what happens during this stage. Apparently the mind goes on a fishing expedition into the subconscious, but the fishing has to be private and random. The conscious mind is not in charge here—all it can do is wait receptively to see what appears. When a solution surfaces, the conscious mind can take over and move ahead.

Incubation doesn't happen just once during the writing process. Like preparation, it's an ongoing process that can occur several times while you're writing a draft as well as between drafts. When you begin to see incubation as essential to the writing process and learn to let it work for you, you should be able to face even difficult writing assignments with confidence. Plan, prepare, write, relax when you need to, and then trust your subconscious to come through for you.

Two cautions, however. First, be ready to seize the moment when a solution surfaces. Be prepared to write it down or to get back to your computer immediately. Second, don't wait indefinitely for lightning to strike. If time is running out and your subconscious is still snoozing, put the conscious mind back on the job and start writing. Chances are good that whatever has been brewing under the surface will emerge and you can move ahead with your work.

In Chapter 6 I'll suggest ways to go about revising your draft when you have been through one or more periods of writing and allowing time for incubation.

EXERCISES

1. List the various writing tasks that people in the following professions might have to do. If necessary, talk to acquaintances in these professions or to faculty who help prepare students for them.

engineering	law
nursing	medical research
banking	politics
public relations	college teaching
advertising	restaurant management

2. List all the experiences you have had that you might find useful in writing a paper on one of these topics. Include experiences such as seeing movies and television shows, reading magazines and books, or taking a related course.

   The changing profession of medicine

   The impact of television talk shows on the political process

   New political consciousness among women

   The major increase in the number of sports vehicles sold in the United States in the last five years

3. Explore a possible topic for a paper—for example, "Mountain Biking" or "Home Schooling"—by asking these questions about the topic and writing out the answers:

   Who? What kind of people are participating?

   What? What is involved in the activity?

   Why? Why do they participate?

   When? When is the activity popular, or when did it start?

Where? Where does the activity take place?

How? How is the activity carried out?

4. Write a 100-word summary of the main ideas you would include in a paper on one of these topics:

The art of buying at a discount

Starting a small business while in college

Preparing one's self to get accepted into law school, graduate business school, or a senior honors program

Finding the right part-time job for a college student

You could make a detailed outline for the topic rather than write a summary.

5. Get together a group of three or four people and brainstorm for twenty minutes on one of these topics. For each subject, ask one person to write down every idea on the board or on paper.

Defensive driving

Call-in radio talk shows

Campus politics at your school

Promising careers for the next ten years

Sexual harassment in secondary schools

SUGGESTED WRITING ASSIGNMENTS

1. At your campus bookstore, any large bookstore chain, or in the periodical room of your library, you'll find a vast selection of special interest magazines on subjects ranging from guns and bicycles and parenting to skiing and astronomy. Choose one that focuses on a special interest of yours and write an article that would fit well into the content of the magazine. Your article should probably be no longer than 1,000 words, but it could be shorter if such a length seems to fit the format of the magazine.

Before you start, on a separate sheet write an analysis of your audience and purpose. See Chapter 4 for more details on doing such an analysis. Also study the articles in the target magazine to get an idea about what kinds of articles they publish and of the tone and style that seems to be favored by the editor. Hand in a copy of a typical article with your first draft.

2. For the student newspaper on your campus, write a guest editorial on one of the topics given below or on a similar topic based on some controversy that has recently made headlines at your school. The editorial should run from 500 to 700 words and include factual information as well as opinion.

   On a separate page, specify which portion of the paper's readers you are trying to reach—remember faculty, state legislators, and administrators make up an important part of the audience for a campus newspaper. Also spell out what you hope to accomplish with this editorial.

   Topics:

   A. A faculty proposal to require two three-hour courses in ethnic studies as a degree requirement at your school.

   B. An administrative proposal to do away with sabbatical leaves for the faculty on the grounds that business and industry usually don't give sabbaticals.

   C. An administrative proposal to impose a computer user fee of twenty dollars a semester on all students, regardless of how much or how little they use computers. The administration says that in order to expand and upgrade on-campus computer facilities such a fee is necessary.

   D. A student government proposal to open a professionally staffed job counseling and placement office on campus, open only to juniors and seniors.

3. Write a review of a book, a new movie, or a new television show to be published in your local campus or city newspaper. The review should be from 400 to 700 words. Before you start, analyze your audience. Who do you think reads reviews such as the one you're going to write, and what do they hope to get from the review? What is your purpose in writing it?

4

WHAT IS YOUR WRITING SITUATION?

> Always assume your readers are intelligent although they may be uninformed.

When you begin any writing task that's important to you, it's worth your time to stop and assess your specific writing situation. Ask yourself, "What's involved here? What are the components of this task and how can I manage them?" One good way to take stock of those components is to ask yourself four questions.

ASSESSING YOUR WRITING SITUATION

Audience: *Who* is my audience?

Purpose: *Why* am I writing?

Persona: *How* do I want to present myself?

Message: *What* do I want to say?

AUDIENCE

Analyzing Your Audience

If someone were to ask me the most important advice that I would give any writer, I would say without hesitation, *"Remember your audience! Know who your readers are and what they want and need from you."*

The advice seems obvious, but most college writers, graduate students as well as undergraduates, have trouble thinking beyond the captive audience of their instructor to an audience of real-life readers. Yet the writing you do in college should prepare you for the writing you'll be doing later in your profession for readers who have high expectations and who will be unhappy if they're not met. That's why every writer needs to learn how to write for different audiences and how to analyze those audiences.

Most of us already know a great deal about analyzing audiences in everyday situations. We protest an unauthorized charge on a credit in a different tone and style than we would use in writing a neighborhood newsletter, and use different strategies in writing a fellowship application than we would in writing a newspaper editorial. In less personal writing situations, however, keeping our minds on the audience can be difficult because we have to *de-center*, or try to look at our subject from other people's point of view.

Learning to view an issue through someone else's eyes is one of the hardest exercises I know. But acquiring that ability is also one of the most valuable skills anyone can master, useful for parents, counselors, executives, lawyers, and physicians as well as for writers. The following questions can help you develop that ability.

GUIDELINE QUESTIONS ABOUT AUDIENCE

Attitudes and beliefs:

> What are my readers' values?
> What kind of arguments will they respect?
> What attitudes about my topic will they have?
> What is their age, class, education, and sex?

Previous knowledge:

> How much about the topic do my readers know?
> What additional information do they need?
> How will they react to specialized terminology?

Readers' expectations:

> What do my readers want and need from my piece?
> What questions will they want answered?
> How much explanation is appropriate?

Such an analysis helps to make your readers come alive for you and creates an over-the-shoulder reader to keep in mind as you write. Notice that this analysis is easier to do for an explanatory paper such as the one in the model topic than it is for an exploratory paper. With the exploratory paper, you might have to find your reader after you've done a draft. (See the discussion about writer-based and reader-based prose in the next chapter.)

Model Topic: Preliminary Analysis of Audience

Audience: Elementary teachers, librarians, and principals, very concerned about the reading skills and tastes of their students.

Attitudes and beliefs: These educators in elementary schools are mostly women and see the special need for girls to have strong role models in their reading. They should respond favorably to my thesis, particularly to an argument that gives examples. These are young to middle-aged teachers, well-educated, and committed to teaching.

Previous knowledge: Their knowledge will vary. Librarians are most likely to realize how few role models there are of women leaders and heroines. Teachers and principals will recognize the problem when it is pointed out to them, but probably haven't thought much about it. They need more specific information.

Readers' expectations: They expect a logical, thoughtful argument supported with familiar examples. They will have questions about how and why the situation developed and what they can do about it. They need substantial evidence to help them to understand the breadth of the problem.

PURPOSE

Analyzing Your Purpose

Once you know who your readers are, think specifically about why you are writing. While you're in college, your first response may be a variation of a comment by the eighteenth-century essayist Samuel Johnson, who said, "Nobody but a blockhead ever wrote except for the money." That is, you're writing for a grade. Well, of course—that's a given.

But if you're serious about becoming a good writer, you have to move beyond such a limited, essentially negative answer and ask yourself what your specific purpose is for this particular paper. If you're not sure, you'll have trouble focusing your paper and, when you finish, no way of judging whether you've accomplished what you set out to do. Using a set of guideline questions can help you here too.

GUIDELINE QUESTIONS ABOUT PURPOSE

Kind of writing:

   Is the paper mainly exploratory or explanatory?
   Do I want to inform, entertain, persuade, or move to action?

Goals:

   What specific objective do I have?
   What change, if any, do I want to bring about?
   Is my goal immediate or long range?

Desired response:

   How do I want my readers to respond?
   What action, if any, do I want them to take?

Working through these questions will not only help you decide what you want to accomplish in your paper; it will also help you generate material. After your first draft, particularly in an exploratory paper, you may shift or modify your purpose. While it's important to plan ahead and start out with a goal, don't get too committed to that purpose. Allow for intuitive discovery as you write.

Model Topic: Preliminary Analysis of Purpose

Kind of writing: This will be primarily an explanatory paper. I want to inform my readers about the lack of strong role models for girls in traditional literature and persuade them that change is necessary.

Goals: My specific objective is to make my readers think about the problems that traditional literature raises when it presents stereotyped and dated images of male and female roles to young readers. I would like for them to think about ways to present such literature in a new context and to supplement it with other material. My goal is immediate.

Desired response: I want my readers to understand the problem and take action. I will propose several steps to improve the situation.

PERSONA

Presenting Yourself

Every time you write for your readers, you assume a *persona*. Like an actor in front of an audience, you take on a role that makes a particular impression on your readers. You can come across as a passionate advocate for a cause, an established authority on some issue, a compassionate observer of social injustice—any number of roles are possible. Even if you don't consciously choose a role, some persona will come through—perhaps one that is arrogant and condescending. Thus it's important for you to get in the habit of thinking about your persona so you control it.

Creating Your Persona

A writer can control the extent to which the audience is aware of his or her personality in a piece of writing. Sometimes the author is virtually invisible—for instance, a scientific report or a technical analysis written in the third person with abstract language and technical terms reveals little of the persona behind it. Subtly, however, by the act of disappearing from the document and maintaining distance from the reader, the writer *is* playing a role, that of the objective observer and reporter. In very personal writing in which you are drawing on your own experience and expressing opinions, you may want to use *I* frequently, use contractions, and appear close to your reader. In less casual writing—say an editorial for a newspaper—you would want to maintain more distance, avoid contractions, and set a serious tone. When you want to come across as an authority, you establish that persona by showing confidence and expertise.

Ethical Appeal

The key element of an effective persona is what the Greek rhetoricians called *ethos* or ethical appeal. The strongest ethical appeal comes from having established a reputation for integrity and sound judgment, which is how writers like the historical essayist Garry Wills and the psychologist Carol Gilligan earned their respected positions. But unknown writers can also convey ethical appeal in several ways. Here are some useful strategies:

Do extensive and careful research

Get the facts straight

Use quotations and authority to support your claims

Show respect for those who disagree with you

Be aware of and respect your audience; don't patronize them

Avoid extreme claims

The following guidelines will help you think about how you can establish an effective persona when you write.

GUIDELINE QUESTIONS ABOUT PERSONA

Credibility:

What facts do I need to show I've done my homework?
Are my claims reasonable and do I support them? Have I acknowledged that there may be other points of view?

Tone:

Is my tone suitable for my topic and my audience?
Have I established the appropriate distance between me and my readers?
What emotional attitude do I project? Would a reader find me angry, bitter, superior, or sarcastic? Is that what I want?

Voice:

Do I project a confident and knowledgeable image?
Do I sound genuinely concerned about the issue I'm writing about?

Bear in mind that you probably won't be able to fully plan your persona ahead of time because it develops from the choices you make as you draft, revise, and polish. Nevertheless, as you write it's a good idea to be thinking consciously about the image you want to present to your reader.

Model Topic: Preliminary Analysis of Persona

Credibility: I want to come across as someone who knows traditional children's literature, has worked with teachers and librarians in presenting such literature, and knows the sexist impact of the typical hero legends.

Tone: I want to sound concerned but not angry. I will acknowledge the problems in finding appropriate literature and show respect for teachers, librarians, and publishers who deal with the problem every day.

Voice: I will acknowledge a personal stake in the paper because of my strong interest in women's issues. I will sound reasonable and confident that my audience is also interested.

MESSAGE

As the last step in analyzing your writing situation, decide on the message you want to give your readers. It's not necessarily the same as your purpose. Although you'll refine your message as you write and revise, starting with a clear message in mind will help anchor your draft as you work.

Here are two variations of a possible message for the model paper.

Model Topic: Preliminary Message

1. The traditional children's classic books show almost no women as heroes or leaders, making it difficult to find role models of strong independent women for girls in elementary school.

2. In order to counteract the stereotyped view of women presented in most classic children's books, today's elementary classroom teachers and librarians need to find and promote books that will furnish positive role models of strong females for both boys and girls. They also need to pressure publishers to produce more appropriate books.

EXERCISES

1. Here is a sample showing how one might go about analyzing the audience for a specific writing situation:

   The writing situation: A young person applying to the board of elders of a church for a tuition scholarship to a college affiliated with that church.

Audience analysis: A group of mature men and women who want to spend their church's limited resources wisely. They want to be sure that the person who gets the scholarship is an active church member who has a good academic record and can demonstrate that he or she needs financial help to go to college. They would also like to know whether the applicant plans to work while in school and what career plans he or she has.

Write a similar analysis for the audience for these writing situations:

A. A letter to a local service club such as the Rotary Club or the Optimists asking the members to donate $5,000 to a fund you are raising to update the computers in your child's third-grade class.

B. A letter to your local representative in Congress urging him or her to support a bill subsidizing child care for single mothers who are returning to school.

C. A brochure for middle school students that promotes a one-day early career awareness fair at the public library. The goal of the fair is to persuade ten- to twelve-year-olds to enroll for science and math courses in middle school so they will be prepared to take precollege courses in high school.

D. A letter to the city council supporting a proposal before them that would create a twenty-mile paved bike trail around the city.

2. Here is a sample showing how one might analyze a reader's reasons for reading a particular piece of writing:

An article on buying antique clocks: The readers of this article would read it to find out where to shop for such clocks, how to tell if they were genuine, what features to look for in good antique clocks, and how much they might have to pay for the clock that they might want to buy.

Write a similar analysis of readers' reasons for reading the following:

A. An article on what one should take into consideration when buying a cellular telephone.

B. An article on reading levels of students in the city's public schools.

C. A magazine profile of a popular country western star.

3. Here is an example of the way one might analyze a writer's purpose in a specific writing situation:

An article on white-water canoeing: The writer of this piece would probably want to let readers know what white-water canoeing offers to people interested in outdoor activities, what kinds of skills it requires, where one might go to participate in the sport, and how much it costs.

Make the same kind of analysis of writer's purpose for the following writing situations:

A. An article for parents on the pros and cons of buying computers for preschool children.
B. A letter to your state representative urging him or her to support or oppose a bill that would make it mandatory for people to vote in state and national elections in order to keep their driver's licenses.
C. A brochure on the benefits of exercise, to be distributed to a company's employees.

4. Here is an example showing how one might analyze the persona he or she wanted to create for a writing situation:

Driver writing to a judge to appeal a six-month suspension of a driver's license because of too many speeding tickets: The writer wants to communicate the image of a sober, industrious person who has learned his lesson and who must be able to drive in order to keep working.

Analyze the persona a writer might want to create in these writing situations:

A. A lawyer is writing to a school board to explain why it cannot fire a teacher who has worn a bikini in a bathing beauty contest.
B. A board member of the Battered Women's Center is writing to a local company to solicit a contribution for the center.
C. A citizen is writing a letter to the editor of the local paper urging support of the school bond election that is coming up in two weeks.

SUGGESTED WRITING ASSIGNMENTS

As a part of each assignment, write a one-paragraph analysis of your audience (including a statement about where your paper would be published and what your readers would want to know), a one-paragraph analysis of your purpose in writing, and a two- or three-sentence analysis of the persona you want to project in your writing.

Topic 1: Assume that you are in charge of publicity for an organization you belong to and have been asked to write a news release to announce *one* of the following events. Remember that when you write a news release, you hope to get a newspaper to publish it free; therefore, one of your audiences is the newspaper editor who decides whether to publish and the other is the group of newspaper readers you are hoping to reach. The news release should be around 250 words.

Events from which to choose:

A. The inauguration of the *Van for the Twenty-First Century*, a technology lab that will make regular rounds of all the area schools to show youngsters and their teachers some the coming opportunities in technology.
B. A low-cost twelve-week seminar for newly divorced men and women that will meet every Friday evening at a local church and be led by the associate pastor of that church, the Reverend Lucy Appleby.
C. A Halloween carnival sponsored by the Lions Club and featuring clowns, contests, pony rides, and face painting, the funds to go to the Lions' Fund for the Blind.
D. The first meeting of a new branch of Adult Children of Alcoholics.

Topic 2: Some law schools ask their applicants to submit as part of their application an essay answering this question: "Why do you think the admissions board of our law school should look favorably on your application?" In no more than 600 words, write such an essay. Before you write, make a careful analysis of your audience and the persona you want to present.

5

DRAFTING YOUR PAPER

 The act of writing harvests ideas from the top of your consciousness and brings new ones to the surface.

First drafts can vary greatly, depending on the kind of writing you are doing, on how important the writing is, and, of course, on your temperament and habits as a writer. Some writers can do a good job on a simple writing task in only one draft if they take pains with it and then edit it carefully. For more complex writing assignments, however, I think it helps to consider a first draft a *discovery draft*. Often a first draft is little more than an exploration. You can develop and focus it later.

WRITER-BASED AND READER-BASED PROSE

Sometimes it helps to think of your first draft as "writer-based" prose, written more as something to get yourself started than as an essay aimed toward a specific group of readers. This idea of writer-based prose can be useful not only when you're discovering your content but also when you are writing the first draft of an argumentative paper on an issue about which you feel strongly. Under those circumstances, you're likely to use forceful, emotional language even though you know you'll have to tone it down later.

In a writer-based draft you can get the anger out of your system and blister your opponents with terms like *disgraceful* and *outrageous* and not worry about whether you're being biased or irrational. But once you have vented your frustration, you need to go back to your draft and consider how you can revise it into "reader-based" writing that your audience would be likely to pay attention to.

For example, here's how writer-based and reader-based first paragraphs might look for the model topic about the need for books with female heroes:

> WRITER-BASED: Traditional children's literature is just sexist as it can be. In book after book of myths and legends, handsome brave men do daring deeds while the women—if there are any—sit around as victims waiting to be rescued. Or else the women are wicked queens or awful witches. It's obvious publishers and librarians don't care about girl students or the role models that such stories present them. The publishers are mostly men anyway, interested in publishing something safe so they can make money, and the librarians don't want to take the time to look for other books.

This is off-the-top-of-the-head stuff, written from exasperation. The writer sounds irrational and hasty, as if she may not have thought carefully about her facts. Such a beginning is all right to help her get started, but her angry tone is likely to alienate the very publishers and librarians she wants to convince. Now let's see how the writer could change the same paragraph into reader-based prose in a second draft:

> READER-BASED: Many of us fondly remember the tales of heroism and courage we heard in our youth—Hercules and his twelve labors, Jason's quest for the Golden Fleece, Theseus slaying the Minotaur. They're marvelous tales, and children love them. Recently, however, some of us have begun to think about the impact these traditional stories may have on girls—and on boys too. The stories portray women either as victims waiting to be rescued or as wicked queens or evil witches. Except for Hippolyta, queen of the Amazons, these classic tales for children show no strong women, no women leaders, no women performing feats of courage and daring.

This opening paragraph does a good job of laying out the main idea, but now the author has softened the angry tone that would put the reader on the defensive and instead set out to engage the reader's interest.

Not all drafts must be writer-based, of course. Often you can be thinking about your readers when you start to write and not let that concern interfere with generating content. But when you have trouble starting a paper or when you're doing exploratory writing, focus on expressing your ideas in writer-based prose at first; you can shift your approach later.

SOME SUGGESTIONS ABOUT OPENINGS

I want to emphasize again what I said in Chapter 3: *Don't take openings too seriously.* You can dig yourself into a hole trying to write the perfect opening, and it's not worth it. Get something down. You can fix it later.

In Chapter 9 I will make specific suggestions about ways to write good openings. Right now I want only to show some of the patterns professional writers often use to get started.

Illustrations

You might begin an essay with an example that previews the main point you are going to make. For example:

> Bernard Martin is at the stove, slicing garlic and ginger into a wok of sizzling peanut oil. With his black hair, widow's peak, glasses, and baggy sweats, he resembles a shy, rumpled Jack Nicholson. There's no hint of the anger that drives this former fisherman now staring into the future with no fish. Outside his kitchen window are Newfoundland's fog-shrouded fishing grounds. The austere scene—rocky cliffs, black water, and wooden boats—evokes sea ballads, not ecological plunder.
>
> —Susan Pollack, "The Last Fish," *Sierra,* July/Aug. 1995: 49

Such openings work well because they focus on specific details that are apt to be interesting to your reader and they give the reader a strong signal about what to expect in the rest of the essay. They also give you a concrete anchor from which to start writing.

Quotations

A quotation relating directly to your topic can become a good opening for a paper. For example, if you were going to write an article about an athlete's disenchantment with playing college football, you might begin:

> The English wit Oscar Wilde once said, "There are two tragedies in life: one is not getting what you want; the other is getting it." That irony resonates with George Hillary now that he has finished his first year playing football for Jefferson College, a year in which he tore a rotator cuff in his shoulder, clashed disastrously with the line coach, and went on scholastic probation.

Here's a professional example:

> "That book was wrong about us. There was a gun battle at Toronto, but we wasn't gunfighters and we wasn't thugs like Bonnie and

Clyde. All we wanted was the money. We was just businessmen like doctors and lawyers and storemen. Robbin' banks and trains was our business." Willis Newton's voice shrilled as he took exception to a book that had described the Newton boys—Willis and his three brothers—as "daring and desperate outlaws who had engaged in many gun battles with the law."

—Claude Stanush, " 'Every time a bank was robbed, they thought it was us,' " *Smithsonian,* Jan. 1994: 75

Starting off with a quotation immediately gives your writing a personal touch and suggests that you are well educated and alert and have good resources to draw on.

Tip: Unless you're aware of a particular quotation that fits your needs or know where to find one, don't spend much time looking for just the right one. It takes too long.

Anecdotes

An opening anecdote can work especially well because it catches the readers' attention with a visual image of people doing something and pulls them into the writing by arousing their curiosity. This anecdote about President Harry Truman's mother from an article on famous men and their mothers provides a good example:

Early in the evening of August 14, 1945, in the living room of her yellow clapboard house in Grandview, Missouri, a small, spry woman of 93, talking to a guest, excused herself to take a long-distance call in another room. "Hello, hello," the guest heard her begin. "Yes, I'm all right. Yes, I've been listening to the radio. . . . I heard the Englishman speak. . . . I'm glad they accepted the surrender terms. Now you come to see me if you can. All right. Good-bye."

"That was Harry," she said, coming through the door. "Harry's a wonderful man. He has a noble disposition and he's loyal to his friends. I knew he'd call. He always calls me after something that happens is over."

—David McCullough, "Mama's Boys," *Psychology Today,* Mar. 1983: 32

(It's interesting that in 1983 David McCullough was already writing about ex-president Harry Truman, who became the subject of his Pulitzer Prize–winning biography, published in 1992.)

Scene-Setting Descriptions

This strategy works well to set the stage for an article. For example:

> A rising sun was just beginning to illuminate the harsh beauty of the Badlands when an early-rising prairie dog emerged from one of the thousands of small dirt mounds decorating a swale of the Great Plains. By midmorning, the ground was alive with the golden-tan, foot-long rodents, which are only now becoming recognized as an ecologically crucial species with an uncommon power to affect the lives and surroundings of other creatures.
>
> —William K. Stevens, "Prairie Dog Colonies Bolster Life in the Plains," *New York Times,* 11 Jul. 1995: B5

Here's another:

> Sitting alert in the backseat of the Lincoln Town Car that has ferried him from Manhattan to Mount Vernon, [Denzel] Washington peers out of the tinted window and confronts the ghosts of his childhood.
>
> "You see that lady right here?" Washington asks in a hushed voice as Mohammed, our driver, navigates past a high-rise housing project that has seen better days. He points out a plumpish, graying, sad-eyed lady in conversation with another woman on a concrete sidewalk. "I think that's Mrs. McCutcheon. That's one of the guys I grew up with— I think that's his mom. I don't know what he's doing right now. He's one of my friends who went to prison for a while." Washington tells Mohammed to stop. "Let me see."
>
> —Lloyd Grove, "A League of His Own," *Vanity Fair,* Oct. 1995: 244

Generative Sentences

Another good way to start a paper is with a *generative sentence*, one that generates expectations in the reader's mind. For instance, here is a sample paragraph with an opening generative sentence:

> *Increasingly, doctors graduating from the best medical schools are choosing to practice only in the nation's largest cities, raising some serious questions about the quality of health care available to tens of millions of American people who live in small towns and rural areas.* One can understand the doctors' point of view. Trained in the best teaching hospitals and used to having sophisticated technology at their fingertips, they're reluctant to practice medicine in a town that may be a hundred miles from the nearest CAT-scan machine or intensive care unit. Yet no organization or agency is working to find ways to make the practice of rural medicine easier or more rewarding and, as a result, a very large part of our population has almost no medical care.

This opening sentence tells the reader what to expect from the essay and promises to generate specific additional information about the issue.

Here's a generative sentence opening a paragraph by a professional writer:

> *The social problems of urban life in the United States are, in large measure, the problems of racial inequality.* The rates of crime, drug addiction, out-of-wedlock births, female-headed families, and welfare dependency have risen dramatically in the last several years, and they reflect a noticeably uneven distribution by race. . . . [L]iberal social scientists have nonetheless been reluctant to face this fact. Often analysts make no reference to race at all when discussing issues such as crime and teenage pregnancy, except to emphasize the deleterious effects of racial discrimination or of the institutionalized inequality of American life.

> —William Julius Wilson, *The Truly Disadvantaged*
> (Chicago: U of Chicago P, 1987) 20

In this opening sentence the writer promises the reader that he will discuss the problems of racial inequality, particularly the manifestations he mentions. This generative sentence and the one in the previous example signal to readers that the writer is going to follow one of the most common thought patterns in informative writing: general to specific.

COMMON PATTERNS OF ORGANIZATION

Readers expect to find a pattern of organization when they read, especially when a writer presents an argument. Thus it's useful for writers to be aware of common patterns in argument and other expository writing, because such patterns can provide the organizing framework for a first draft. They are

- Reasoning from evidence

- Assertion and support

- Definition

- Cause and effect

- Comparison

- Classification

- Narration

- Process

Reasoning from Evidence

Writing that takes this form is roughly patterned on the so-called scientific method; that is, the writer gathers evidence, examines it, and draws conclusions. Here a columnist does just that by studying a report of the annual Report Card on Children's Health. After examining the evidence, she draws conclusions and writes her story:

> A new assessment of children's health in America shows an increase in drug and alcohol use among teens and an overall decline in children's health that has disturbing implications for society. The study, being released today by the American Health Foundation, shows an increase in cigarette smoking, as well as teen-age use of cocaine, crack, marijuana, and alcohol. Among the 68 areas of child health rated in the study, nine received lower grades than in 1994 while three improved. In other key areas the report shows poor performance and little improvement.

> —Rachel L. Jones, "Children's Overall Health Declining, Report Says," *American Statesman* (Austin), 2 Oct. 1995: A12

Here is another example of an argument constructed from statistical evidence:

> The last two decades have seen advances in the education and health of women around the world, yet hundreds of millions of women in both rich and poor nations are still significantly undervalued economically, denied access to political power, and kept down by crippling inequities under the law, according to a [United Nations] report issued today. . . . Seventy percent of the world's poor are women, and women make up 80 percent of its refugees.
> The report says that worldwide women have only 14 percent of top managerial jobs, hold 10 percent of national legislative seats, and 6 percent of cabinet-level positions. Only in the Nordic countries, led by Norway, have women reached the level of 40 percent or more in government ministries, in large part because of strong affirmative action policies, the study concludes. The United States, which is given the second highest overall human development ranking . . . falls to fifth place when income and health disparities between men and women are taken into account. If women's access to political power is factored in, the United States falls to eighth place.

> —Barbara Crossette, "U.N. Documents Inequities for Women," *New York Times*, 8 Aug. 1995

You can use this writing pattern in two ways: either you can give the evidence first and then generalize from it or you can state your conclusion first and then give the evidence on which you base it. In most cases, I prefer to state the argument first and then present the evidence. With that format you get your readers' attention and prepare them to accept the evidence more readily.

When you're arguing from evidence, keep these guidelines in mind:

1. *Use sufficient evidence.* Any writer needs to be careful not to fall into the common fallacy of overgeneralizing from scanty evidence, but usually you can make commonsense judgments about how large the sample needs to be. If you wanted to generalize about students' political beliefs at a college of 3,500 students, you would need to interview at least 200 students. Citing just three examples of dishonest officials as proof of corruption throughout the state would hardly be convincing, but if those three officials were all on the city council of one town, they could indeed demonstrate corruption in that town.

2. *Use a random sample.* The randomness of your sample is even more important than its size. You must be careful to choose a sampling method that will give you an accurate cross section of the population you are writing about. One way is to select every tenth person or every fiftieth person from a directory or list. But that list has to be relevant to the kind of information you want. If you were trying to find out how air travelers in your city feel about the local airport facilities, calling every fiftieth name in the phone book would not give you an accurate sample because many people don't travel. Instead you would have to choose a cross section of travelers who passed through the terminal on three different kinds of traveling days—perhaps on a business day, on a Saturday, and on a holiday weekend.

   When you want to get a random sample for other kinds of broader-based surveys you have to be sure that your sample includes representative groups chosen according to race, sex, income, education, occupation, and age. In general, the broader and more serious your claim is, the more carefully you have to plan your sampling strategies if you want to get convincing results.

3. *Use accurate evidence.* Be sure your facts are accurate. The force of this kind of reasoning comes from the *weight of facts,* and if your evidence seems flimsy or if skeptical readers spot a significant error, you'll quickly lose credibility. Be careful also to cite your sources. Unscrupulous writers can and do make up statistics to suit themselves, so you need to reassure your readers that your evidence comes from reliable sources that can be checked. In both articles cited above, the writers quickly reassure their readers by showing their sources are reliable.

> **Tip:** Present your evidence clearly, using all the tricks you can to make it readable (see Chapter 12 on document design, pp. 191–237). Readers quickly tire of facts, figures, and data if they're not skillfully presented.

Assertion and Support

We all use another common thought pattern, that of *assertion and support*. We do that when we make a claim, then back it up with reasons. Here's an example:

[ASSERTION]

Educators and parents need to go beyond traditional children's literature, which is often sexist, to find books that give girls portraits of women leaders and heroes

[SUPPORT]

because strong role models play a crucial part in a child's personality development.

Such arguments, typical of those that lawyers present in court, can be classified as *informal logic*. They don't go through all the steps of formal deduction or proof, but they make a rational appeal to common sense. Notice that there are deductive elements here:

Major premise: Girls need to read about strong females in the roles of leaders and heroes in order to develop autonomy in their lives.

Minor premise: Traditional children's literature has few positive role models for girls.

Conclusion: Therefore educators and librarians need to look beyond traditional literature to find books in which women and girls are leaders and heroes.

You can't *prove* an argument like this; the only thing you can do is state your claim persuasively and support it with sound evidence. You do that in a number of ways:

- Make your key assertion early but don't overstate your case. When you make absolute statements, such as "The traditional myths and legends are all sexist and unsuitable for children," you risk raising the hackles of your readers before you get started. If they can think of one contradictory example, you've damaged your credibility.

- Select your supporting reasons with your audience in mind. That's not as cynical as it sounds. It doesn't mean you falsify or distort your evidence. It does mean you consider your readers' interests and biases and, among the many reasons you can give, you choose those you think will appeal to them, just as you adapt your tone and style.

- Cite authorities and studies to support your case. Go beyond your own opinions to read in the relevant area and find articles confirming your points. When you give statistics, cite their source.

- Keep a civil tongue in your head (so to speak). If you want to convince readers, they have to feel that you respect them. Nasty labels like "bloodsuckers," "sleazeballs," "fascists," and "big spenders" only make you look like a juvenile calling names. True, some entertainers are making fortunes indulging in such tactics, but they're working in another medium, one not noted for good taste or judgment.

    When I write critical essays, I remind myself that one day I may meet the person whom I am criticizing, and I want to be able to look him or her in the eye and not be ashamed of what I've said. I believe the public debate that democracy requires should be conducted in civil, restrained language.

Definition

Another natural thought pattern that one can use to organize writing is *definition*. We use definitions when we want to persuade, explain, or evaluate. Often they form the basis of essays or even whole books. The historian Barbara Tuchman, for example, wrote her book *The March of Folly* to define "woodenheadedness" in national affairs. Plato's *Republic* is a definition of justice.

The most common methods of defining are these:

- Attributing characteristics:
    A quality day-care center must have separate rooms for different age groups of children, an area for outside exercise, professionally trained personnel, and carefully chosen toys and playground equipment.

- Analyzing parts (this can overlap with attributing characteristics):
    The student body at today's urban colleges is richly diverse, made up of retired people as well as full-time students, of immigrants from

all over the world as well as native-born Americans, and of welfare parents as well as young, affluent students.

■ Giving examples:
Typical urban universities are the University of Illinois at Chicago, Northeastern University in Boston, the four-year colleges in the City University of New York system, and the University of Louisville in Kentucky.

■ Stating function:
The function of the public urban college or university is to make quality education accessible at a reasonable cost to those large numbers of citizens who cannot or do not want to leave their home areas.

Definition is a particularly useful pattern of organization when you write a paper or an argument in which you are *judging* or *evaluating.* You can use it to create a standard or yardstick for the way something ought to be, then apply that standard to an existing institution or situation and show how it should be changed. In a 1990 article in the *New York Times,* educational leader Albert Shanker used the French system of child care as a model by which the United States might judge its own system. He listed the French system's characteristics as

■ Being available to all children regardless of family income

■ Employing highly trained personnel who are well paid

■ Providing universal preventive health care

■ Offering a variety of care options

He then went on to argue that by failing to provide comparable care, the United States is cheating its children. Definition plays a crucial role in this kind of argument about moral principles or ethical issues.

Cause and Effect

A cause-and-effect pattern is one of the first options you should consider for organizing a paper. A fundamental mode of thinking, it can be used in a number of ways. For example, it would work well in explanatory papers on topics like these:

What are the effects of diabetes on pregnancy?

What was President Lyndon Johnson's role in passing the breakthrough civil rights legislation of the 1960s?

What impact has sharply increased sports vehicle sales in the 1990s had on gasoline consumption in the United States?

It would also work well in exploratory papers on topics like these:

What is the relationship between increased educational opportunities for women and declining birth rates in developing countries?

Has legalizing gambling in thirty-seven states undermined the work ethic in the United States?

What would the effect be of restricting welfare payments to single mothers who had more children while on welfare?

Cause-and-effect arguments are particularly useful when you want to convince readers who you suspect may not share your values. Rather than argue from the controversial basis of what's moral or right—controversial because your readers may not agree with you—you'll do better to make a pragmatic argument. Talk about good and bad effects, about what works and what doesn't.

For example, you may feel strongly that your neighborhood should be recycling papers and bottles yet notice that few families are participating in the program that invites them to fill and set their blue recycling bins at the curb every Monday morning. It's become almost a moral issue with you, and you'd like to knock on doors and shake your finger at everyone who isn't participating. But you know such an approach isn't likely to do much good. What might work is an article in your neighborhood newsletter pointing out that since the city has a "pay-as-you-throw" trash collection policy, families could save up to 50 percent on their city services bill every month by recycling instead of throwing out their newspapers and bottles.

In constructing an argument, then, look for ways to show your readers that what you propose will have good effects, that it will solve an important problem. In fact, cause-and-effect arguments are often problem-solving arguments and, as such, have wide appeal.

Tip: Cause-and-effect arguments become suspect when they suggest easy solutions to hard problems.

Circumstantial Arguments

Sometimes you may want to make a cause-and-effect argument in terms so compelling that your audience will almost have to agree with you. In that situation you can construct a *circumstantial argument,* one in which you claim that the chain of cause and effect is so strong that if A occurs, B is inevitable. When you want to make this kind of argument, choose language that conveys great urgency. Here are some typical phrases:

"Under the circumstances, we have no other choice . . . "

"We are forced to take these steps . . . "

"Given this situation, we must . . ."

"We have no alternative . . ."

For example, in writing an environmental impact statement, you could point out that if a manufacturer continues to use a local lake for cooling, the water temperature will rise enough to cause an increase in algae and pollute the lake. Or in arguing for an increase in the dues of an association you belong to, you could stress that increased costs for rent, utilities, and paper will bankrupt the organization if it does not get more income. Carefully constructed arguments from circumstance are hard to refute, so if you think your case is a particularly strong one, reach for those phrases that signal a crisis.

Comparison

Another good way to employ common thought patterns in your writing is to draw *comparisons.* In drawing a straight comparison, you simply show likenesses or differences that illustrate and strengthen the points you are making. For example:

- To prepare an analysis of the advantages and disadvantages of instituting "flex-time" as company policy, you could cite the experiences of several other companies that have adopted flex-time.

- To persuade your readers that they should begin an exercise program, you could give figures that compare the blood pressures of exercisers and nonexercisers.

- To argue the benefits of a free-market system as compared to controlled systems, you could compare the productivity of farmers in the United States to that of farmers in countries that have state-controlled farm programs.

Hard-fact comparisons like these are particularly effective when you are writing a report for a business or professional audience who want data to help make a decision. Straight comparisons also work well when it's important to your readers that they be perceived as meeting standards and staying up to date on everything. For example, college administrators often respond quickly to the suggestion that their programs or faculty might not be as good as those of comparable institutions and will do what they can to keep up with other colleges and universities.

While hard-fact comparisons can be convincing, often they are also dull. They work best if you present them with colorful charts and graphs. Fortunately that's not hard to do these days with so many sophisticated programs available to help you produce graphic demonstrations. See Chapter 12 on document design for suggestions.

Analogies

For a more striking kind of comparison, turn to analogy. You can use an opening analogy to catch the readers' attention and bring them to a flash of recognition. For example, here is a lovely analogy that immediately draws the reader into the article:

> Like Galileo's observation that the earth revolves around the sun, the A. C. Nielsen Company's report of an unexpectedly sharp drop in the national television audience last winter has altered the accepted view of reality. And like the telescope Galileo used, a new instrument—the "people meter"—provided the new information. The big three networks are fighting the conclusion and trying to force the messenger to recant. But like those who believed the sun circles the earth, they seem fated to find themselves on the wrong side of the revolution.
>
> —Randal Rothenberg, "Black Hole in Television," *New York Times,* 8 Oct. 1990: D1

And look at this:

> They are the P. T. Barnums of the flower kingdom, dedicated to the premise that there is a sucker born every minute: a sucker, that is, with wings, a thorax, and an unquenchable thirst for nectar and love. They are the orchids, flowers so flashy of hue and fleshy of petal that they seem thoroughly decadent. And when it comes to their wiles for deceiving and sexually seducing insect pollinators, their decadence would make Oscar Wilde wilt.
>
> —Natalie Angier, "The Grand Strategy of Orchids," *The Beauty of the Beastly* (Boston: Houghton, 1995) 44

The ability to write such vivid analogy is partially a talent, of course, but it's one worth trying to cultivate. Good writers are always looking for the apt comparison, the right image that will clarify the unfamiliar by linking it to the familiar. In fact, Angier, a science writer for the *New York Times,* puts it like this in the introduction to the Pulitzer Prize–winning book from which the above quotation comes:

> In delving into the science of molecular biology, I'll do anything to come up with similes or metaphors. I do it for myself, to make the abstract concrete, and I do it in writing to keep the plot going.

Remember, however, that analogies can't prove a thesis; they only clarify and strengthen it.

A Fortiori Reasoning

Another useful pattern of comparison is the *a fortiori* argument (pronounced ah-for-shee-or-ee). The term means "from the stronger." When we use this kind of reasoning we claim that if a person or institution can do one difficult thing, then it is logical to expect it can do a similar but easier thing—that is, reasoning from the stronger case, we assume they can do the lesser. This kind of comparison underlies comments such as "If our city can pass a bond issue to build a new ten-million-dollar stadium, it should be able to pass a less expensive bond issue to build new primary schools."

The from-the-stronger approach to developing an argument relies on the kind of commonsense reasoning that all of us use when we appeal to the readers' sense of what is logical and consistent. For instance:

- If we can spend billions of dollars to prosecute and imprison drug dealers, why can't we spend a few million to strengthen our drug prevention and rehabilitation facilities?

- Gambling in the United States is a forty-billion-dollar industry; then why do we say we can't afford a national health-care system?

- If people have to pass a test and get a license to drive a car, shouldn't they also have to pass a test and be licensed to be parents?

One must be careful, however, not to let *a fortiori* arguments deteriorate into oversimplification of the issues. Often such arguments become little more than outraged complaints about priorities, and they can be hard to develop effectively. Issues of apparently conflicting priorities are usually more complex than they seem. So although these arguments can be good for capturing an audience's attention, it's not a good idea to depend totally on *a fortiori* comparisons.

Narration

Although we usually think of narration as simply storytelling, writers of nonfiction use it in many ways. Scientists and psychologists use narration for case studies, and professionals often base their reports on narratives. Many writers use personal narrative as the foundation for powerful arguments. The following paragraph begins an essay by an African American woman in which she explains why she feels she has to tell her story in order to refute the easy stereotypes that have marked much discussion about welfare:

> Growing up on welfare was a story I had planned to tell a long time from now, when I had children of my own. My childhood on Aid to Families with Dependent Children (A.F.D.C.) was going to be one of those stories I would tell my kids about the bad old days, an urban legend equivalent to Abe Lincoln studying by firelight. But I know now I cannot wait, because in spite of a wealth of evidence about the true nature of welfare and poverty in America, the debate has turned ugly, vicious, and racist. The "welfare question" has become the race question and the woman question in disguise, and so far the answers bode well for no one.

> —Rosemary Bray, "So How Did I Get Here?"
> *New York Times Magazine*, 8 Nov. 1993: 51

Bray goes on to tell an extended, moving story about her mother's struggle to raise four children on welfare in Chicago in the 1960s. Three of those children went to college: Bray herself graduated from Yale and went on to become a reporter for the *New York Times*.

Wendell Berry, William Raspberry, Maya Angelou, and Maxine Hong Kingston are among the many writers who use personal narratives as the basis for argument, reporting, or social commentary. Good biography, of course, also comes from good storytellers. David McCullough, author of *Truman*, *The Great Bridge* (the story of the Brooklyn Bridge), and *Mornings on Horseback* (the biography of young Theodore Roosevelt), is a master. The historian Barbara Tuchman made the story of one French noble family the unifying motif of her major book, *A Distant Mirror: The Calamitous 14th Century.*

When you build a paper around narrative, remember that good narrators use concrete, vivid language to *show* their readers what is happening. They strive for visual elements to add *presence* to their writing. See more in Chapter 8 on some ways to achieve those visual effects.

Process

A *process* paper is a "how-to" paper; it could range from a sheet of directions for assembling a doghouse to a book titled *365 Days to a More Beau-*

tiful You. Typically, the person doing a process paper leads the reader through a series of steps chronologically, explaining and illustrating, sometimes with diagrams. These days, with more desktop publishing tools readily available to people who write with computers, writers can turn out effective process papers that are more illustration than text. One sees these frequently in newspaper articles that seek to explain complex procedures.

Much of the day-to-day writing that goes on in technology, business, and the professions is process writing, and to function effectively in those fields, most people have to master the art of writing clear process papers. In some fields, such as engineering and computer science, achieving clarity is not easy, and executives in those professions often require that their people take special courses in technical or scientific writing. For the most part, however, writers who have trained themselves to write clear and direct expository prose can also become good process writers of nontechnical papers. Many of the suggestions in other chapters for organizing and developing your writing will help you with process writing.

CHOOSING AND COMBINING METHODS

It's useful for every writer to know about and be able to recognize the common patterns of organization. It's also useful to know that certain patterns are likely to work well in certain situations, as I pointed out earlier in recommending cause-and-effect arguments when you know your audience may be hard to convince. I also habitually use assertion-and-support patterns or reasoning-from-evidence arguments for skeptical readers who I know place great stress on logic.

But I also know that many experienced writers seldom stop to think about what kinds of argument or patterns they are going to use when they write. Rather they rough out what they're going to say, gather their material, make notes, and start writing. They could probably identify the patterns they're using—an argument from circumstance or an extended definition, for instance—but they're not conscious of those patterns as they work. And they seldom write according to just one pattern, but move from one to another as the topic seems to demand.

So don't feel that you need to pick a pattern for your writing and stick to it as you work; combine them when it seems useful to do so. Know what the patterns are and what their possibilities are: just don't feel enslaved by them. Use them creatively—to help you generate material and to give structure to your writing. Use them pragmatically—to put your argument in its most persuasive light.

KNOWING WHEN YOU HAVE AN ADEQUATE DRAFT

So how do you know when you have an adequate first draft? First drafts can vary a great deal because writers differ so much in skill and temperament and because those of us who are plodders are likely to spend considerable time on a first draft even though we tell ourselves not to. But I believe it's possible to set up criteria for an adequate first draft, one that is ready to be reread and revised.

First, an adequate first draft shows that the writer has invested time and thought in the paper. It's a good-faith effort that takes the assignment seriously and makes an intelligent, earnest response to it. The writer who tosses off a superficial draft because he or she is in a hurry or because it won't be graded is working in bad faith. Other readers, including an instructor, don't want to spend their time critiquing a draft into which the writer has put very little effort.

Second, an adequate first draft is reasonably complete. The main idea should be clear and should be at least partially developed with some examples and support. An outline with a few paragraphs doesn't qualify as a draft, nor does a polished opening followed by a description of the rest of the paper. A first draft might lack a solid conclusion, but it should be substantial enough for the reader to understand fully the argument the writer is making and how that argument will be developed.

Third, an adequate first draft must be legible and easy to read. Your instructor and those you are working with in a revision group deserve a clear, readable copy. You can't expect them to waste time figuring out what you're saying. So double-space, leave wide margins, print a dark copy that can be photocopied, and number your pages.

EXERCISES

1. Working with two or three other students in a small group discussion, consider what illustrative examples or anecdotes a writer might use as an opener for papers on these topics:

    A. Advantages of starting one's college education at a community college.

    B. The reason some professional athletes command multimillion-dollar salaries.

    C. Why television soap operas are popular on many college campuses.

    D. The purpose of instituting multicultural courses in a college curriculum.

2. Here is an example of a generative sentence that could help you get started writing a paper about the admission process for many prestigious colleges:

Many prestigious colleges such as Michigan, UCLA, Yale, and Johns Hopkins rely too heavily on objective machine-scored tests that cannot measure motivation, perseverance, or creativity and that may be culturally biased against minority candidates or nonnative speakers.

Construct a similar generative sentence that could provide the basis to start writing on one of these topics:

A. Your reasons for choosing the profession you plan to enter.

B. An explanation of the Internet.

C. The place of high school football or basketball in your home town.

D. Your response to extremely violent movies such as *Pulp Fiction, Assassins,* or *The Terminator.*

3. Review the sections on arguing from evidence and assertion/support arguments. Then working with two or three other students, write down the claim you would make for each of these topics and jot down ideas about what kind of supporting evidence you could use:

A. Computer hackers who disrupt a university computer system should (or should not) be charged with a felony offense.

B. Professors should (or should not) be allowed to require their own textbooks in courses they teach.

C. The disparity between the multimillion-dollar salaries of athletes and entertainment stars and the income of the average college-educated worker is (or is not) a problem.

4. Write out cause-and-effect arguments that you could use to support or oppose these propositions:

A. Several states are recommending the passage of concealed weapon laws that allow individuals who take a prescribed training course on gun safety to carry a concealed gun on their persons or in their cars.

B. In recent budget negotiations, a committee of your state legislature has proposed cutting the appropriation for research at state universities by 7 percent; write to the committee giving your reasons for agreeing or disagreeing with the proposal.

C. The Federal Communications Commission should put tighter regulations on advertising beer and wine.

5. Working with two or three other students, create short narratives or anecdotes that could be used to start a paper on one of these topics:

   A. The drinking problem that is becoming serious among both men and women on many campuses.
   B. The increasing number of students who, because of financial pressures, must spend six or seven years completing a degree.
   C. The need for stricter measures to rid areas around your college of itinerants who congregate there.

SUGGESTED WRITING ASSIGNMENTS

Before you start your draft, write a preliminary analysis of your audience and purpose, using the guideline questions from the previous chapter (pp. 40 and 42). Put these analyses on a separate sheet to be turned in with your draft.

Topic 1: Collect several brochures from various places around your campus and community; some good sources are the offices of campus agencies such as the Student Financial Assistance Office, Student Dean's Office, Student Union, and the University Credit Union. Other possible sources are doctors' offices, banks, grocery stores, and so on. With other students in your class, analyze these brochures to see how they present information.

Now draft a brochure for an agency or institution, giving as much information as you can squeeze into no more than 500 words. The writing should be clear, simple, and lively so the audience can read the brochure quickly and absorb the information easily. Several possible topics are listed below, but you might also get an idea from one of the brochures you examine.

   A. A brochure on how students can establish good credit ratings.
   B. A guide to student recreation for budget-minded students.
   C. A brochure on health services available to women students.
   D. A brochure on how to look for on-campus jobs.
   E. A guide to popular music spots for students.

For ideas about arranging your text and for possible graphics, see the sample brochure in Chapter 12.

Topic 2: Draft an argument for or against one of the propositions below, using one or more of the patterns of argument discussed in this chapter. Your audience for this should be your campus newspaper, and your argument should not run over 500 words, the maximum for the "guest opinion" column.

A. Your college should (or should not) require each student to take two courses in cross-cultural studies before he or she can receive a degree. Such courses might be in African American or Latin American literature or history, in women's studies, in sociolinguistics, or in Middle Eastern history or art.

B. Your college is proposing to increase student fees for the coming year but has promised that it will consult with students on how those fees will be spent. Argue for your priorities for spending such fees.

C. A student organization called Students Older Than Average (SOTA) is protesting the spring round-up parade on campus, which features elaborate floats that are partially subsidized by student activity funds. They argue that they get no benefits from the floats because most of them aren't on campus over weekends. They want the proportion of the activity fund that they contribute, several thousand dollars, to be spent for a campus lounge where commuting students could relax between classes. Argue for or against their proposal.

6

REVISING

Experienced writers who care about doing good work plan on revising almost everything they write. They don't expect to sit down and write a report or an essay and be finished with it in one or two sessions. Rather they see revision as an essential part of any important writing project, something they plan on as part of their writing schedule. Often, particularly with exploratory writing, they expect to develop a piece of writing *through* the revision process. They depend on revising to help them accomplish three goals:

1. It will help them generate additional material as they work.
2. It will help them focus their message.
3. It will help them polish and tighten their writing.

When you begin to look at revising this way, as a process by which you continue to develop a piece of writing rather than one by which you correct it, you should find it easier to write. No longer do you have to get everything right the first time. A draft is just a draft, something to work with, not something you're committed to. It also helps to know that experienced writers have some reliable and systematic strategies for revising, and that those strategies can be learned. This chapter discusses those strategies.

This chapter assumes that when you begin revising, you have an adequate first draft, one that meets the criteria given on p. 66 in Chapter 5 on drafting.

THE REVISION PROCESS

Different Kinds of Revising

Not all revising is the same. Because different revision goals call for different processes, I divide revising into three stages.

1. *Large-scale or global revising.* This can involve

   ■ Shifting or narrowing the focus of your paper

   ■ Redirecting the paper to better suit the audience

   ■ Modifying the main purpose of your paper

   ■ Making substantial cuts or expanding certain sections

   ■ Reorganizing the paper to change its emphasis

These are substantive changes that significantly affect content.

2. *Small-scale or local revising.* This can involve

   ■ Adding examples, anecdotes, and details for color or interest

   ■ Combining, rearranging, or changing sentences

   ■ Cutting excess words and phrases; getting rid of clutter

   ■ Adding charts, illustrations, or graphics if appropriate

   ■ Rethinking and perhaps rewriting the opening and closing paragraphs

   ■ Improving word choice, particularly verbs

   ■ Strengthening transitions

   ■ Improving tone and polishing style

These changes affect style, not content. They're important because you want your paper to engage and favorably impress your readers, but they don't alter your thesis.

3. *Editing and proofreading.* This involves

- Checking details for accuracy and consistency.

- Improving the appearance of your writing by dividing it into paragraphs, inserting headings, and breaking up long passages with subheadings, diagrams, or lists

- Eliminating obvious repetition

- Checking spelling and punctuation

- Proofreading for spelling, grammar, and typographical errors

The major distinction among these three kinds of revision is this: Authors themselves should do the large- and small-scale revising because only they know what they want to say and how they want to say it. It really violates a writer's work to have someone else make significant changes, even though outsiders can and often do make useful suggestions.

But an outside editor can make the editing changes because they are corrections, not revisions. Nevertheless, writers should usually do their own editing. The surface details focused on in editing are very important to audiences, and you can't depend on someone else to edit your writing as carefully as you would. See Chapter 10 for guidelines about editing.

A PLAN FOR REVISING IN STAGES

After you've finished your first draft, consider how important this particular document is to you—is it an essay you're going to submit for a scholarship application or a major term paper for a course? If you feel that the paper is very important, allow yourself enough time for several drafts. Don't sell yourself short by waiting until the last minute and turning in a paper that's less developed and edited than it could be.

Revision Strategies: Stage One

1. Working from a printed copy, read the draft slowly and thoughtfully. What strengths do you feel the paper has? What obvious gaps do you see? Make notes about possible changes. Review any comments you've had from your fellow writers and/or your instructor, and make notes about which of their suggestions you want to incorporate into your revision.

2. Keep reminding yourself that you are going to make only major

changes in this first round and don't let yourself get bogged down in details. DON'T start out doing a sentence by sentence, paragraph by paragraph revision.

3. Start by looking at your main idea and focus. Is your main point clear? Have you kept your topic narrow enough to be adequately developed in the space you have?

4. Specifically define your audience and think about what questions they would expect you to answer. Have you answered those questions? Are you giving your readers fresh information that will interest or inform them?

5. Review the organization of the paper. Does your development follow a pattern that will be quickly apparent to your readers? Could you improve the paper by rearranging some of your points?

6. Ask yourself how well you have supported your thesis or your argument. Do you need additional evidence to strengthen your argument?

Revision Strategies: Stage Two

You should now be working from a solid second draft that is tightly focused and written to a specific audience. Your main idea should be clear and adequately developed with good support and examples, and you should be fairly well satisfied with the way your paper is organized. At this point go through these steps:

1. Do you need more examples to illustrate some points or an anecdote or analogy to add a concrete image? Would an illustration or chart enhance the paper?

2. Reread your sentences to see if you can cut out excess words or repetition. Try to get rid of strung-out phrases or heavy-duty noun phrases. Get rid of clutter. (See pp. 11–12 in Chapter 2.) Can you rearrange or revise some sentences to make them agent/action sentences? Are there places where you should add people to your writing?

3. Consider the language you've used, particularly verbs. Can you use stronger, more direct verbs in some places? Is your language lively and concrete?

4. Do you have tight connections between sentences and between paragraphs? Do you need to improve transitions?

5. Reread your opening and closing paragraphs. Does the opening paragraph engage the reader immediately and forecast what's ahead? Does the last paragraph give the reader a sense of closure? Revise either or both if necessary.

MODEL PAPER

Here is the first draft of a model paper that a student might write for an upper-division class in English education or in women's studies. It is primarily an explanatory, persuasive paper that reflects considerable research and thought.

AUDIENCE: Readers of the *Hornbook Magazine*, a publication of the International Reading Association that is read by public and school librarians, elementary teachers, and professors of elementary education and reading. They are interested in ideas that will help them provide good reading for children and that will promote literacy. Parents who sometimes see this journal are a secondary audience since they are concerned about finding stories that furnish good role models for their daughters and sons.

PURPOSE: To point out the need for more books that provide good models for girl readers. Because we all understand our world through the stories we read and hear, it's very important that girls read and hear more stories about strong women leaders and heroines in positions of power who have behaved valiantly and had an impact on their worlds. Unfortunately, almost all of the traditional literature about heroes focuses on men; women play subordinate roles or are cast as witches. In this paper I want to persuade teachers, librarians, and publishers to promote and initiate stories about women heroes and to see that they become part of the reading curriculum for elementary schools. The paper should be no more than 1,500 words, the limit specified by the magazine editor.

WANTED: STORIES ABOUT VALIANT WOMEN

For the past two years, I have been a volunteer reader in an Austin elementary school that focuses on making every child a reader. They have had remarkable success because teachers and volunteers in the school work together to communicate the joy of books to these children, many of whom come from homes where there are few readers and fewer books.

MALE ROLE MODELS DOMINATE TRADITIONAL MYTHS AND LEGENDS. In choosing stories to read to these second and third graders, the librarian and I agreed to begin with the traditional myths and legends that form part of the cultural heritage of the Western world. There's abundant material—beautifully illustrated collections that feature Hercules and Odysseus, Prometheus and Jason, Theseus and Bellerophon, as well as King Arthur, Robin Hood, John Henry, Pecos Bill, William Tell, and Johnny Appleseed. As the school year went on, however, I became uncomfortably aware how few women appeared in the stories. Even boys in the classes began asking, "Why aren't there any women in these stories?" My explanation that most women stayed home in those days sounded lame indeed.

Worse, when women do appear in the stories, often they are victims waiting to be rescued like Andromeda and Eurydice; villainous witches like Medusa and Grendel's mother; or, at best, helpers like Ariadne and Medea. Possible exceptions such as the fleet-footed Atalanta and Hippolyta, the Amazon queen, don't appear in the most popular collections. So the girls in these classes heard nothing of brave and valiant women—no stories that would help them envision themselves as heroines and leaders, women who might aspire to fame and honor.

Yet we know that all of us are molded by the stories we hear and read. Hero legends shape boys' ideas of what it means to be a man. The hero must leave home to search for a prize, risking his life and overcoming obstacles to get his reward. But there are no comparable hero legends for girls, no adventure stories showing girls who take risks and persevere to earn honor and fortune. Lacking such stories, girls' ideas are shaped by the myths of romance, as Debold, Wilson, and Malavé point out in their book *Mother Daughter Revolution*. The women in romantic legends focus their lives on men and depend on their beauty to get ahead. A shining prince will rescue Snow White from the wicked stepmother because she is so beautiful; Prince Charming will carry Cinderella away from her life of drudgery because she is innocent and lovely while her stepsisters are ugly and cruel. That modern myth maker, Walt Disney, has kept to this tradition; in his stories—*Sleeping Beauty, The Little Mermaid, Snow White*—women are rescued or they give up their own identity to get their man.

Where then are today's girls going to find the models of leadership and strength they need if they are to become leaders and achievers? While there are a few outstanding contemporary books that show girls as brave and enterprising—*The Island of the Blue Dolphins* and *Julie of the Wolves*—there are almost no storybooks for young girls that show valiant women from the past, women in roles of power and leadership.

HISTORICAL MODELS AVAILABLE FOR STORIES ABOUT VALIANT WOMEN. With a little research, one can find abundant historical material on such women. Boudicca, the queen who led her tribe against the Romans in first-century Britain, is the best known, but there are many others. Some of them are Semiramis, who captured the throne of Babylonia in the ninth century B.C.; Zenobia of Palmyra, who led her troops to capture half of Asia Minor in the third century A.D.; the Rani of Jhansi, who led her people against the British in the Indian rebellion of 1857; and Queen Jinga of Angola, who successfully fought the Portuguese invaders of her country in the seventeenth century.

Fine stories could also be written about the legendary Amazon queens Penthesilia and Hippolyta as well as about the heroic Vietnamese sisters, Trung Trac and Trung Nhi who, in A.D. 39, led their country's first uprising against the Chinese. As the historian Antonia Fraser says in the opening chapter of her book *The Warrior Queens*, "many women have found in the crucible of war the fiery process which has guaranteed them passage into the realms of honorary men." Valiant women appear in several biblical stories, and later history offers two outstanding models of courageous women in the great medieval queen, Eleanor of Aquitaine, and the warrior maiden, Joan of Arc.

THE CONVENTIONAL WISDOM ABOUT STORIES FOR BOYS AND GIRLS. Why then have editors, authors, and publishers neglected these important historical sources of inspiring stories for girls? There's no single reason, of course, but the answer lies partly in the conventional wisdom that has long influenced the publishing establishment. That wisdom holds that girls will read books for boys, but boys won't read books for girls—thus why not play it safe and publish those books boys will like, particularly since another tenet of conventional wisdom holds that since it's harder to get boys to read, it's important to cater to their tastes.

It's time to challenge such excuses for not providing girls with the stories they need. First, since there have been no legends of adventure and heroism that feature women leaders, we don't at all know that boys wouldn't read such books if they were well written and attractively done. For example, *The Island of the Blue Dolphins*, which features a courageous girl heroine, is an international best-seller. Second, meeting girls' need for strong role models that will help them envision themselves as leaders and achievers is as important as catering to boys' preferences in order to entice them to read.

What can be done? First, as educators we must take the lead in urging publishers to seek out and promote books that feature valiant and dynamic women in leadership roles. In recent years we've had good success in getting publishers to include many more multicultural books in their offerings—the range of offerings is now quite impressive. If we ask for more books about women leaders, we should have similar success. Then we need to talk to the organizations that award the Caldecott and Newbery awards for outstanding children's books and suggest that they join us in asking publishers for more books about valiant women.

As educators we need too to weave stories about heroic women into the curriculum of elementary schools and into the literature for adolescent girls. It is in the early grades that girls begin to absorb their pictures of what the world is like—to give them no heroines in those years is to deny them access to the models they need. Adolescent girls also badly need stories about achieving women. A study by the American Association of University Women shows that when girls enter middle school, they often lose the confidence and independence they have in their preadolescent years and begin to depend on fashion magazines like *Seventeen* and *Glamour* for their success models. Too often the message from those models equates success with getting a man.

We need also to connect with the parents of children and remind them that stories about brave, adventurous women should be a part of every modern child's cultural heritage. Without such stories, girls and boys have trouble imagining a world where women can aspire to power and leadership, where they can achieve the power and the glory with which we reward those citizens who serve their countries. All our children need role models, but until now those that embodied courage and daring have been almost exclusively male. It's past time to move beyond such a limited vision.

Stage One Revisions

On rereading this paper and getting comments from another reader, the first major change the author decided on was to *reorganize* the paper and move the main point into the first two paragraphs. The next change was to *shift the focus.* The second reader suggested putting more emphasis on the need to change the school curriculum to include books about strong women.

Then the author decided she should *give the audience more information* about some of the examples she uses, realizing that she was assuming her readers knew a great deal about history and legend. She also needed to *give more specific answers to the second reader's questions* about what should be done.

Stage Two Revisions

After the author made these changes, she went through the second draft again and decided on these small-scale changes. First, and most important, she needed *a stronger, more engaging opening paragraph and a better closing paragraph.* The opening paragraph in the first draft takes too long to get to the topic and the last paragraph in the first version seems weak and clichéd. Next she *cut out excess phrases* such as "with a little research," "of course," and "at all" and substituted "Girls begin early to absorb their pictures" for "It is the early grades that girls begin." She also *cut the quotation* from Antonia Fraser, deciding that it added little to the argument, and she *deleted personal information* about reading to children.

MODEL PAPER REVISED

[To avoid repetition, this version of the model paper incorporates the first and second revisions as well as final editing changes. See p. 147 in Chapter 10 for comments on final editing changes.]

NEEDED: STORIES FOR GIRLS TO LIVE BY

Stories are central to all our lives. The myths and legends of our culture interpret that culture for us and give us a sense of our own possibilities. How can young people imagine that they might become heroes or leaders or explorers if they have never heard stories about heroes and leaders and explorers? Unfortunately, however, the myths and legends of our Western culture offer young girls little sense of their possibilities. The traditional literature taught and promoted in our schools and in our books is male-centered and offers few role models that encourage girls to excel or to become leaders.

Consider the tales of heroism and courage that so many of us heard and loved as youngsters. Hercules and the twelve labors, Jason's quest for the Golden Fleece, Theseus slaying the Minotaur, Odysseus killing the one-eyed monster Polyphemus—these represent just a few. Beautifully illustrated books filled with these stories and dozens of others crowd the shelves in bookstores and libraries.

NEGATIVE IMAGES OF WOMEN FILL TRADITIONAL MYTHS AND LEGENDS: Yet if one looks at the roles that women play in these tales, they're patronizing and negative. Women are victims waiting to be rescued—Andromeda chained to the rock waiting for Perseus to free her and Eurydice trapped in Hades until Orpheus comes for her; or they are malevolent creatures—Medusa, the Gorgon whom Perseus kills, and Electra, who persuades her brother to kill their mother. At best, they are helpers like Ariadne, who guides Theseus through the labyrinth and Medea, who helps Jason steal the Golden Fleece. Even a possible winner like the fleet-footed Atalanta loses her race because she allows herself to be distracted by the golden apples her opponent uses to trick her.

The list of hero legends goes on—Siegfried, King Arthur, Robin Hood, William Tell, Pecos Bill, John Henry, Tarzan, to name just a few. Stories like these show boys what it means to become a man. The hero must leave home to search for a prize, risking his life and overcoming great hazards to win fame and fortune. But there are no comparable tales about girls becoming women, none that show strong women performing feats of courage and winning prizes.

Yet we know that all of us are molded by the stories we hear and read. Lacking such stories, girls' ideas are shaped by the myths of romance, as Debold, Wilson, and Malavé point out in their book *Mother Daughter Revolution*. The women in romantic legends focus their lives on men and depend on their beauty to get ahead. A shining prince will rescue Snow White from the wicked stepmother because she is so beautiful; Prince Charming will carry Cinderella away from her life of drudgery because she is innocent and lovely while her stepsisters are ugly and cruel. That modern mythmaker, Walt Disney, has kept to this tradition; in his stories—*Sleeping Beauty*, *The Little Mermaid*, *Snow White*—women are valued because of their beauty, they are passive victims waiting to be rescued, or they give up their own identity to get their man.

Where then are today's girls going to find the models of leadership and strength they need if they are to become leaders and achievers? While there are a few outstanding contemporary books that show girls as brave and enterprising—*The Island of the Blue Dolphins* and *Julie of the Wolves*, for example—there are almost no handsome storybooks for young girls that show valiant women from the past, women in roles of power and leadership.

HISTORICAL MODELS AVAILABLE FOR STORIES ABOUT VALIANT WOMEN: Such women did exist—and one can find abundant material on them. Boudicca, the queen who led her tribe against the Romans in first-century Britain, is the best known, but there are many others— Semiramis, who captured the throne of Babylonia in the ninth century B.C.; Zenobia of Palmyra, who led her troops to capture half of Asia Minor in the third century A.D.; the Rani of Jhansi, who led her people against the British in the Indian rebellion of 1857; and Queen Jinga of Angola, who successfully drove the Portuguese invaders from her country in the seventeenth century.

Fine stories could also be written about the legendary Amazon queens Penthesilia and Hippolyta as well as about the heroic Vietnamese sisters, Trung Trac and Trung Nhi, who in A.D. 39 led their country's first uprising against the Chinese. Valiant women appear in several biblical stories, and more modern history offers two outstanding models of courageous women in the great medieval queen, Eleanor of Aquitaine, and the fifteenth-century warrior maiden, Joan of Arc.

THE CONVENTIONAL WISDOM ABOUT STORIES FOR BOYS AND GIRLS: Why then have editors, authors, and publishers neglected these important historical sources of inspiring stories for girls? One answer comes from the critic and professor Carolyn Heilbrun. In her book *Writing a Woman's Life* she says, "Power consists to a large extent in deciding what stories will be told, [and] male power has made certain stories unthinkable." The answer also lies partly in the conventional wisdom that has long influenced the publishing establishment. That wisdom holds that girls will read books for boys, but boys won't read books for girls—thus why not play it safe and publish those books boys will like? That view is reinforced by another tenet of conventional wisdom that holds that since it's harder to get boys to read, it's more important to cater to their tastes than it is to seek out books for girls.

It's time to challenge such excuses for not providing girls with the stories they need. First, since there are so few legends of adventure and heroism that feature women leaders, we don't know that boys wouldn't read books about heroic women if they were well written and attractively done. *The Island of the Blue Dolphins* was an international bestseller even though a courageous girl is the sole protagonist. Second, just as recent authors are turning to tales and legends of various ethnic groups to introduce young readers to customs and cultures other than their own, today's authors need to honor women leaders of the past in order to expand the consciousness of both boys and girls about what women can do. When boys learn early that women can play a vital role in history, they're more likely to grow up to accept women leaders in all areas of their lives.

HOW THE SITUATION CAN BE CHANGED: What can be done? The first step should be to enrich the curriculum in the elementary schools by adding stories about strong, achieving women not only to the library shelves but to the history, science, and language art courses. Such stories must become part of the curriculum. It is in the early grades that girls begin to absorb their pictures of what the world is like—to give them no heroines in those years is to deny them access to the models they need. If girls were to hear stories about Queen Boudicca of Britain, Queen Jinga Mphandi of Angola, and Sacajawea, the woman guide for Lewis and Clark, they would be less likely to respond to the Hercules myth as one second-grade girl did by saying, "Oh, I'd like to have a husband like that."

Adolescent girls also badly need stories about achieving women. A study by the American Association of University Women shows that when girls enter middle school, they often lose the confidence and independence they have in their preadolescent years and begin to depend on fashion magazines like *Seventeen* and *Glamour* for their success models. Too often the message from those models echoes the romantic myth and equates success with getting a man. If teenage girls had the opportunity to read about women heroes like Eleanor of Aquitaine and the Rani of Jhansa, they might see that women can do well on their own.

Finally, as educators we must take the lead in urging publishers to seek out and promote books that feature valiant and dynamic women in leadership roles. In recent years we've had good success in getting publishers to include many more multicultural books in their offerings so that the curriculum would resemble the diversity of the student population. The range of multicultural offerings is now quite impressive. If we ask for more books about women leaders, we should have similar success. Publishers will produce what the public wants, and if educators insist on more books about women in strong roles, those books will appear. We should also confer with organizations that award the Caldecott and Newbery awards for outstanding children's books and explain our concerns. If they were to join us in asking publishers for more books about valiant women, our argument would be even more persuasive.

Through magazines and school organizations, we need also to connect with the parents of children and remind them that stories about brave, adventurous women should be a part of every modern child's cultural heritage. Without such stories, girls and boys have trouble imagining a world where women can aspire to power and leadership, where they can earn the status and rewards that traditionally have been given mostly to men. One way to change a culture is to change the stories it lives by. It's time to begin.

REVISING IN PEER GROUPS

In many writing classes today, students work together in peer groups to help each other with revising. Such groups work well for a number of reasons:

1. Working in peer groups gives each writer a chance to write for an immediate audience other than the instructor.

2. Audience becomes a more real concern for writers who know they'll be discussing their drafts face-to-face with their readers.

3. Working in peer groups gives writers a chance to discuss their drafts with someone who does not have the power of a grade over them. This situation makes for a more open and productive exchange of opinion.

4. Writers working in groups can get immediate feedback on a draft, getting constructive responses as they develop their papers.

5. Working with other writers increases many writers' confidence. They find that other writers also struggle to get started and that most writers' first drafts are less than excellent.

6. Working in groups can also help writers now and later when they must work on a project with other writers. Working in groups, writers learn the skills necessary for succeeding in a collaborative enterprise.

Guidelines for Working in Writing Groups

Working in groups can be difficult at first. Sometimes students are reluctant to comment on each other's work, protesting, "Who am I to criticize other people's writing?" My answer is, "Don't think of peer review as 'criticizing' someone's writing. You're responding to it as an interested reader who has questions and suggestions and may have useful feedback to give the writer."

Giving others good feedback means avoiding two extremes. You shouldn't say everything is wonderful for fear of hurting someone's feelings, nor should you be hypercritical, picking on surface errors. Neither response is helpful. Instead, try to give the kind of feedback you would like to get yourself—a thoughtful response that reflects sympathy with what the writer is trying to do.

When you start to work in groups, observing certain ground rules will help to get a productive conversation started:

1. Establish the rule that no one starts out by apologizing for his or her draft or by making excuses. By definition, drafts are works in progress that the writer intends to develop, and making excuses only wastes everyone's time.

2. Concentrate first on *what* the writer is saying and make a serious effort to understand his or her central idea and purpose. Don't let yourself get distracted by word choice or minor grammatical errors.

3. Remember that a draft conference is not the place to argue with a writer about his or her ideas. You may strongly disagree with what a writer is saying, but your job now is to help that writer express those ideas effectively.

4. When you are responding to a first draft, focus on large-scale concerns. Save comments on style and surface features until you're responding to the second draft.

Responding to Drafts

In my class I use response sheets for responding to students' drafts instead of writing on the papers themselves. I have found this keeps me focused on large-scale concerns and on the priorities I want to emphasize in the class. To make the most of the response sheets below, fill one out for each draft you receive from other members of your small groups, and use them as the basis for discussion in group conferences. With this system, each student leaves his or her draft conference with written and oral comments to draw on in revising.

RESPONSE SHEET FOR LARGE-SCALE REVISION

Author's name _____

Title of draft _____

Name of person responding to draft _____

1. What strengths does this paper have? What works well?

2. To what extent does the writer seem to be keeping the audience in mind? Any suggestions for improvement?

3. What does the writer's purpose seem to be? Any suggestions for improvement?

4. How well does the draft focus on a central topic? Any suggestions for improvement?

5. What questions might a reader have after reading the draft?

6. What additional examples might improve the paper?

7. What are two suggestions that could be made for the next draft?

8. General comments?

RESPONSE SHEET FOR SMALL-SCALE REVISION

Author's name _____

Title of draft _____

Name of person responding to draft _____

1. What is especially interesting or effective about this draft?

2. What good stylistic features do you find? Suggestions?

3. What seems to be the central idea of the draft?

4. How well does the draft seem to address its audience?

5. Comment on the opening paragraph. Suggestions?

6. Comment on the organization of the draft. How well unified is it?

7. What suggestions, if any, might one make about cutting at some places?

8. At what places, if any, might additional details or examples help?

9. Comment on the conclusion.

10. Questions and general comments.

REVISING UNDER PRESSURE

Admittedly, I've presented an idealistic model for revision in this chapter, one that is painstaking and time-consuming. Nevertheless, I think it's one that many authors try to follow when they are writing for publication. But you won't always have time to write three drafts of a paper or tinker with your sentence structure and word choice in order to turn out really polished work. That's particularly true on the job, where you may be asked for a report or analysis in twenty-four or forty-eight hours: no extensions granted. What happens to revising under such circumstances? Do you resign yourself to turning in a sloppy piece of writing?

Absolutely not, if you can possibly help it. Bad writing costs too much, especially on the job. That's why you should develop writing habits that will serve you well when the pressure is on. Here are some practices that will help:

1. Always plan to do two drafts. Try to write the first one quickly, running a mental check to see that you're covering the essentials. Print out a copy and read it carefully, making notes as you go. As you revise, consider whether you need to rearrange some things and delete others. And think about your audience! Are you giving them what they need? Then make a final copy, checking on spelling and mechanics as you go.

2. When you're not under pressure, work on internalizing some sentence patterns that strengthen and clarify writing. For instance:

   ■ Start your sentences with an acting subject.

   ■ Put people in your sentences.

   ■ Avoid passive verbs.

   ■ Use short, strong verbs when possible.

   ■ Avoid long introductory clauses.

   ■ Avoid strung-out noun phrases.

   The more conscious you become of these ingredients of good writing, the stronger your first drafts will be. See Chapter 8 for more suggestions.

3. Because you're not going to have time to move from writer-based prose to reader-based prose, keep your audience in mind as you write your first draft. Ask yourself,

- Am I over-explaining, telling them what they already know?

- Am I using clear language, not jargon?

- Does my writing have a straightforward, easy-to-follow pattern?

- Am I answering the questions they will have on the topic?

4. Be confident that you can turn out good work quickly. Thousands of writers from copywriters to newspaper journalists turn out amazingly good work almost on demand—it can be done. And the more effort you put into careful revision when you have time, the better you will get at revising under pressure.

WHEN TO STOP REVISING

Writing teachers and writing textbooks constantly stress the conventional wisdom that all good writing is rewriting, and mostly they're right. Everything we know about the writing process suggests that writing is generative, that it develops through stages, and that writers improve their work as they work through drafts and try out various options. For most writing tasks, however, one can reach a point of diminishing returns with revising. Even on important work, that point probably comes at the third or fourth draft.

If you have put serious efforts into three drafts and made significant changes as you worked, tinkering with words and sentences in the process, I doubt that writing another two or three drafts will improve your work substantially, at least not in proportion to the amount of effort invested. Don't let yourself be like the "bleeders" I described in Chapter 3, compulsive revisers who can't let their work go. For these reasons, consider carefully before you go on to a fifth or sixth draft:

1. When you have read and reread something a dozen times, you lose your distance from it and can no longer see its flaws.

2. You may be blocking your growth as a writer by worrying too much over the problems that one writing assignment presents. You would learn more by moving on to the challenge of a different project.

3. You run the danger of becoming a perfectionist who can't turn loose a piece of writing because it's not exactly right. But nothing is ever "exactly right," and you cannot improve your writing unless you are willing to expose it to the judgment of others.

Ultimately, you have to do some cost accounting about your revising. How much do you care about doing really good work? Are you willing to put in the extra eight or ten hours that it might take to turn a draft that would earn a B paper into an A paper? Are you willing to write and rewrite, get feedback, and rewrite again and perhaps again? Is the time that process requires a good investment for you?

Writers who ask themselves these questions often have second thoughts when they realize how much time and effort they will have to invest to revise solid, competent writing into first-rate writing, and they may decide to settle for less than the best because they have other priorities. That's a legitimate and often sensible decision. It's good to know, however, that most satisfactory writers *can* become good writers. Whether they have the time, energy, and will to do so is another matter. But anyone who decides he or she wants to be an excellent writer is going to have to work at revising. It can pay off handsomely.

7

HOLDING YOUR READER

If there's any way for your readers to get lost, they will.

Writers need to work consciously to keep their readers engaged and on track as they read. Once lost, they are hard to recapture. For that reason, it's useful to have some specific strategies for holding readers. I'll identify and explain seven of those strategies in this chapter.

But you should also remember that the most important way of holding your readers involves a principle, not a strategy. The principle is this: *Most readers will stay with you as long as they are learning something.* As long as you can give them information that interests or entertains them and teaches them something they didn't know before, you are likely to keep them reading.

SEVEN STRATEGIES FOR HOLDING YOUR READER

1. Make your writing visually attractive.
2. Choose a good title.
3. Write a strong lead.
4. Keep your writing tight and unified.
5. Achieve frequent closure in your sentences.
6. Chunk your writing into units and blocks.
7. Avoid antagonizing your readers.

MAKE YOUR WRITING VISUALLY ATTRACTIVE

When a potential reader picks up something you have written, its body language should say "Read Me." Of course different readers read the body language of print in different ways. A long passage of print with few breaks or illustrations won't usually put off well-educated and experienced readers, but it can easily discourage young or inexperienced readers. And when impatient readers—and there are lots of them—encounter pages of unbroken print with little visual appeal, they're likely just not to bother. So the writer who wants to be read needs to think about the first impression his or her paper, report, or article makes. Chapter 12 gives you much more information about this concept as does the section of this chapter about chunking your writing into units.

To get you started thinking about the visual impact of your writing, here are some general suggestions:

- Put your title, headings, and subheadings in a bold, easy-to-read type font. (See Chapter 12 to learn more about fonts.)
- Leave ample white space around titles and illustrations and between columns and paragraphs.
- Use charts and graphs to reinforce and dramatize statistical information or comparisons.
- Use illustrations and graphics to enhance your text when appropriate.
- Keep paragraphs fairly short, particularly when you're using a two- or three-column layout.
- Be constantly aware of ways to break your writing into units, using headings, boxes, borders, shading, and so on.

> **Tip:** You may want to postpone focusing on the body language of a document until you get to the small-scale revision or to the editing stage. When you're still drafting, such concerns may be premature.

CHOOSE A GOOD TITLE

Titles play a crucial part in getting off to a good start with your readers. In fact, your prospective readers will often decide whether or not to read what you write solely on the basis of its title. That's why it's so important that your title be clear, accurate, and, if possible, interesting. It should also do certain specific things.

First, it should predict the paper's content. Titles like "The Roots of Country Music" or "How to Get the Most Car Stereo for Your Money" are direct and accurate enough to immediately attract readers who are interested in those subjects. When you are writing a paper for a college course, a good title gets you a favorable start with your instructor. A title like "Irony in Shakespeare's Histories" is so broad it would immediately trigger an instructor's skeptical instincts; one like "Richard's Manipulation of Women in *Richard III*" makes a better impression because it shows the reader exactly what you intend to do.

Second, a title should catch the reader's interest. Provocative titles sometimes work well—it depends on the writing situation. If you're doing an opinion piece for the local or campus newspaper, you might want to catch your reader's eye with a title like "Does Sex Education Cause Sex?" You could title a paper for a political science class "Toxic Cash: How Lobbyists Poisoned the EPA." Be careful though. Some professors might object to opinionated titles. Questions can also work well for titles: for example, "What's Behind the Gender Gap Among Voters?"

Third, a title, particularly for academic papers or reports, should reflect the focus of the article. This one, "The Strange Disappearance of Civic America" (*American Prospect*, Winter 1995), does that. So does "Dolphin Courtship: Brutal, Cunning, and Complex" (a chapter from the book *The Beauty of the Beastly* by *New York Times* science writer Natalie Angier). A subtitle after a colon helps to make a title very specific. Here's an example: "This Pen for Hire: On Grinding Out Papers for College Students" (*Harper's*, June 1995).

Finally, if you're writing something that you hope to publish, include in it key words that will make it easy to find through a computer search. For example, an article on ways to start a small business while you are in college should have the words *small business* and *college* in it—perhaps "How to Work Your Way Through College by Starting a Small Business." A report on Margaret Sanger should have her name and some reference to her accomplishments—perhaps "Margaret Sanger, Family Planning Pioneer." Test your title for papers like this. Put yourself in the place of the cataloger or file clerk who may some day have to classify your paper but doesn't have time to read it. Will he or she be able to easily decide from the title where it should be filed?

In most instances resist the impulse to give your writing cute, facetious, or deliberately ambiguous titles. They're tempting, particularly if you like jokes, but they're risky. You may mislead your readers or annoy them because they don't share your sense of humor, and, of course, such titles are the ones most likely to be misclassified.

WRITE STRONG LEADS

The most important sentence in any article is the first one. If it doesn't induce the reader to proceed to the second sentence, your article is dead. And if the second sentence doesn't induce him to continue to the third sentence, it's equally dead. Of such a progression of sentences, each tugging the reader forward until he is safely hooked, a writer constructs that fateful unit the "lead."

—William Zinsser, *On Writing Well*, 5th ed.
(New York: HarperCollins, 1994) 142

Leads can make or break you with your reader. Even if you're not competing for that fickle audience of magazine readers, you can still lose your readers' attention if you write weak openers. Editors, managers, and members of admission committees are also busy and impatient people, and when manuscripts, reports, or application letters come across their desks, they make preliminary decisions in two or three minutes. You have that long to convince them that what you are going to say will be interesting or informative or useful to them.

"But," you say, "that's not really true of professors. They have to read what I write." Well, yes and no. Professors are busy and impatient too, and although they may have to read your papers, they don't have to like them or take much interest in them. If your writing begins with a long dull paragraph or if you fail to make your main point clear, you stand to lose your reader—even when it's your instructor. If he or she can't grasp your main idea by the middle of the second page, you're in trouble.

Because your lead is so crucial, think carefully about how you handle those first few paragraphs. You don't necessarily have to come up with a startling or gimmicky opening to catch your reader; in fact, in many writing situations, such an opening would be inappropriate and could do more harm than good. But keep in mind that every opening should do these things:

- Engage the reader's attention

- Make a promise or commitment

- Give readers a reason to continue reading

- Set the tone for the writing

Experienced writers write leads that meet these requirements in a number of ways; two of the most common are *leads that promise to intrigue* and *leads that promise to inform*.

The writer who wants to intrigue can do so with an anecdote, a quotation, an analogy, or an allusion of some kind. For instance, for a magazine article about the savings and loan debacle of the late 1980s, an author begins with this elegant first paragraph:

> Ever since the first Florentine loaned his first ducat to his first Medici, it has been one of the most shopworn clichés of the financial industry that the best way to rob a bank is to own one. This maxim, like all maxims, is rooted in a basic truth about human nature: to wit, if criminals are given easy access to large sums of money, they will steal, and under such tempting circumstances, even honest men may be corrupted. To forget this is to invite madness and ruin. In our time, such madness and ruin has visited in the form of the savings and loan scandal.
>
> —L. J. Davis, "Chronicle of a Debacle Foretold: How Deregulation Begat S&L Scandal," *Harper's*, Sept. 1990: 50

Davis attracts his readers with a promise to tell them about the circumstances that led to the savings and loan crisis.

Natalie Angier opens an article about scorpions with this intriguing paragraph:

> To the ancient Chinese, snakes embodied both good and evil, but scorpions symbolized pure wickedness. To the Persians, scorpions were the devil's minions, sent to destroy all life by attacking the testicles of the sacred bull whose blood should have fertilized the universe. In the Old Testament, the Hebrew King Rehoboam threatened to chastise his people, not with ordinary whips, but with scorpions—dread scourges that sting like a scorpion's tail. The Greeks blamed a scorpion for killing Orion, a lusty giant and celebrated hunter.
>
> —Natalie Angier, "Admirers of the Scorpion," *The Beauty of the Beastly* (Boston: Houghton, 1995) 97

The reader's attention is immediately engaged.

Here is a promise-to-inform lead from a *Smithsonian* article on astronomy:

> Ever since the human mind first grasped the immensity and complexity of the Universe, Man has tried to explain how it could have come into being.

The article goes on to explain the Big Bang theory of the origin of the universe and the formation of galaxies.

Here's another promise-to-inform lead:

> The fundamental crisis in black America is twofold: too much poverty and too little self-love. The urgent problem of black poverty is primarily due to the distribution of wealth, power, and income—a

distribution influenced by the racial caste system that denied opportunities to the most "qualified" black people until two decades ago.

—Cornel West, *Race Matters* (Boston: Beacon Press, 1993) 63

Which kind of opening is better, the one that intrigues or the one that informs? The answer, as always, is "That depends." Each time you write you have to decide according to what you perceive as your readers' expectations and according to your purpose in writing. Intriguing openers can capture fickle readers and persuade them to go on reading, but they can also annoy readers if they delay too long in getting to the point. Although the straight informative opening may not seem as interesting, often it is safer, particularly for documents in business or industry, because readers there generally want to go straight to the point. You'll have to make the judgment call.

All this being said, the fact remains that many writers have trouble with opening paragraphs precisely because they are so important. For that reason, I talk about them in much more detail on pages 137–39 in Chapter 9 on crafting paragraphs.

TIGHTEN YOUR WRITING WITH TRANSITIONS

Writing that is highly readable has a quality called *linearity;* that is, the reader can move steadily through it in a straight line without having to puzzle about what the writer means or double back to reread. Think how often you have bogged down in dense, difficult writing. If you could quit reading, you probably did. If you couldn't, you plowed on but groaned and cursed the writer who was making life so difficult for you. You don't want your readers to feel that way, particularly not readers who are in a position to penalize you for giving them so much trouble.

There are a number of strategies you can use to keep your writing unified so that your readers can move steadily along. They include the patterns of organization given in the earlier chapter on drafting as well as the transition devices discussed here. These are

- Links and nudges
- Directional signals
- Repeated words
- Conjunctions at the beginning of sentences

Links and Nudges

Links are the terms that hold writing together by signaling connections; *nudges* are the terms that give writers a little push from one point to another. You should have a stock of such terms at your fingertips to draw on.

Links	*Nudges*
also	this
moreover	then
for example	first
in addition	consequently
however	therefore
in spite of	next
nevertheless	thus
although	hence
similarly	since
not only	as a result
because	

For instance, here is a student paragraph with both links and nudges italicized:

> *Like* a rat that avoids electric shock, a child avoids contact with those who hurt him. *So* avoiding punishment, *except* as a last resort, is advisable. Punishment instills hate and fear and soon becomes an "aversive stimulus." *Also, because* the only real effect of it is to suppress a response temporarily, no permanent weakening of the unwanted behavior takes place. *And* as soon as the effect, *or* the sting of the spanking, wears off, the child repeats *it*.

Here is another paragraph in which the links and nudges are italicized; this one comes from the book *It Takes a Village,* by Hillary Rodham Clinton:

> *When* it comes to everyday life, *however,* parents have to concentrate on instilling self-discipline, self-control, and self-respect early on,

and *then* must allow their children to practice those skills the way they would let them exercise their muscles or their brains. *As* my mother taught me, *even* very young children can be given a sense of strength in the face of cruelty. Part of *that* strength comes from experiencing appropriate discipline.

—Hillary Rodham Clinton, *It Takes a Village*
(New York: Simon & Schuster, 1996) 15

Repeated Words

Although many of us try to edit out repetitious language when we revise our writing, repeating keywords, phrases, or stylistic patterns in a piece of writing can help focus your readers' attention on points you want to emphasize. This student paragraph furnishes a good example of using repetition as links within a paragraph:

Walt Disney's monumental idea for creating an *amusement park* began when he took his young daughters to an *amusement park* in Los Angeles. The girls were entertained while riding on the merry-go-round, but Walt was bored sitting on a bench eating peanuts. He realized the need for a place where children and their parents could have fun together. Impetus for his new *park* came from his own hobby, constructing his own backyard railroad. Trains were his boyhood passion . . . and he began to talk about building a railroad that would link the Burbank studios, then linked this idea to his conception of a new kind of *amusement park*. He realized that transportation and nostalgia were the key factors in making his *park* different. In July 1955, his dream became a reality with the opening of Disneyland.

The black poet Nikki Giovanni uses repetition very purposefully in this paragraph from her book *Racism 101*:

The fact of slavery is no more our fault than the fact of rape. People are raped. It is not their choice. *How the victim becomes responsible* for the behavior of the victimizer is well beyond my understanding. *How the poor are responsible* for their condition is equally baffling. *No one* chooses to live in the streets; *no one* chooses to go to sleep at night hungry: *no one* chooses to be cold, to watch their children have unmet needs. *No one* chooses misery, and our efforts to make this a choice will be the damnation of our souls. Yet such thinking is one of the several troubling legacies we have inherited from [W. E. B.] DuBois.

—Nikki Giovanni, *Racism 101* (New York: Morrow, 1994) 51

Using Conjunctions to Begin Sentences

The prejudice that many writers have against beginning a sentence with *and* or *but* seems to have grown out of the notion that because these words are called "conjunctions," they must always appear between two other words. Not necessarily. They are also strong signal words that tell readers what to expect next. Notice how the following writers have used *and* and *but* for this purpose:

> *Harvard Business Review* subscribers . . . recently rated "the ability to communicate" as the prime requisite of a promotable executive. *And,* of all the aspects of communication, the written form is the most troublesome.
>
> —John S. Fielden, "What Do You Mean I Can't Write?"
The Practical Craft, ed. Keith Sparrow and
Donald Cunningham (Boston: Houghton, 1978)

> If we hear a well-constructed, grammatical sentence, the ideas fall easily and quickly into the slots of our consciousness. *But,* if we hear a conglomerate, ungrammatical hodgepodge, we have to sort it out at an expenditure of time and effort.
>
> —Everett C. Smith, "Industry Views the Teaching
of English," *The Practical Craft*

But works especially well as the opening word of a paragraph that you want to highlight, because it states an important qualification or contrast to the content of the previous paragraph. Notice the effect in these examples:

> For the most part, readers are assumed to be ideal readers, fully prepared to relate to the fiction or poetry on the author's terms. This expectation is as it should be; it is appropriate for what we regard as creative writing.
>
> *But* a different expectation exists in business and technical writing where readers are busy executives who want the important findings up front, or are privates last-class who need information at a level they can understand, or somewhere in the bewildering range between.
>
> —Keith Sparrow and Donald Cunningham, "What Are Some
Important Writing Strategies?" *The Practical Craft*

> By contrast, a vigorous speech for Henry Wallace . . . touched off another noisy demonstration. . . . Wallace's delegate strength for the first ballot appeared to be gaining.
>
> *But* Hannegan, Flynn, Kelly and the others had been working through the night, talking to delegates and applying a good deal of pres-

sure to help them see the sense in selecting Harry Truman. No one knows how many deals were made . . . but by the time morning came, Postmaster General Frank Walker had telephoned every chairman of every delegation.

> —David McCullough, *Truman* (New York:
> Simon & Schuster, 1992) 318

These examples, selected from articles on business and technical writing and from a Pulitzer Prize–winning historian, should convince you that it is not a sin, or even a grammatical lapse, to start a sentence with *and* or *but*.

ACHIEVE FREQUENT CLOSURE IN SENTENCES

Another way to help your readers keep moving along is not to make them wait too long to discover meaning. Try to construct your sentences in a way that the reader can come to frequent *closure*: that is, the phrases and clauses that make up the sentence make sense in themselves. When you do so, your readers can process meaning as they read rather than having to wait until the end of the sentence before they can understand any of it. For instance, here is a confusing sentence from a student paper:

> Furthermore, *that the United States has the best medical technology in the world, yet ranks sixteenth among countries in successful births per pregnancy* results because a distressing number of women cannot afford early prenatal care.

The strung-out twenty-two-word subject in this sentence keeps readers in suspense for so long that they miss the verb, "results," on the first reading. If the writer had rearranged the ideas into units that had meaning in themselves, readers would not get lost. Here is a rewritten version with the units of thought marked off:

> Even though the United States has the best medical technology in the world, / it ranks below fifteen other countries in successful births per pregnancy / because a distressing number of women cannot afford early prenatal care.

Because readers can assimilate information more efficiently when it is divided into small units, in most situations you shouldn't let your sentences get too long and complex. But long sentences in themselves don't cause reading problems if they're constructed to come to frequent closure. That's evident in this 108-word sentence from a professional writer and educator. I've marked off the natural units of meaning.

> In the time I spent with her, / Pat committed to finding a few hundred dollars / so that teachers could take their students on a field trip; / con-

ferred with a reading teacher about her school's attempt to remodel its curriculum; / thought through with two other teachers at two other schools / the possibilities of starting small academies, / one of which would focus on health care; / worried that a principal was not delegating enough responsibility to her teachers; / worried, too, / that teachers were jumping on the small school bandwagon / without considering all the planning that would be necessary / —and worried, / therefore, / that some of their efforts would fail from limited foresight.

—Mike Rose, *Possible Lives* (Boston: Houghton, 1995) 156

CHUNK YOUR WRITING INTO UNITS AND BLOCKS

Another way of segmenting your writing to make it easier for your readers to follow is called *chunking;* that is, breaking up long units of writing into parts so that they will be easier to process. If you include too much information in one sentence or one paragraph, you risk overloading the mental circuits by which readers process information, and your readers either give up or have to go back to reread the material two or three times to absorb it.

Chunking is the principle behind grouping the digits in telephone numbers and social security numbers. Would you ever remember your sister's telephone number if it were written 2143889697? Or your social security number if it were written 328939775? If, however, the numbers are split into groups, they are fairly easy to process and remember: **214-388-9697** and **328-93-9775**. When numbers are written like this, you process each unit separately and put it into short-term memory before you come to the next unit—that's the secret of memorization.

You can chunk your writing to break up long sentences that are overstuffed with information or to divide paragraphs that include so many items that the reader gets lost. One way to do that is to break long sentences into shorter ones. For instance, here is a sentence so overstuffed that it's almost impossible to follow:

> With the tension in Iraq cutting off substantial oil imports and its announced intention to last out the boycott however long it takes, the worldwide increase in oil prices and the probable effect of armed conflict on new exploration, and the ongoing determination of both auto manufacturers and several branches of government to resist any real efforts to move toward substantial conservation measures, an energy crisis of some magnitude seems imminent.

However, if we cut up the sentence and reorganize it into manageable chunks, it becomes easy to follow:

For at least three reasons, an energy crisis seems imminent. First, the tension in Iraq is cutting off imports and its government says it will hold out against the boycott. Second, oil prices have increased worldwide and the prospect of armed conflict discourages new exploration. Third, U.S. auto manufacturers and several branches of government seem determined to resist any real efforts to push oil conservation.

Another excellent way to chunk an overloaded sentence or paragraph is to break the information into lists. For example, here's a sentence so overloaded that a reader would get lost halfway through:

The factors that keep individuals interested in their jobs are interesting responsibilities, wide range of duties, challenge, stimulation, recognition, chance to make a difference, status, relationship with others, being one's own boss, freedom to act, high-quality organization, and compensation.

Impossible! Now let's redo the sentence by creating a list:

These are the factors that keep individuals interested in their jobs:

interesting responsibilities	status
wide range of duties	relationship with others
challenge	being one's own boss
stimulation	freedom to act
recognition	high-quality organization
chance to make a difference	compensation

Whenever you find that you're loading a sentence or paragraph with more than three or four points of information, consider breaking it out into a list. (Notice how often I have done that in this text.) Such rearrangement can make a great difference in how your reader will respond to your writing.

For additional, more specific advice on breaking your writing into units, see Chapter 12 on document design, pages 191–237.

AVOID ANTAGONIZING YOUR READERS

My last suggestion on ways to hold your readers is psychological rather than editorial: Remember you will lose readers if you make them uncomfortable or angry. Most people are not willing to read or listen to someone who is attacking them or criticizing their beliefs. If you really want your audience to read what you are writing, you need to consider their emotions as well as their strictly intellectual reactions.

Sometimes, to be sure, you are writing for two sets of readers, particularly when you're writing an argument. Some of your readers—that group whose position you're criticizing—aren't likely to change their minds. You shouldn't worry too much about making them angry—it's probably inevitable. You should, however, take pains not to anger the other group— those readers who are undecided on the issue and whom you hope to influence. It's important to distinguish between these two segments of an audience when you're constructing your argument.

To avoid threatening readers whom you want to influence, keep these principles in mind:

- *Respect your audience.* Assume that your readers are intelligent and rational people of goodwill and that they will respond to reason. Rather than attacking their positions, try to discover what common interests or common goals you may have and work from there.

- *Use objective language.* Strong, biased words such as *disgraceful, vicious,* and *intolerable* are likely to trigger defensive reactions from readers who do not already agree with you. Their first response will be to argue rather than to pay attention to your point of view. For more suggestions, see the section on biased language, pages 116–21 in Chapter 8.

- *Learn to write provisionally, not dogmatically.* Learn to use the *subjunctive mood,* a much-neglected but extremely useful verb form that allows you to speculate, hypothesize, or wish, as well as to express a courteous and inquiring attitude in your writing. The careful writer should understand what the subjunctive forms are and when they should be used. They are used when one wants to express a point conditionally or to express wishes. For example:

    If Castle *were* in charge, he *would handle* the protesters well.

    I wish I *were* not *involved* in that proposal.

    If that *should* happen, the supervisor *would want* us to know.

    You *would be* a great help if you *were to join* us.

Occasionally *had* is combined with a subjunctive verb to talk about events that didn't take place. For example:

Had I thought of it, I *would have* written.

Had he known what he was getting into, he *would have* been appalled.

The subjunctive form of a verb should be used in clauses beginning with *that* when the main verb expresses desires, orders, or suggestions. For example:

The lawyer requested that her client *be given* a new trial.

We believe there should *be* a recount of the votes.

If you use these words in phrases like "If I were," "It might be that," and "We could consider," you create an atmosphere of cooperation and courtesy in which your readers can pay attention to what you are proposing because they are not forced to defend themselves.

EXERCISES

1. Working with other students in a small group, discuss these titles chosen from the table of contents of an essay anthology. How useful are they as forecasters of what the reader would find in the essay? As a group, decide which three titles are the most informative. Which three are the least informative?

   On Being Black and Middle Class

   Home

   The Stunt Pilot

   How to Get Out of a Locked Trunk

   Heaven and Nature

   On Seeing England for the First Time

   The Stone Horse

   The Killing Game

   Vital Signs

   On the Pilgrim's Path to Lourdes

2. Working in a group, try to draft titles that are both informative and provocative for papers written on these topics:

   A. Exercise as a major component in a weight-reduction program.
   B. A review of women students' paintings in a local art gallery.
   C. A comparison of child-care policies in France with those in the United States.

3. Working with other students in a group, evaluate these opening paragraphs taken from papers by advanced student writers. What is your response to these leads? Do they make you want to go on and read the papers themselves? What suggestions, if any, would you make to improve them?

A. Mike Frazier, manager of the 1984 U.S. Olympic Cycling Team, said to me in Dallas recently that many riders testing out as superior athletes statistically are consistently beaten by riders of less athletic prowess but superior skills. An interesting statement in light of the great physical exertion the sport requires. For instance, the 1990 Branders Jeans Tour of Texas covers more than 700 miles in eight days, including one rest day. During the 60-mile stage I saw the riders burned, according to Frazier, enough calories for two marathons.

B. Every year, our highways needlessly slaughter many thousands of people. And every year, people are reminded that wearing their protective safety belts would dramatically increase their chances for survival. And yet people continue to ignore such advice and suffer the consequences. In an attempt to solve this problem, this country has gone as far as to install systems that virtually force occupants of automobiles to wear protective safety belts. What happened? People resisted to such a degree that the legislation was finally repealed. So, obviously, another solution is needed if the population is to reap the benefits of being protected from their cars. Airbags are such a solution.

4. Write an opening paragraph for one of the topics given in Exercise 2 above. Then get together with two or three other students who have written on the same topic. Discuss the differences in your paragraphs and see if you can combine efforts to write one paragraph that all of you can agree on.

5. Here are two long but fairly readable sentences from professional writers. Mark each of them off into units of closure that reveal how the content is organized:

Once that fact is recognized, it may be possible to think again about the proper building blocks of a meritocracy—measures that do not seal fate at an early age, that emphasize performance in specific areas, that expand the pool of talent in more than a hit-or-miss way, and whose limits are always visible to us, so that we are not again deluded into thinking we have found a scientific basis for the order of lords, vassals, and serfs.

—James Fallows, "The Tests and the Brightest," *Atlantic*, 3 Feb. 1980: 48

In the last year, for instance, environmental organizations have suffered a sharp falling off in their direct-mail receipts not only because of the recession but also because the average donor no longer believes that the environment is threatened, while women's organizations, buoyed by anger from the Anita Hill–Clarence Thomas hearings and the looming battle over *Roe vs. Wade*, have experienced an upsurge in contributions.

—John B. Judis, "The Pressure Elite," *Ticking Time Bombs*, ed. Robert Kuttner (New York: New Press, 1996) 175

SUGGESTED WRITING ASSIGNMENTS

As a part of each writing assignment, write a detailed analysis of your audience that specifies characteristics they have that you need to keep in mind as you write, problems that such an audience might present, and what the audience would expect to get from your paper. Also analyze your purpose in writing, specifying what you hope to accomplish in the paper. If appropriate, include an accurate and descriptive title for your paper.

Topic 1: Imagine that you write for the entertainment section of a local news-paper or magazine. One of your weekly jobs is to eat at one of the major restaurants in the city and write a 300- to 500-word review of your experience there for the Saturday paper. Although all the better restaurants advertise in the paper or magazine, your editor wants an honest review that will let potential customers know what they can expect if they eat there. You are gradually building a reputation as a fair and reliable judge of restaurants and so you should keep that in mind as you write. Don't forget to mention prices.

Topic 2: The regents of your college or university are having hearings to deter-mine whether they should tear down the low-rent student housing that was built forty-five years ago from secondhand army surplus buildings. The hous-ing is unsightly and needs repairs; some of the regents have said that they think it is unsafe. If it is torn down, however, the apartments that would replace it would rent for almost twice as much as the present units, and the campus would be without any low-rent housing for at least two years.

   Prepare a ten-minute talk (no more than 750 words) against tearing down the buildings to be delivered at the meeting that the regents are going to hold. You will be the spokesperson for the married students who now live in the uni-versity housing.

Topic 3: Write a letter to the vice president for marketing of a major firm such as General Foods or Ralph Lauren trying to persuade him or her that the firm should no longer run a particular television commercial that you find offensive. Specify what you find offensive and why and try to give the vice president a good reason for dropping the commercial.

8

WRITING CLEARLY

The essence of good writing lies in the details.

If you want people to enjoy and profit from what you write, you need to work at writing clearly. It's tempting to think that clear writing must come easily to good writers like *New York Times* science writer Natalie Angier or Truman's biographer David McCullough. Almost certainly that's not the case. Most successful writers work very hard to achieve a graceful, lucid style; they know that in order to write clearly, they must concentrate and pay careful attention to details.

Just as the person who wants a flexible, lean, and smoothly functioning body has to work at it constantly, so the writer who wants clear, taut, and effective writing has to work at it constantly, revising and editing again and again. And as fitness-minded people need strategies for maintaining their bodies, so writers need strategies for producing clear writing. In this chapter I suggest several strategies; I try hard to practice them myself.

WRITE CONCRETELY AND SPECIFICALLY

Your readers will understand your writing more easily if you use concrete and specific language to make the abstract and general clear. *Abstract language* consists of words that refer to intangible qualities, concepts, ideas, or attitudes. We cannot grasp the abstract through our senses; we can only *conceive* of it mentally. Words like *loyalty, intelligence, philosophy, value,* and *evil* are abstract.

Concrete language consists of words that refer to the tangible and physical: that is, objects or qualities that we can know through our senses. We *perceive* the concrete. Words like *bottle, hot, kitten, car,* and *computer* are concrete.

But most words do not fall so neatly into these either/or categories. Instead we have to classify them according to a scale, place them somewhere on what semanticists call the *ladder of abstraction.* It is from that metaphorical ladder that we derive the term *level of abstraction;* we are also referring to that ladder when we talk about *high-level* or *low-level* abstractions. Here is how the ladder works:

   7. methods of communication
      6. telecommunication
         5. computer networks
            4. the Internet
               3. World Wide Web
                  2. Web site
                     1. http://www.paris.org

The phrase at the top is highly abstract and comprehensive; the phrase at the bottom is very concrete and individual. Each step down is a subdivision of the previous step.

Tightly related to the concepts of *abstract* and *concrete* are the categories *general* and *specific. General language* consists of words and phrases that refer to large classes of people, institutions, or activities or to broad areas of study or activity. Words and phrases like *college, housing, the medical profession,* or *the American people* are general.

Specific language consists of words and phrases that refer to individual instances or persons or to particular details and examples. Phases like *Queen Elizabeth, chocolate chip ice cream,* and *Masterpiece Theater* are specific. When someone says "Use specific details," that person is asking for individual examples. One could also describe the ladder of abstraction illustrated above as a scale that goes from the general to the specific.

At times, all writers have to generalize and use abstract language. If we didn't, we could never get beyond citing examples (specific acts of violence, say, such as a drive-by shooting) to arrive at a generalization about the larger problem (violence in our society). But if you want to help readers grasp your ideas quickly, learn how to use the personal, the concrete, and the specific to illustrate your points.

For example, an astronomy writer who wanted to help his readers understand the abstract idea of black holes used a concrete analogy of watching streams of traffic pour into a domed stadium. A writer who is writing about violent Mafia movies could illustrate the general class with specific films such as *Goodfellas, Casino,* and *The Godfather* I, II, III.

Use Specific Examples

When you use specific examples, you strengthen and clarify your writing in several ways.

First, you add the *weight of facts* to your writing and anchor it to reality. An article about the growing menace of teenage gang wars needs specific details such as information about the semiautomatic weapons gang members carry in New York and Los Angeles and the number of innocent victims killed in Houston in 1995. Such details are easily available from papers like the *Houston Chronicle* or the *Los Angeles Times,* or you can find magazine articles by doing a key word search in your library.

Second, specific details make your writing more interesting to your readers because they can learn from it. If you were writing an essay deploring the poor child-care system in the United States, it's easy enough to generalize about the problems, but you could make your readers see your point more clearly by giving specific details about the French system, which Hillary Rodham Clinton describes in her book about rearing children, *It Takes a Village.*

Third, specific details and facts enhance your credibility and make potentially skeptical readers pay more attention to your ideas. Most of us who are concerned with social problems can spin out broad generalities about issues such as racial injustice, the need for educational reform, and inadequate financing for drug rehabilitation programs, and our readers will agree with us. But an interested audience wants a writer to move quickly past generalities and platitudes and get down to details. The writers who hold their attention and earn their respect are the ones who show by specific comparisons, examples, and statistics that they have done their research and know their subject.

Of course, when you use specific and concrete details, you also take risks. When you give an example to illustrate a general statement, your readers may disagree with that example. For instance, if you claim that we must increase teachers' salaries to improve public school education, you're probably safe, but if you go on to claim that the experienced teacher who makes $35,000 a year is underpaid, a reader may challenge that statement. If you claim that in order to reduce the budget deficit, we must have tax reform, your readers will probably agree. That's a safe generality. If, however, you propose a national sales tax as the best solution, some readers will immediately disagree. But those are the chances you must take if you are going to move beyond generalities to gain your readers' attention and respect.

Make Your Readers *See* Something

When possible, make your reader see something. Most of today's readers are visually oriented, accustomed to a television-movie-billboard culture that stresses images, and they expect communication that engages their senses as well as their intellect. The strength of the visual appeal undoubtedly accounts for the breakthrough success of the Macintosh computer in the 1980s. New users took to it instantly and were able to master its programs because it literally showed them what to do by using graphics and images—sketches of desktops and file folders, paint brushes and trash cans, rulers and clocks and calenders—all designed to teach through the eyes and through association with familiar objects. Nearly all software programs now use similar icons.

You can do the same thing in your writing, not by long descriptions but by bringing in anecdotes, narratives, and allusions that engage your readers' visual imagination. Here are two professional examples; notice how they engage your senses:

> My father was a farmer with no use for fashions. He married and went into business for himself in the spring of 1946, raising laying hens, vegetables, and berries on a seven-and-a-half acre truck farm. Small-scale horticulture was his real interest. For the rest of his life, he devoted as much time and care to his gardens and orchards and beehives as to his row crops. The eggs he sold to the local plant, the berries and vegetables to the local grocers. It was hard labor, done mostly with his hands and a two-wheeled garden tractor, and it afforded a very meager living.

—Paul Gruchow, "Remember the Flowers," *Sierra*, Nov./Dec. 1990: 83

> Long voyages waxed longer for lack of [knowledge about] longitude, and the extra time at sea condemned sailors to the dread disease of scurvy. The oceangoing diet of the day, devoid of fresh fruits and vegetables, deprived them of vitamin C, and their bodies' connective tissues deteriorated as a result. Their blood vessels leaked, making the men look bruised all over, even in the absence of any injury. When they were injured, their wounds failed to heal. Their legs swelled. . . . Their gums bled, too, as their teeth loosened. They gasped for breath, struggled against debilitating weakness, and when the blood vessels around their brains ruptured, they died.

—Dava Sobel, *Longitude* (New York: Walker, 1995) 14

Here is an example that is comprehensible but less likely to engage readers' interest because they can't *see* anything happening:

> Regardless of the color, gender, or ethnicity of leaders and their constituencies, they must present the public with a balanced view of various

social categories. A description of the inequities that continue to exist need to be balanced with a discussion of the progress to date. . . . Commonalties among groups must again be part of our public discourse which currently highlights only diversity. We will not persist as a nation if we cease to believe that we have at least as much, and probably more, in common with one another than we have differences dividing us. To restore this sense of community in the absence of an external enemy, once provided by the "threat of communism," should be a major goal of our national leadership.

—Janet Saltzman Chafetz, "Minorities, Gender, Mythologies, and Moderation," *Responsive Community*, Winter 1993/94: 41

At first reading, one's mind hydroplanes right over the surface of the paragraph because there is not a single concrete or visual word in it. The reader can't *perceive* anything. The words *ethnicities, constituencies*, and *commonalities* do not refer to anything a reader can, at first reading, connect with people or reality. Although the content of the passage isn't particularly difficult, it's dull reading because the writing is so abstract.

Unfortunately, many students who encounter this kind of abstract writing assume that the harder something is to read, the more important it must be. They may also be afraid that they will be asked to write that kind of difficult and abstract style in order to get ahead in their professions. My survey of business and professional people shows that such fears are seldom justified. Again and again, such leaders show that they value clear writing and know how to write clearly themselves. Here is an example of clear writing from a book by Robert Reich, former secretary of labor under President Clinton:

No nation congratulates itself more enthusiastically on its charitable acts than America; none engages in a greater number of charity balls, bake sales, benefit auctions, and border-to-border hand-holding for good causes. Most of this is sincerely motivated and much of it is admirable. But close examination reveals that these and other forms of benevolence rarely in fact help the poor. Particularly suspect is the one-third to one-half of all private giving that derives from Americans in the top income-tax bracket. Studies have revealed that such donations do not flow to social services for society's less fortunate citizens—to better schools, community health clinics, or recreational facilities for impoverished people. Instead, most of the contributions of America's wealthy go to the places where wealthy people are entertained, inspired, cured, or educated—to art museums, opera houses, theaters, symphony orchestras, private hospitals, and elite universities.

—Robert Reich, *The Work of Nations* (New York: Vintage Books, 1991) 279

Downshift from the General to the Specific

Often you need to begin a paragraph by making a general statement, but then you need to shift quickly to a lower level of generality, using more specific and concrete language to clarify and reinforce the original broad statement. Notice that is what Robert Reich has done to illustrate his generalization about charitable giving in America. Here is another example that moves several steps down the ladder of generality:

> I once described to somebody what it is like to be a reporter in Beirut. It's as if you are standing there watching this white light of truth coming at you. But before it hits you it is refracted through this prism of Lebanese factions and fiefs and religious groups, so that before it reaches your eyes it is splayed out in fifteen different directions. Your challenge as a reporter is to grab a little bit of the blue band, and a little bit of the red band, and a little bit of the green band, and try to paint as close a picture of reality as you possibly can.
>
> —Thomas L. Friedman, "From Beirut to Jerusalem to Washington," *The Writing Life* (New York: Random House, 1995) 143

The author has started out with a general statement and expanded on it by giving specific and illustrative details. We call this process *downshifting*; it is a strategy that authors use frequently to make their writing clear. You will learn more about this useful technique in Chapter 9.

Choose Specific and Concrete Subjects for Your Sentences

When you can, use people or specific entities as the subjects of your sentences. When you do so, you give your readers a solid anchor early in the sentence and make the rest of it easier to follow. For instance, compare these two versions of the same sentence:

ORIGINAL: The affordability of hotels is one major factor that draws tourists to Baja California.

REVISION: Many tourists come to Baja California because of its cheap hotels.

The second version is easier and quicker to read because it begins with a specific and personal subject rather than an abstract concept and uses an active verb, "come," rather than the uninteresting verb "is."

Here is another pair:

ORIGINAL: Voluntary employee participation in the plan is requisite for its success.

REVISION: Employees must participate willingly in the plan if it is to succeed.

Readers understand the second version more quickly.

If you choose concrete, specific subjects for your sentences, you will almost automatically select stronger verbs to go with them. Abstractions can't *do* anything; therefore, you usually have to combine them with "is" verbs. For instance, if you begin a sentence with a subject like "desirability," you almost have to write "The desirability of the program is in question," or "Its desirability cannot be determined." Both are dull sentences because the reader cannot visualize either the subject or the verb. Abstract subjects also tend to attract passive verbs (see pp. 114–15).

Use Actor/Action Sentence Patterns

You can cut down the number of abstract subjects in your sentence if you try consciously to write *actor/action* sentences: that is, sentences in which your reader can tell immediately *who* is doing *what* to *whom*. For example, here are two versions of the same sentence:

> ORIGINAL: The instinctual response of a child who is accused of something is to deny responsibility.

> REVISION: Children instinctively deny responsibility when they are accused of something.

The reader understands the revised version more quickly because someone (children) is doing something (denying).

Here is another example:

> ORIGINAL: Technological expansionism and the increase in computers in the United States have led to more consumption of energy and less availability of resources for future generations.

> REVISION: As we expand our electronic technology in the United States and build more computers, we use more energy and leave fewer resources for future generations.

In the first sentence no actors appear so the reader can't tell who is doing what. The phrases "technological expansionism" and "increase in computers" don't indicate somebody is doing something. But when you identify the actor in the sentence as "we" and link it with the action verbs "expand" and "build," the sentence becomes much clearer.

Put People in Your Sentences

Putting people in your writing will do more to clarify and strengthen it than any other single strategy. When you bring people into your writing, you get rid of many of the abstract terms that cloud it; you're more likely to use strong, active verbs; and you usually make it more visual. For instance, notice the difference in these pairs of sentences when people are introduced into the revisions:

ORIGINAL: One barrier to fundamental change in the health-care system is the entrenched perception of national health insurance as an additional expenditure program.

REVISION: Because most people think of national health insurance as a program to spend more money, they resist real change in the health-care system.

The original sentence is stuffed with abstract phrases held together with one weak little verb: *is*. The reader can't see anything and gets no sense that people are involved. The revision, however, starts right off with "people" as the subject and follows with active verbs: *think* and *resist*. Thus the revision is much easier to read and understand.

Here's another example:

ORIGINAL: A workforce with a large proportion of functional illiterates is a problem for all who are dependent on a productive economy.

REVISION: When many workers can scarcely read and write, everyone suffers because we all depend on a productive economy.

The original sentence is readable, but impersonal and abstract. Because the revised sentence starts with people, it uses stronger verbs and emphasizes the human beings who are involved.

If you want to put more people in your writing but still get nervous about using *I* and *you* in your papers, remember that some outstanding writers use *I* regularly. For example, the respected essayist Lewis Thomas uses *I* frequently; the scientist Carl Sagan uses *I*, *we*, and *you* in his 1995 book *The Demon-Haunted World*; and you'll find many instances of first- and second-person pronouns in serious books and magazine articles. They're not necessarily taboo and can sometimes be used to excellent effect. You can avoid such pronouns if you want to sound very formal, but that doesn't mean you can't find other ways to add people in your writing. It's still a good idea.

Avoid Too Many Nominalizations

I call abstract words that are likely to clog your writing "heavy-duty nouns"; that's my term for nominalizations, nouns created by tacking endings onto verbs and nouns. Here are just a few examples:

capability	immediacy
recognition	modernity
competitiveness	accountability
viability	inclusiveness
enhancement	utilization
marketability	continuation

When you find your writing has filled up with words that end with *-ity, -tion, -ness, -ance, -ment,* and *-ism,* consider how you can thin them out. Some are absolutely necessary, of course, but not as many as you think. These clunky words have no life, no character—they're flabby terms, and used too often, they'll destroy a clear and readable style. Take a look at a textbook or article you find hard to read, and you'll find it filled with these unlovely, heavy-duty nouns. If you look back at many of the examples of poor writing I've used in this book so far, you will find that most of them are loaded with nominalizations.

SUMMARY OF STRATEGIES FOR MAKING YOUR WRITING CLEAR

1. Use concrete terms and specific examples.
2. Make your reader see something.
3. Downshift from the general to the specific.
4. Use actor/action sentence patterns.
5. Put people in your sentences.
6. Avoid too many nominalizations.

CHOOSE VERBS FOR CLARITY

Verbs are the lifeblood of writing. Because they affect not only clarity but also the tone and rhythm of anything you write, it's worth giving them special attention when you write and when you revise.

Use *To Be* Verbs Sparingly

Although you must occasionally use some form of the verb *to be* to convey certain ideas, style-conscious writers use it sparingly. It's a verb that connects and describes rather than acts, and it can easily get lost or over-whelmed by other words. For example:

> ORIGINAL: Greater deregulation and liberalization of the global marketing system and a subsequent lowering of international trade barriers that have barred competition *is* the goal of the conference.

> REVISION: The conferees *want* to deregulate and liberalize the global marketing system and thus *lower* the international trade barriers that have barred competition.

In the first sentence, the verb *is* gets lost in a thicket of abstract words; in the revision, the verbs *want* and *lower* describe actions so the sentence is clear.

In this paragraph by the professional writer Gordon Parks, notice how he carefully chooses active verbs to give a compelling image of the musician Duke Ellington:

> For me, and many other black people then, his importance as a human being *transcended* his importance as a musician. We had been *assaulted* by Hollywood grinning darky types all of our lives. It was refreshing to be a part of Duke Ellington's audience. Ellington never *grinned*. He *smiled*. Ellington never *shuffled*. He *strode*. It was "Good afternoon, ladies and gentlemen," never "How y'all doin'?" We wanted to be seen by the whites in the audience. We wanted them to know that this elegant, handsome, and awe-inspiring man playing that ever-so-fine music on that golden stage before that big beautiful black band was black—like us. (emphasis added)

> —Gordon Parks, "Jazz," *Esquire*, Dec. 1975: 140

Many kinds of writing—technical reports or critical analyses, for example—need only to be clear, not colorful. Nor do I recommend that you try to eliminate all *to be* verbs from your writing. But when you want to make your writing more interesting to read and easier to follow, opt for verbs that do something. And when you revise, check to see if you have overused *to be* verbs or begun too many sentences with "It is . . ." or "There are . . ."

Choose Economical Verbs

Your writing will be clearer and more effective if you make a habit of choosing one-word, direct verbs rather than strung-out verb phrases that incorporate nouns and adjectives. For example:

Why write . . .	*When you could write* . . .
be cognizant of	recognize
put the emphasis on	emphasize
is reflective of	reflects
make an attempt to	try
have an understanding of	understand
make a comparison to	compare
grant permission to	allow

Stretched-out verb forms, although not wrong, slow writing down and make it more formal. One such phrase here and there does little damage, but too many of them clog writing.

Prefer Active to Passive Verbs

A *passive verb* is a verb form that shows the subject receiving rather than doing the action. For example:

> Gun control *is considered* one of the major political issues of the 1990s.
>
> The gang members *were warned* that they would be prosecuted.

Cultivate the habit of revising passive verb constructions out of your writing when you want to strengthen and clarify it. Passive verbs not only make writing impersonal and rather stuffy, but they make it harder to read for several reasons.

First, with passive verbs, the reader often takes longer to find out what is going on.

Second, sentences with many passive verbs usually have fewer people and more heavy-duty nouns; thus they're harder to read.

Third, passive verbs cause vagueness because they conceal the agent in a sentence. Consider sentences like these:

> In many countries, bribes *are considered* a legitimate business expense.
>
> Outside agitators *are being blamed* for the trouble.
>
> The candidate has already *been selected.*

The reader who wants to know facts—*who* considers bribes legitimate? *who* is blaming outside agitators?—becomes impatient with such evasive statements.

Use Passive Verbs Carefully

Sometimes a writer needs to use passive verbs. The two principle uses are

1. To focus the reader's attention on the action rather than on the agent
2. To express action when the agent is unknown

For instance:

Pompeii *was buried* by a volcano 2,000 years ago.

The operation *has been duplicated* in several hospitals.

Hundreds of subway passengers *were overcome* by smoke.

Writers working on technical or scientific prose often need to use the passive voice to focus their readers' attention on a process or a mechanism rather than on the persons involved. If you are doing such writing, it's a good idea to check a sample passage from a document in that field. If it uses predominantly passive verbs, you may want to follow the same pattern. But even in technical writing, some editors are encouraging writers to use the active voice occasionally.

CHOOSE ADJECTIVES AND ADVERBS CAREFULLY

When you can, try to convey your meaning with nouns and verbs rather than relying heavily on adjectives and adverbs. Keep these hints in mind:

- Use modifiers sparingly. Remember what Mark Twain said: "As to the Adjective, when in doubt, strike it out."
- Avoid hackneyed pairings such as *common* courtesy, *fundamental* difference, *final* destination, and *absolutely* essential.
- Edit out extravagant adjectives such as *marvelous, terrific, fabulous,* and *fantastic* and use sparingly such overworked adjectives as *really, very,* and *definitely.*
- Avoid overstating your case by adding qualifying terms such as *probably, for the most part, in many cases,* or *generally.* For example, you'd have trouble proving the statement, "By the year 2000, only college graduates will be able to compete in the job market," but you could make your point by writing, "*For the most part,* by the year 2000, only college graduates will be able to compete in the job market."

ADD METAPHORS FOR CLARITY

Metaphor, along with analogy, serves as an invaluable device for illustrating and clarifying abstract concepts because it helps readers to *see* the writer's meaning. It also explains the unfamiliar by drawing from the familiar.

Here is an example from a British scholar-journalist who enlivens a historic account with a vivid metaphor:

> What I had seen [the night of 18 August 1991] was the conspirators' candle, the spark carried through the night by men who supposed that they were reviving the Revolution and saving the Soviet Union. Instead, they lit a fire that destroyed everything they honored. . . . At first, for a day or so after the plotters had captured Gorbachev at Foros, the flame of conspiracy seemed to burn bright and straight, and the terrified land was quiet. But then a very few men and women gathered in the streets of Moscow and Leningrad, raising their bare hands against the tanks. They blew the flame back over the conspirators, until it consumed not only the plotters themselves but all the dried-out palaces and prisons and fortresses of the Revolution behind them.

> —Neal Ascherson, *Black Sea* (New York: Hill & Wang, 1995) 13–14

One of the bonuses of using metaphor is that you can simultaneously enrich and condense your writing. For instance, the sociologist David Riesman illustrated his theories of inner-directed and outer-directed personalities by writing that inner-directed people make decisions by consulting internal gyroscopes that have been preset by parents and society; outer-directed people make their decisions by putting out radarlike signals to test the attitudes of people around them. Not only does his metaphor add a visual element to his writing, but it communicates more economically than a detailed, theoretical explanation would. Thus good metaphors are a kind of shorthand.

CONTROL FOR BIAS IN YOUR LANGUAGE

Except for those who write scientific and technical articles, few writers would claim that they eliminate bias completely from their writing. Nor would they want to. If they are going to write colorful and engaging prose that involves people, they must use images and metaphors, and images and metaphors are seldom neutral. For example:

I was the smallest of boys, late to grow, living in a society of girls who shot up like mutants and were five-foot-nine by the age of twelve. Nowhere was the disparity sharper than at the dances I was made to attend throughout my youth. The tribal rules required every boy to bring a gardenia to the girl who invited him, which he would pin to the bosom of her gown. Too young to appreciate the bosom, I was just tall enough for my nose to be pressed into the gardenia I had brought to adorn it. The sickly smell of that flower was like chloroform as I lurched round and round the dance floor. Talk was almost out of the question; my lofty partner was just as isolated and resentful.

—William Zinsser, introduction, *Inventing the Truth*
(Boston: Houghton, 1995) 7

And in a highly partisan and entertaining book, the political consultant James Carville writes like this:

The bottom line is that, if we're serious about [welfare] reform, we've got to help people climb up the first rung of the economic ladder to get them toward independence. And we've got to make that first rung look more appealing. If I were a welfare recipient, I don't know that I'd be much interested in climbing up onto that rickety first rung the way things are now. With a pathetically lousy minimum wage, no health care, and no day care, welfare makes a lot more sense than many jobs. We've got to change the incentives. If you work, you should not be poor!

—James Carville, *We're Right, They're Wrong*
(New York: Random House, 1996) 22

Zinsser writes to evoke a nostalgic image from his childhood; Carville writes to persuade readers to think about the issues raised by welfare reform. Each uses biased language effectively, but he also uses it responsibly. And that's the key: responsibility, along with a strong sense of audience and purpose.

When you're writing in college, in business, or for mainstream, reputable newspapers or magazines, avoid expressing these kinds of bias:

- Sexist bias: discrimination against and stereotyping of either women or men
- Racial or ethnic bias: prejudice against individuals or groups because of their race (e.g., whites, Asians, African Americans) or their ethnic, religious, or cultural heritage (e.g., Jews, Muslims, or Amish)
- Bias toward age, physical condition, or sexual orientation
- Bias toward certain classes or social groups

Avoid Sexism in Language

As leaders and shapers of public opinion have always known, language shapes thought, and in recent years the women's movement has made all of us more conscious of how deeply language affects attitudes toward women. To avoid sexist language, keep these guidelines in mind:

- Rather than using *he* and *him* when you make general statements, use *he* or *she* and *him* or *her*. Often you can write around the problem by using plural nouns.

Why write . . .	*When you could write . . .*
Anyone concerned about *his* health should stop smoking.	People concerned about *their* health should stop smoking
The astute leader always listens to *his* men.	The astute leader always listens to *his* or *her* followers.
An astronaut must like and trust *his* team members.	An astronaut must like and trust *his* or *her* team members.
	or
	Astronauts must like and trust their team members.

- Avoid using the term *man* or *men* to refer to everyone in a group.

Why write . . .	*When you could write . . .*
A *man* must learn to compromise if *he* wants a career in politics.	*People* must learn to compromise if *they* want careers in politics.
Men show their best qualities in times of crisis.	*Men and women* show their best qualities in times of crisis.
Policeman, mailman, chairman, or *businessmen*	*Police officer, mail carrier, chairperson,* or *business executives*

- Edit out language that stereotypes certain professions in sexist ways. For instance, don't suggest that all nurses, librarians, and secretaries are women or that engineers, physicians, and navy officers are all men. Also, avoid subtle implications that men and women behave in stereotyped ways—for instance, that only women like to shop or that only men like to hunt and fish.

■ When writing to or about a married woman, try to find out what name she prefers and use it—to many women, that name is very important. Following are the possibilities:

husband's name	Mrs. John W. Kleberg
first name + husband's last name	Brenda Kleberg
first name + maiden name + husband's name	Brenda Coles Kleberg
first name + hyphenated last name	Brenda Coles-Kleberg
maiden name	Brenda Coles

Many women, single or married, prefer the title *Ms.* to either *Miss* or *Mrs.* If you're not sure which designation a woman prefers, it's best to use *Ms.*

Avoid Racial and Ethnic Bias

Much of the time you don't even need to mention someone's race or cultural heritage. For instance, if you're writing an article about a scientist, that person's credentials are relevant but his or her race is not. So mention race only if you make an important point by doing so. Then keep these guidelines in mind:

■ **Use specific and accurate terminology.** For those whose forebears come from another country, combine descriptive terms with American: *Japanese American, Cuban American,* and so on. The term *Asian* is so broad that it's almost useless; use *Chinese, Japanese, Indonesian, Filipino,* and so on. The term *Oriental* is no longer used to describe specific races. The term *Hispanic* is also very broad; when you can, use *Mexican, Peruvian, Colombian, Spanish,* and so on.

The terms *Native American* and *American Indian* are both acceptable for native-born Americans; for natives of the Arctic regions, the term *Inuit* now is preferred over *Eskimo.*

■ **As far as you can, use terminology preferred by the people you're writing about.** At this time, the terms favored by many whose ancestors came from Africa seems to be *African American,* but *black* is still widely used. If you're in doubt, ask a friend from that group or consult a respected newspaper such as the *New York Times* or the *Los Angeles Times.* I believe the term *people of color* is vague and unhelpful.

■ **Be careful not to slip into subtle ethnic or racial stereotypes.** Might someone construe something you've written to mean that Irish are hot-tempered or Italians are connected with crime or Scots are tight-fisted? If so, consider revising to avoid unintended bias. Sometimes it helps to get someone else to read your paper to look for such slips.

Avoid Bias Connected with Age, Physical Condition, or Sexual Orientation

When you're working with language, treating people fairly means not demeaning people for characteristics over which they have no control. Among those characteristics are age, physical handicaps, and sexual orientation.

- **Use respectful terms for people who are sixty-five or older, and recognize that individuals in that category vary as much as those in any other group.** Many such individuals do not want to be called *elderly* or *old* or even *senior citizens*. Your best bet here is to be specific; write "late sixties" or "early seventies." Avoid patronizing comments like "For a seventy-five-year-old, he's remarkably alert." Of course, that doesn't mean that you can't recognize truly unusual accomplishments, as a *New York Times* article did in reporting on the Russian ballerina Maria Plateskaya performing on her seventieth birthday.

- **Use the terms *boys*, *girls*, and *kids* only for people under eighteen.** College students and young working adults deserve to be called men and women. The term "college kids" is both patronizing and, these days, highly inaccurate.

- **When it's relevant to mention a person's disability or illness, use specific language and avoid words like "crippled" or "victim."** Terms like "visually impaired" or "paraplegic" are simply descriptive and are acceptable. A useful formula is to mention the person first and his or her disability second: "my friend Joe, who is diabetic" or "Anne's father, who has multiple sclerosis."

- **Mention a person's sexual orientation only when it is pertinent to the topic you're discussing, and use specific, nonjudgmental language when you do.** *Gay* and *lesbian* now seem to be the terms preferred by those whose sexual orientation is toward their own sex. Although members of these groups may sometimes use the term "queer" in their own literature, that term is clearly offensive when used by a person outside such groups.

- **Edit out language that suggests negative class connotations such as** "red neck," "wet back," "welfare mother," "fraternity boy," "country club set," or "Junior Leaguer." Be careful too with terms that have become code words suggesting racial or social stereotypes; two such terms are "underclass" and "cultural elite."

Keep a Sense of Humor and Proportion

You can keep offensive bias out of your writing and still create vivid, engaging articles that inform and entertain your readers. Magazine and newspaper writers do it all the time. Here is an example:

> In the rush to judge Andy Collins [former director of the Texas Department of Correctional Justice], the media and the politicians have failed to judge his accomplices in the great prison scandal: themselves. So eager were they to sate the public's bloodlust for locking up criminals and throwing away the key that they helped create a climate of hysteria in which corruption could flourish. The dust from the prison expansion has settled now, and we are left in a sorry mess indeed. The state prison system, which before the buildup was so overcrowded that it had to turn inmates loose after only a few months behind bars, now has 146,000 prison beds but only 129,000 inmates.
>
> —Robert Draper, "The Great Texas Prison Mess,"
> *Texas Monthly*, May 1996: 129

Words like "sate," "bloodlust," "climate of hysteria," and "sorry mess" are definitely biased, but given the facts of the case and Draper's audience— primarily Texans who want to know more about a state scandal—such strong language seems justified. Such language would be inappropriate in an academic paper, but for an article in a mainstream and well-respected magazine, it works well.

Maintain a Civil Tone

Finally, always remember that the language that you use reflects who you are. So even when you're using strong language for strong purposes, keep it civil. People who call those who disagree with them by names like "environmental wacko" or "fascist" or "pinko" reveal themselves as extremists who have little interest in honest argument or productive discussion. Their language reveals them as so self-centered that they care about appealing only to those who already agree with them. They're contemptuous of anyone else. So if you want to be taken seriously, show respect for your readers even when you disagree with them. That's the only way you'll get them to consider your point of view.

EXERCISES

1. Working with two or three other students, discuss ways to revise these sentences using more concrete and specific language:

   A. Your accepting our recommendation would mean elimination of homeless elements on our city streets.
   B. A knowledge and understanding of the law is a necessity for those who want an alteration of it.
   C. The result of the election is an indication that the legislator has an environmentally aware constituency.

   When you are finished, write a clear version of each sentence.

2. Revise these sentences, and put in people or a person as the subject of each one:

   A. The load of responsibility on the lender is great.
   B. A stringent self-evaluation is needed to remedy your problem.
   C. The anxiety that accompanies choosing a profession is a major cause of stress.

3. Working with two or three other students, discuss ways in which one could revise these sentences using more vigorous verbs:

   A. There are several advantages that will be achieved by this ruling.
   B. Vitamins are substances the body requires in small amounts.
   C. There are many things to examine when looking for a used car.

   When you are finished, write a stronger version of each sentence.

4. Revise these sentences to replace passive verbs with active verbs. Get rid of any nominalizations you think are weakening the sentences.

   A. Uneducated women often feel serious apprehension when they are forced into the job market for the first time.
   B. Such information should be made available to consumers before they ask for it.
   C. What should be considered is the capability and suitability of the individual for each job.
   D. It is recommended by administrators that accountability be made a major factor in giving salary bonuses.

E. The requirements were put into effect by a group of uninformed people before the problem had been fully studied.

5. Photocopy a magazine article in which the author uses metaphor or allusion and bring it to class. Analyze what you see as the writer's reason for using allusion and metaphor. Do you think the technique is effective?

6. Working with two or three other students in a group, discuss how you might revise the following passages to get rid of inappropriate biased language:

A. The artist must follow his own intuition if he is to do lasting work, whether he is a painter or a sculptor. The man who tries to imitate or do what is currently chic will not make his mark on the culture.

B. The nurse who wants to work with the day-to-day patients in a hospital will often find that she has been replaced by nurses' aides because the hospital administrator has been forced to cut his expenses.

C. Policemen, teachers, and mailmen are often well paid in large cities that have strong public employee unions.

D. One can depend on good restaurants in Cincinnati because many Italians and Greeks settled there.

E. As a 6 foot, 8 inch African American, Jarvis will probably be going to college on a basketball scholarship.

F. The editor of an on-line magazine that will be launched next year is a gay man with wide experience in magazine publishing and television talk shows.

G. Those girls have been playing bridge together once a week for at least twenty-five years.

H. Although the photographer has passed her seventy-fifth birthday, she still travels and does outstanding work.

SUGGESTED WRITING ASSIGNMENTS

As a part of each assignment write a detailed analysis of your audience and specify the characteristics they would have that you need to keep in mind as you write, the problems such an audience might present, and what the audience would expect to get from reading your paper. Also analyze your purpose in writing, specifying what you hope to accomplish with the paper. If appropriate, include an accurate and descriptive title for your paper.

TOPIC 1: Observe carefully a street, neighborhood, building, or small area in your city, and write an objective report on it that might be used for a paper in an urban sociology class or course on city government. Use concrete and specific but neutral language; appeal to the senses as much as possible, and avoid using vague adjectives. Think about what kind of information your reader would want to get from the report and what use that information might be put to outside class. Some possible topics for description might be the following:

A. A school building that needs to be modernized.

B. A vacant lot that could be converted into a playground.

C. A block close to campus that is being invaded by X-rated bookstores and porno movie houses.

D. The county courthouse that was built in the last century.

TOPIC 2: The generous retirement pay of people who have served twenty years or more in the armed services costs U.S. taxpayers a substantial amount of money. For example, a colonel may retire at forty-two and receive more than $1,500 a month retirement pay while holding down another job; a four-star admiral may retire at the age of sixty with a pension of more than $70,000 a year. These benefits also have the advantage of being tied to the cost of living so that they increase as the price index rises.

Assume the persona of someone who defends or opposes these benefits and write an article expressing your views. Think carefully about the consequences of your argument and support your points. Direct your paper to a specific audience, perhaps a congressional committee that is considering budget cuts or the readers of your local newspaper.

TOPIC 3: Write a short article for young people from ten to fourteen years old explaining the basic concepts of some subject on which you are well informed or in which you are very interested. Assume that your readers are bright youngsters who read well and who enjoy learning something new. Try to explain your ideas or give your information in terms they will understand, using concrete examples and analogies. Keep your focus narrow enough so that you can treat the subject in no more than 1,000 words. Here are some suggestions for topics:

A new discovery in geology, astronomy, archeology, or other science

What it takes to be a dancer, lawyer, journalist, or other professional

How weather forecasting is done

How airplanes fly or ducks swim or whales breathe

How to budget and spend a clothes allowance

How to buy one's first horse

Choosing a sport to participate in

How to take care of a dog in hot weather

Remember that your audience doesn't have to read your article and will do so only if you keep them interested. It would be a good idea to look at some children's magazines or the column for young people in magazines such as *Sierra* to get a feel for what kind of writing appeals to youngsters and what qualities articles for them are likely to have. *And remember not to preach.*

9

CRAFTING PARAGRAPHS

"A paragraph should contain no unnecessary sentences,
for the same reason that a drawing should have no
unnecessary lines and a machine no unnecessary parts."
—*William Strunk,* The Elements of Style

Writers and editors break writing into paragraphs so that readers will be able to read and to grasp meaning more quickly. We don't actually think in paragraphs in the way that we think in sentences—they're not natural to us. That's why all of us sometimes have trouble deciding when to start a new paragraph or deciding just how long an individual paragraph should be. But writers who care about their readers need to develop strong paragraphing skills.

How do you develop those skills? Partly through practice and partly through intuition. The more you write and the more audience conscious you become, the stronger your feel for paragraphing will become. It may help if you think about paragraphing from two points of view: first from an outside view and then from an inside view.

THE OUTSIDE VIEW OF PARAGRAPHING

When writers and editors break writing into paragraphs for the sake of appearance, they do it for outside reasons. They know that a printed page has its own body language, that it gives off signals to its potential readers before those readers ever read a word. (See Chapter 12 on document design.) Paragraph length strongly affects that body language. Long paragraphs, especially if they are in small print and have narrow margins and few subheadings, say to the reader, "I am hard to read."

For this reason, editors and audience-conscious writers insert frequent paragraph breaks in order to make a page reader-friendly. It's the principle of "chunking" again (see pp. 98–99). They do it to break up the material into manageable segments so that readers won't feel they are getting too much information at one time. If that seems patronizing, think about your own reactions to long paragraphs—don't you find them rather intimidating? I do. I have rejected more than one book when I was browsing in the library or bookstore because its paragraphs ran to more than a page.

Writers who are the most audience conscious make decisions about paragraphing according to what they know about a specific audience. If they are writing for an audience of limited education and reading skills—say the readers of *Family Circle* or *TV Guide*—they will write shorter paragraphs than they would for a narrower audience whom they assume to be educated and skilled readers—for example, the readers of *Scientific American* or the *New York Times*. They will also use shorter paragraphs when they are writing for young readers.

Of course, the terms "short paragraph" and "long paragraph" are relative, but in general, a short paragraph is one that runs from three to six sentences of medium length. A paragraph of seven or eight sentences, depending on their length, is medium to long. Any paragraph of more than ten sentences, or one that covers more than half a printed page, is definitely long, and you should consider breaking it up. As you can tell by glancing over this book, I believe strongly in short paragraphs. When I can divide a paragraph without compromising its unity, I do.

If you are writing something that's going to appear in columns—for example, a newspaper editorial or an article for a newsletter—keep your paragraphs short. When you squeeze several sentences into a narrow column, you get a paragraph that looks long even if it isn't.

Guidelines for Breaking Paragraphs

First, don't worry about paragraph length when you're still drafting your paper or even when you're working on the first revision. When you're adjusting paragraph length, you're dealing with matters of style, and you'll do better to put such decisions off until you're revising at that level.

Remember, though, that no careful writer chops his or her writing into paragraphs arbitrarily just to make it look better. You must observe some principles and guidelines, or you will wind up with divisions that confuse your readers more than they help them.

The traditional rule of thumb is that you start a new paragraph whenever you come to a new idea. That's fine for certain kinds of writing. For example, if you're writing a paper that lists several reasons or classifies a number of examples, you can probably build a new paragraph on each point or example. Paragraphing can be easy when your paper falls into such natural divisions.

But it's not always easy to tell when you've come to a new idea—and what if it's a complex idea? Thus you need something to go by that's more specific than the rule of thumb above. When you think a paragraph is getting too long and you want to break it, here are some clues that may signal a place where you could break it:

PLACES WHERE YOU MAY BREAK A PARAGRAPH

- **A shift in time.** Look for sentences beginning with words like *first, next, formerly, at that time*, and so on.
- **A shift in place.** Look for sentences beginning with words like *elsewhere, in the meantime, on the other side of*, and so on.
- **A shift showing contrast.** Look for sentences beginning with words like *however, on the other hand, nevertheless*, and so on.
- **A shift in emphasis.** Look for sentences beginning with terms like *if that happens, in spite of, another possibility*, and so on.

There are no firm rules on these matters. You'll just have to use your judgment and ask yourself, "What would work best with my audience?" For instance, here is an example of a long paragraph that could be broken up into more manageable chunks without its unity being affected:

"People say that Arthur [Ashe] lacks the killer instinct." (Ronald Charity is commenting.) "And that is a lot of baloney. Arthur is quietly aggressive—more aggressive than people give him credit for being. You don't get to be that good without a will to win. He'll let you win the first two sets, then he'll blast you off the court." Ronald Charity, who taught Arthur Ashe to play tennis, was himself taught by no one. "I was my own protégé," he says. Charity is approaching forty and is the head of an advertising and public-relations firm in Danville, Virginia. Trim, lithe, in excellent condition, he is still nationally ranked as one of the top ten players in the A.T.A. / In 1946, when he began to play tennis, as a seventeen-year-old in Richmond, there were—male and female, all ages—about twenty Negroes in the city who played the game and none of them played it well. Charity, as a college freshman, thought tennis looked interesting, and when, in a bookstore, he saw Lloyd Budge's *Tennis Made Easy* he bought a copy and began to teach himself to play.

When he had absorbed what Budge had to say, he bought Alice Marble's *The Road to Wimbledon,* and, finally, William T. Tilden's *How to Play Better Tennis.* "It just happened that I could pull off a page and project into my imagination how it should be done," he says. / Blacks in Richmond could play tennis only at the Negro Y.W.C.A., where Charity developed his game, and, a little later, four hard-surface courts were built at Brook Field, a Negro playground about two miles from the heart of the city. Arthur Ashe, a Special Police Officer in charge of discipline at several Negro playgrounds, lived in a frame house in the middle of Brook Field. When Arthur Ashe, Jr., was six years old, he spent a great deal of time watching Ronald Charity play tennis, and would never forget what he felt as he watched him. "I thought he was the best in the world. He had long, fluid, graceful strokes. I could see no kinks in his game."

—John McPhee, "Levels of the Game," *The John McPhee Reader,*
ed. William Howarth (New York: Vintage Books, 1978) 178–79

Notice that the first place I broke this paragraph (indicated by a slash) comes at a shift in time—the narrative moves from the present back to 1946. The second place where it could be broken comes at a change in space—the narrative moves from talking about tennis books to the tennis courts at the Y.W.C.A.

Use One-Sentence Paragraphs Sparingly

Unfortunately, some mass-market writers let their enthusiasm for short paragraphs carry them to the extreme of habitually writing a series of one- and two-sentence paragraphs that are really not paragraphs at all. They are only separated sentences. For example:

"Frankly, it's not profitable to service your [Internet] account anymore," a technical support representative explained.

It seems that the company regrets that it offered me a so-called Unix shell account several years ago and now wishes me to cancel it and sign up for the more profitable (to them) Netcruiser service.

To drive the point home, the Netcom technician informed me that the company no longer accepts telephone calls from shell account customers who need technical support. Rather, all questions have to be submitted by electronic mail.

—Peter Lewis, "Looking Around to Find a New Internet Home,"
New York Times, 21 May 1996: B6

Although writers for newspapers probably write these one-sentence paragraphs because the narrow columns of a newspaper make a paragraph of normal length look long and intimidating, this kind of paragraphing chops a piece of writing into arbitrary divisions that are hard to follow. The reader senses no pattern or unity to the writing.

You shouldn't assume, however, that you can never write one-sentence paragraphs. Sometimes they serve well to introduce a major point, or they can make a kind of announcement to which the writer wants to draw attention.

Here are two examples from professional writers. In the first, the author uses the one-sentence paragraph to dramatize a major point in her narrative of an accident:

> Hobo ran ahead, then back, brushing snow crystals and fur against my leg. I put a hand on my skin to warm it and dragged nylon ski pants over the road behind me. Mom said to have them along in case the bus broke down, but she knew I would not wear them, could not bear the plastic sounds they made between my thighs.
> No light was on in our home.

> —Natalie Kusz, "Vital Signs," *The Best American Essays, 1990,* ed. Justin Kaplan (New York: Ticknor & Fields, 1990) 155

In this narrative selection by a well-regarded writer, two one-sentence paragraphs add dramatic effect:

> I waited in the backyard, waited out there with beer and guilt and guesses at how much I was going to owe the landlord for my miscalculation about what a number seven [shotgun] shot would do to such a big animal with all that fur on her flesh. Jim came in his pick-up; his twelve-year-old daughter was with him, and when she climbed down from the cab he held up his hand.
> "You'd better wait here," he said, and she got into the cab again.
> He squatted over the ewe, felt her chest, and told me she was dead.

> —Andre Dubus, *Broken Vessels* (Boston: Godine, 1991) 8

So you see a one-sentence paragraph can be effective. If you use one, however, be sure you are doing it consciously and for a definite purpose. They are attention getters, and most of the time you will do better to avoid them, sticking with the principle that a paragraph is a group of sentences that pertain to and develop a single idea.

THE INSIDE VIEW OF PARAGRAPHING

When you consider a paragraph from the internal point of view, its essential quality should be *unity.* A paragraph should have a central idea, and everything in the paragraph should relate to and develop that idea. The reader should find no surprises, and every sentence should fit with the others. Moreover, the sentences should follow each other in logical order so that one could not move the sentences around at random: each one needs to be in its particular place to advance the internal development of the paragraph.

How does one go about developing these unified paragraphs? People who write a lot probably develop their paragraphs mostly by intuition, developing their points with examples and explanations. If you were to ask them to explain how they write their paragraphs, they probably couldn't tell you. Nevertheless, much of the time professional writers are producing paragraphs that fit certain patterns that follow natural thought processes. Apprentice writers can learn something about good paragraph development by studying those patterns and analyzing how they are developed.

Commitment/Response Paragraphs

One important pattern for paragraphs is that of commitment and response. That is, the first sentence of the paragraph makes a *commitment* to the reader, makes a statement that sets up certain expectations and leads the reader to expect that they will be fulfilled. In some cases, the commitment sentence could be called a *topic sentence.* Whatever you label it, it works by making a promise to the reader and following through on it. Commitments in a paragraph can take many forms, as the following examples show. (I have italicized the commitment sentence in each one.)

Commitment/response pattern 1: Begin with a *generative sentence,* a lead that suggests additional details will follow:

> *Within hours of my arrival in September, 1960, New York astonished and delighted me.* The astonishment was instant. I stepped from the plane at what is now called John F. Kennedy airport but was then called Idlewild into a sea of water, my first encounter with an East Coast hurricane. The scene inside the airport resembled a Brueghel run wild. Sodden people lurched in all directions, colliding in their frantic search for lost luggage and nonexistent taxis. Some laughed and told war stories of other major storms. Others interrogated all comers, anxious for news.

> —Jill Ker Conway, *True North: A Memoir*
> (New York: Vintage Books, 1995) 3

Commitment/response pattern 2: Open with a *question* that will be followed by an answer:

> *But do the [new] drugs cost too much?* The Clinton administration says they do, and in some cases, the prices are astonishing. The current wholesale price for one patient's annual supply of Clozaril [a drug for

treating schizophrenia] is about $4,000. Some people would call that a fair trade, considering that it saves more than $40,000 in annual hospital costs; others call it price-gouging. Centocor priced Centoxin, a promising treatment for often-fatal septic shock, at more than $3,000 for each dose during its initial marketing. Negative test results shot down the drug, but not before the price set off a wave of outrage.

> —Janice Castro, *The American Way of Health*
> (New York: Little, Brown, 1994) 145

Commitment/response pattern 3: *Begin with the first sentence of a narrative* and signal that the rest of the story will follow:

> *One morning I arrived early at work and went into the bank lobby where the Negro porter was mopping.* I stood at a counter and picked up the Memphis *Commercial Appeal* and began my free reading of the press. I came finally to the editorial page and saw an article dealing with one H. L. Mencken. I knew by hearsay that he was the editor of the *American Mercury,* but aside from that I knew nothing about him. The article was a furious denunciation with one hot, short sentence: Mencken is a fool.

> —Richard Wright, *Black Boy* (New York:
> Harper & Row, 1937) 214

Commitment/response pattern 4: *Begin with a quotation* that introduces your topic:

> *"Within the first hour [after the attack at Pearl Harbor],"* Grace *Tully recalled, "it was evident that the Navy was dangerously crippled."* And there was no way of knowing where the Japanese would stop. The president's butler Alonzo Fields recalls hearing snatches of a remarkable conversation between Harry Hopkins and the president that afternoon in which they imagined the possibility of the invading Japanese armies' driving inland from the West Coast as far as Chicago. At that point, the president figured, since the United States was a country much like Russia in the vastness of its terrain, we could make the Japanese overextend their communication and supply lines and begin to force them back.

> —Doris Kearns Goodwin, *No Ordinary Time*
> (New York: Simon & Schuster, 1994) 290

Commitment/response pattern 5: *Downshift* from a general statement to particulars that illustrate it:

> *Every big [Mississippi] plantation was a fiefdom; the small hamlets that dot the map of the Delta were mostly plantation headquarters rather than conventional towns.* Sharecroppers traded at a plantation-owned commissary, often in scrip rather than money. They prayed at plantation-owned Baptist churches. Their children walked, sometimes

miles, to plantation-owned schools, usually one- or two-room buildings without heating or plumbing. Education ended with the eighth grade and was extremely casual until then. . . . The textbooks were hand-me-downs from the white schools. The planter could and did shut down the schools whenever there was work to be done in the fields. . . . Many sharecroppers remember going to school only when it rained.

> —Nicholas Leman, *The Promised Land*
> (New York: Knopf, 1991) 17–18

So writers can choose several different ways to build their paragraphs from a commitment/response pattern. The important point to remember is that the sentences that follow the opening commitment must not frustrate or confuse the reader by failing to follow through.

Other Paragraph Patterns

Writers also use several other paragraph patterns, including some that reflect the common patterns of organization covered in Chapter 5: *reasoning from evidence, assertion and support, definition, cause and effect, comparison, classification, narration,* and *process*. Here are some examples. You will probably notice that many of them are also *commitment/response* paragraphs and many use *generative sentences*.

Reasoning from evidence

This is a particularly useful pattern when you're writing an argument. Notice how the eminent historian Barbara Tuchman goes from specific evidence to a conclusion in this paragraph:

> Over a period of sixty years, from roughly 1470 to 1530, the secular spirit of the age was exemplified in a succession of six popes—five Italians and one Spaniard—who carried it to an excess of venality, amorality, avarice, and spectacularly calamitous power politics. Their governance dismayed the faithful, brought the Holy See into disrepute, left unanswered the cry for reform, ignored all protests, warnings, and signs of rising revolt, and ended by breaking apart the unity of Christendom and losing half the papal constituency to the Protestant secession. Theirs was folly of perversity, perhaps the most consequential in Western history, if measured by its result in centuries of ensuing hostility and fratricidal war.

> —Barbara Tuchman, *The March of Folly* (New York:
> Ballantine Books, 1984) 52

Assertion and support

Most of us use this pattern automatically when we want to convince someone to accept our reasoning. Here the editors of *Texas Monthly* use the pattern to begin an article on the best schools in Texas:

> There are those who argue that it is impossible to compare schools—that each one is unique, and that the important lessons students learn there, about themselves and about life, cannot be measured. We disagree. The fundamental job of an elementary school is to teach kids to read, write, and compute, and those skills can be tested. Education is so important, and the sums the state spends on it are so vast, that measuring the success or failure of each school is a necessity. There is no other way to hold schools accountable for their performance.
>
> —The Editors, "Our Best Schools," *Texas Monthly*, Nov. 1996: 112

Definition

This is a useful pattern when you want to explain a term or a concept that is important to your thesis. For instance:

> Hail is a product of turbulence—of spinning updrafts and downdrafts within a local storm. A droplet of water is whisked aloft to the freezing level, and turns into a pellet of ice. The downdraft returns it to the soggy regions of the cloud, and there it gains a coating of moisture before its next ascent. And so it goes. The hailstone bounces up and down like popcorn in a roaster, growing layer upon layer of alternate snow and ice, until its accumulated weight causes it to crash.
>
> —Jonathan Raban, "The Unlamented West,"
> *New Yorker*, 20 May 1996: 72

Cause and effect

This is another pattern that is useful when you make a claim and want to show the basis of your statement. For example:

> In order to tell us his epic tale, in which everything and everyone ends up in the arms of the blues, [Duke] Ellington had to stay out there for more than five decades, writing for everyone from the clarinetist to the baritone saxophonist, the trumpet player to the trombonist, the string-bass player to the trap drummer. He wrote show tunes for singers, composed musicals, did scores for movies and television, and always kept himself well afloat. Beneath those blue suède gloves were homemade brass knuckles. Duke Ellington learned early that his was a world both sweet and tough and that he had to be ready for anything.
>
> —Stanley Crouch, "The Duke's Blues," *New Yorker*,
> 29 Apr.–6 May 1996: 159–60

Comparison

This pattern works well when you want to develop a point by showing likeness or differences. For instance:

> When girls play together, they do so in small, intimate groups, with an emphasis on minimizing hostility and maximizing cooperation, while boys' games are in larger groups, with an emphasis on competition. One key difference can be seen in what happens when games boys or girls are playing get disrupted by someone getting hurt. If a boy who has gotten hurt gets upset, he is expected to get out of the way and stop crying so the game can go on. If the same happens among a group of girls who are playing the *game stops* while everyone gathers around to help the girl who is crying. This difference between boys and girls at play epitomizes what Harvard's Carol Gilligan points to as a key disparity between the sexes: boys take pride in a lone, tough-minded independence and autonomy, while girls see themselves as part of a web of connectedness. Thus boys are threatened by anything that might challenge their independence, while girls are more threatened by a rupture in their relationships.

> —Daniel Goleman, *Emotional Intelligence* (New York: Bantam Books, 1995) 131–32

In developing an idea by comparison and contrast, it also works well to compare by alternating paragraphs. For instance,

> Ross [Lockridge] was an oak of prudence and industry. He rarely drank and he never smoked. He excelled at everything he did. He had married his hometown sweetheart, was proudly faithful to her and produced four fine children. After a sampling of success on both coasts, he had gone home to the Indiana of his parents and childhood friends.

> Tom Heggen had a taste for the low life. He had been divorced, had no children and shared bachelor quarters in New York with an ex-actor and screenwriter, Dorothy Parker's estranged husband, Alan Campbell. Tom was a drinker and a pill addict. He turned up regularly at the fashionable restaurant "21," usually bringing along a new girl, a dancer or an actress.

> —John Leggett, *Ross and Tom* (New York: Simon & Schuster, 1974)

Classification

Another useful paragraph pattern is classification, which helps you organize your ideas into a pattern you can work from. For example:

> There are, as nearly I can make out, three kinds of conservation currently operating. The first is the preservation of places that are grandly wild or "scenic" or in some way spectacular. The second is what is

called "conservation of natural resources"—that is, of the things of nature that we intend to use: soil, water, timber, and minerals. The third is what you might call industrial troubleshooting: the attempt to limit or stop or remedy the most flagrant abuses of the industrial system. All three kinds of conservation are inadequate, separately and together.

> —Wendell Berry, "Conservation Is Good Work," *Sex, Economy, Freedom, and Community* (New York: Pantheon Books, 1993) 27

Narration

A miniature story is frequently a good way to illustrate a point that you have already made or one that you want to make. It also has the virtue of adding a visual element or a personal element to your writing. For example:

> One morning in November, 1956, Blair [Chotzinoff], who was living in the New York apartment of his sister and brother-in-law, awoke to find the ring he had given [Gloria] Steinem on the table together with a note calling the engagement off. He was devastated and never quite resigned; it took him many years to get over a feeling of worthlessness. When, in the early sixties, Steinem began seeing Tom Guinzberg, publisher of Viking Press . . . , Chotzinoff's parents said he would see that they had been right: she would marry Guinzberg because he was so rich; she had only been waiting for a truly rich man. No, she won't, Chotzinoff said; and right he was.

> —Carolyn Heilbrun, *The Education of a Woman* (New York: Dial Press, 1995) 62

Process

This kind of paragraph is particularly useful when you have been generalizing about a theory and need to explain specifically how it works. For instance, here a gifted writer talks about how he works:

> When I write, I like to have an interval before me when I am not likely to be interrupted. For me, this means usually the early morning, before others are awake. I get pen and paper, take a glance out the window (often it is dark out there), and wait. It is like fishing. But I do not wait very long, for there is always a nibble—and this is where receptivity comes in. To get started I will accept anything that occurs to me. Something always occurs, of course, to any of us. We can't keep from thinking. Maybe I have to settle for an immediate impression: it's cold, or hot, or dark, or bright, or in between! Or—well, the possibilities are endless. If I put something down, that thing will help the next thing come, and I'm off. If I let the process go on, things will occur to me that

were not at all in my mind when I started. These things, odd or trivial as they may be, are somehow connected. And if I let them string out, surprising things will happen.

—William Stafford, "A Way of Writing," *Field,* Spring 1970

OPENING AND CLOSING PARAGRAPHS

Crafting Opening Paragraphs

In Chapter 5 I made several specific suggestions about patterns you might use for opening paragraphs. If you're stumped for an idea for your opener, you may want to read that section again (pp. 51–53). Here I want to say more about why it's so important to write strong opening paragraphs:

- They introduce you to your reader and establish a first impression.
- They announce your topic to your reader.
- They set the tone for your writing.
- They let your reader know what to expect.

Because these are such crucial functions, it's worth your while to spend time rethinking and revising first paragraphs before you submit your final drafts. A strong opening paragraph can help you win your readers' confidence from the start; a poor one will get you off to a stumbling start from which it can be hard to recover.

Tip: Any good opening paragraph in an article or report probably represents the author's fourth or fifth draft. Often you can't even write a good first paragraph until you know how the rest of your paper is going to come out.

Here are two strong opening paragraphs from professional writers. The first, by Cornel West, a black intellectual who is a professor at Harvard University, opens his book on the complexities and challenges of race relations in the United States:

What happened in Los Angeles in April of 1992 was neither a race riot nor a class rebellion. Rather, this monumental upheaval was a multiracial, trans-class, and largely male display of justified rage. For all its ugly, xenophobic resentment, it signified the sense of powerlessness in American society. Glib attempts to reduce its meaning to the pathologies of the black underclass, the criminal actions of hoodlums, or the political revolt of the oppressed urban masses miss the mark. Of those arrested, only 36 percent were black, more than a third had full-time jobs, and most claimed to shun political affiliation. What we witnessed in Los Angeles was the consequence of a lethal linkage of economic decline, cultural decay, and political lethargy in American life. Race was the visible catalyst, not the underlying cause.

—Cornel West, *Race Matters* (Boston: Beacon Press, 1993) 1

The second, by the lead book reviewer for the *New York Times*, uses a vivid comparison and contrast paragraph to begin her book review:

They were the odd couple of American politics: Kennedy the charming aristocrat, debonair, self-confident and beloved; Nixon the perpetual outsider, calculating, self-conscious and maligned. One would be remembered as the martyred king of Camelot; the other as "tricky Dick," the dark prince who resigned the presidency in shame. The two men began together in Congress as friends, and later became bitter rivals for the highest office in the land. They would go down in history, in Nixon's own words, as "a pair of unmatched bookends."

—Michiko Kakutani, "Competition That Made Kennedy and Nixon Foes," *New York Times*, 24 May 1996: B8

Both paragraphs do precisely what first paragraphs are supposed to do:

- They catch the readers' attention immediately,
- help the reader anticipate what is to come, and
- indicate what the tone and style of the piece will be.

Adapting Opening Paragraphs to Audience and Purpose

Although good first paragraphs share the characteristics mentioned in the previous section, you'll want to vary your opening paragraphs according to the kind of writing you are doing. Your good sense should tell you that a provocative first sentence that might be just right for a newspaper editorial or an article in a magazine like *Rolling Stone* won't work well for a business report, a technical paper, or a paper of literary analysis.

When you're writing a straightforward, informative paper—say a business proposal, an environmental impact paper, or a report that summarizes findings—announce your topic immediately in the first paragraph. At

this point your first concern should be not to waste your readers' time—
they're busy, often impatient people who want to read quickly and efficiently. So get to the point. For example, this opening from the model
paper on the need for role models for girls in Chapter 6 gets directly to the
point:

> Stories are central to all our lives. The myths and legends of our cul-
> ture interpret that culture for us and give us a sense of our own possi-
> bilities. How can young people imagine that they might become heroes
> or leaders or explorers if they have never heard stories about heroes and
> leaders and explorers? Unfortunately, however, the myths and legends
> of our Western culture offer young girls little sense of their possibilities.
> The traditional literature taught and promoted in our schools and in
> our books is male-centered and offers few role models that encourage
> girls to become leaders or explorers.

The opening paragraph of a report on recent trends in real estate in a
city might look like this:

CHANGING TRENDS IN REAL ESTATE VALUES IN AUSTIN, TEXAS

> In the 1970s and 1980s, real estate values in Austin were pre-
> dictable. Values were consistently highest in the stable though heteroge-
> neous areas bounded by the University of Texas on the east and Lake
> Austin and the Colorado River on the west. In the mid-1990s, however,
> patterns have begun to change. Now the homes with the highest evalu-
> ation cluster around the edges of the city in gated communities designed
> for buyers in the $500,000 to $800,000 category. The change has come
> because developers building for the high end of the market were able to
> find adequate tracts of land only if they moved out from the city.

Caution: Readers from some cultures, especially those in Asia and the Middle
East, may dislike such direct openings and find them rude. They may believe
people should exchange pleasantries and formal statements of concern before
getting down to business. If you are writing for an audience from such a culture,
try to find out what kind of introductory style they favor and honor it.

Wrestling with Closing Paragraphs

Conclusions are hard. Any writer will tell you that. It's difficult to complete
your explanation or argument and leave your readers satisfied, yet not fall

into clichés or obvious comments at the end. Thus many of us continue to struggle with conclusions, no matter how long we've been writing.

For some writing tasks, endings are almost prescribed, and you can find models that will help you. For example, for technical and business reports, case studies, or proposals, the writer is expected to summarize his or her findings and, if appropriate, make recommendations. Such endings are straightforward and not too hard to write.

In other kinds of writing, such as an argument or an analysis, the writer often needs to restate main ideas or arguments at the end of the paper in order to refresh the reader about points that have been made earlier. Conclusions of this kind resemble the summation a lawyer makes for a jury:

1. It restates the principal claim;
2. it summarizes the evidence; and
3. it recommends a policy or outcome.

For that wide range of other kinds of nonfiction—theater or music reviews, exploratory personal essays, cause-and-effect analyses, or essays on social issues, for instance—it's less easy to find a pattern. I have looked at dozens of such essays and find an amazing variety of good ways to wind up an essay. It's not easy to generalize. Nevertheless, here are three suggestions that you may find useful:

- *Close by summarizing the main points you have made.* This is what Hillary Rodham Clinton does in this concluding paragraph to her book on nurturing children.

  Nothing is more important to our shared future than the well-being of children. For children are at our core—not only as vulnerable beings in need of love and care but as a moral touchstone amidst the complexity and contentiousness of modern life. Just as it takes a village to raise a child, it takes children to raise up a village to become all it should be. The village we build with them in mind will be a better place for us all.

  —Hillary Rodham Clinton, *It Takes a Village*
  (New York: Simon & Schuster, 1996) 278

- *Finish with a recommendation that grows out of the argument you've been making.* This is what Cathy Young does in this last paragraph of her essay "Keeping Women Weak," in which she rejects a kind of feminism that wants to overprotect women and portray them as victims.

  We need a "Third Wave" feminism that rejects the excesses of the gender fanatics *and* the sentimental traditionalism of the Phyllis

Schlaflys; one that does not seek special protection for women and does not view us as too socially disadvantaged to take care of ourselves. Because on the path that feminism has taken in the last few years, we are allowing ourselves to be treated as frail, helpless little things—by our would-be liberators.

> —Cathy Young, "Keeping Women Weak," *NEXT: Young American Writers on the New Generation,* ed. Eric Liu (New York: Norton, 1994) 230

■ *Tie the last paragraph to the first paragraph.* You can give your readers a sense of closure and wrap up your essay by plucking an image or reference from your opening paragraph and including it in your final paragraph. In this article about diving off Australia's Great Barrier Reef the author does just that.

Opening paragraph:

At first I thought (maybe even hoped) that I'd emerge from the waters of Australia's Great Barrier Reef feeling like Lloyd Bridges, the swaggering hero of the old TV series *Sea Hunt.* I'd have met and triumphed over another teeth-gritting physical challenge, and I'd have the scars to prove it. Instead I returned feeling a lot more like Alice after her traipse through Wonderland: awed, slightly dazed, and not at all sure that anyone would take me seriously once I told them what I'd seen.

Closing paragraph:

Emerging from the metaphorical rabbit hole just off the Queensland coast, I found, like Alice, that I "had got so much into the way of expecting nothing but out-of-the-way things to happen that it seemed quite dull and stupid for life to go in the common way."

—Reed McManus, " 'Dive?' He Said," *Sierra,* Nov./Dec. 1990: 71, 80

EXERCISES

1. Read over this paragraph to see where you think you could break it without seriously interrupting the train of thought:

> In outline it was a good plan, but it quite failed to take into account the mentality of buzzards. As soon as they were wired to the tree they all began to try and fly away. The wires prevented that, of course, but did not prevent them from falling off the limbs, where they dangled upside down, wings flopping, nether parts exposed. It is hard to imagine anything less likely to beguile a moviegoing audience than a tree full of dangling buzzards. Everyone agreed it

was unaesthetic. The buzzards were righted, but they tried again, and with each try their humiliation deepened. Finally they abandoned their efforts to fly away and resigned themselves to life on their tree. Their resignation was so complete that when the scene was readied and the time came for them to fly, they refused. They had had enough of ignominy; better to remain on the limb indefinitely. Buzzards are not without patience. Profanity, firecrackers, and even a shotgun full of rock salt failed to move them. I'm told that, in desperation, a bird man was flown in from L.A. to teach the sulky bastards how to fly. The whole experience left everyone touchy. A day or so later, looking at the pictures again, I noticed a further provocative detail. The dead heifer that figured so prominently in the scene was quite clearly a steer. When I pointed this out to the still photographers they just shrugged. A steer was close enough; after all they were both essentially cows. "In essence, it's a cow," one said moodily. No one wanted those buzzards back again.

> —Larry McMurtry, "Here's HUD in Your Eye," *In a Narrow Grave*
> (New York: Simon & Schuster, 1968) 10–11.

2. What commitment do you think the writer makes to the reader in these opening sentences from the paragraphs of professional writers?

"Some of us who live in arid parts of the world think about water with a reverence others might find excessive."—Joan Didion

"The weeks after graduation were filled with heady activities."
—Maya Angelou

"After my confrontation with the Chair of the History Department over my promotion, I began thinking about the situation of other women faculty."—Jill Ker Conway

3. Working with two or three other students, discuss what kind of paragraph you could write to complete each of these opening sentences. Then choose the one that you find most interesting and draft a paragraph together to be shared with the rest of the class.

A. In the 1990s, a new kind of temporary worker is appearing: a high-tech, well-paid specialist who is in great demand to work on short-term projects for major companies such as Microsoft.

B. Violence has become an almost ordinary fact of life in the lives of a distressing number of young children.

C. The average American squanders water in ways that he or she has probably never even thought about.

SUGGESTED WRITING ASSIGNMENTS

As a part of each assignment, write a detailed analysis of your audience and specify the characteristics they would have that you need to keep in mind as you write, the problems that such an audience might present, and what the audience would expect to get from reading your paper. Also analyze your purpose in writing, specifying what you hope to accomplish in the paper. If appropriate, include an accurate and descriptive title for your paper.

TOPIC 1: An organization to which you belong is going to have its annual convention in your city, and you have been asked to serve as local arrangements chair. Among other things, that means that you must write a letter of invitation to the convention that will go out with announcements of the convention. In that letter you want to convince people that they would enjoy visiting your city and to give them information that would help them make up their minds about coming to the convention.

You do not need to mention hotel rates since that information would be in the announcement. You want to point out what special events might be going on in the city at convention time, major points of interest such as art museums or zoos, shopping areas close to the hotel, well-known restaurants, and so on. If you want to keep your letter to one page, you could add a separate sheet with a list of events. Probably your letter should not run to more than 350 or 400 words. Remember that the opening paragraph is particularly important.

TOPIC 2: You are married with a young child and you and your spouse want to move into an apartment nearer your job. In looking for apartments, however, you have discovered that landlords in the neighborhood you want to live in do not allow children. Write a letter to the city council pointing out that such exclusion by landlords is grossly discriminatory and may be unconstitutional. Ask for an interpretation of current city law and suggest that an ordinance against such discrimination needs to be passed if it does not already exist.

TOPIC 3: As part of your duties at the county social services bureau, you have the assignment of writing informative pamphlets that will be available to any clients who come into the office. Your supervisor is particularly eager to have a pamphlet that outlines the options open to young unmarried women who have problem pregnancies, because women who would not want to ask for such a pamphlet would probably pick one up if it were displayed. She asks you to write the pamphlet, specifying that it must use direct but neutral language and be simple enough for young people to understand. The brochure should not be more than 600 words.

10

EDITING

 Careful editing is that last important courtesy to your readers.

Successful writers have learned to be careful and thorough editors. They know that readers make judgments about their writing and about them on the basis of how that writing looks and how well it meets the conventional standards—or most of them, anyway. Thus the more important a document or paper is to you, the more time you should allow for careful editing at the end of the writing process.

STRATEGIES FOR EDITING

- Adjust sentence length and variety
- Check sentence rhythms
- Review word choice
- Improve body language of the document
- Check usage
- Check spelling
- Review specifications
- Proofread

144

I call the first four strategies "tinkering," playing around to improve the way your writing sounds and looks; the last four are more like a mop-up operation. Now that almost everyone writes with a word processor, tinkering or fine-tuning has become practical in a way it wasn't a decade ago. Then few of us were willing to keep polishing sentences if it meant retyping an entire paper; now fine-tuning is easy, and, I think, worthwhile.

Adjust Sentence Length and Variety

When you write a series of long sentences, you slow down your readers. Also, unless such sentences are very skillfully constructed (see pp. 97–99 in Chapter 7), they make your writing seem formal and distance you from the reader. On the other hand, an unbroken sequence of short sentences usually creates a choppy effect—they can sound juvenile.

To avoid either extreme, when you're editing watch to see that you don't have too many sentences of either kind clumped together. If you do, try occasionally to break up the monotony by inserting a short, crisp sentence among several long ones or by combining two or three short sentences into a longer one with a clause or two. When you read passages from nonfiction writers that you like, notice how skillfully the authors manipulate sentence length, even now and then using a minor sentence or fragment when it will work well (see pp. 151–52).

Notice how Henry Louis Gates, Jr., mixes long and short sentences in this passage:

> [Louis] Farrakhan, relaxed and gracious, made sure I was supplied with hot tea and honey. . . . For the rest of a long day, we sat together at his big dining-room table, and it became clear that Farrakhan is a man of enormous intelligence, curiosity, and charm. He can also be deeply strange. It all depends on the moment and the subject. When he talks about the need for personal responsibility or of his fondness for Johnny Mathis and Frank Sinatra, he sounds as jovial and bourgeois as Bill Cosby; when he is warning of the wicked machinations of Jewish financiers, he seems as odd and obsessed as Pat Robertson.
>
> —Henry Louis Gates, Jr., "The Charmer,"
> *New Yorker*, 29 Apr.–6 May 1996: 116

Often you can also improve your writing by varying your sentence patterns. Try inverting standard constructions and moving clauses around. For example, here are some possibilities:

ORIGINAL: New York City officials have talked for years about cleaning up and refurbishing the area around Times Square, and now it looks as if they may finally be going to do it.

VARIATION 1: After having talked for years about cleaning up and refurbishing the area around Times Square, New York City officials may finally be going to do it.

VARIATION 2: New York City officials are finally going to clean up and refurbish the area around Times Square, a project they have talked about for years.

You can also polish your writing by creating parallel sentence patterns. Here's an example:

ORIGINAL: According to many health professionals, exercise comes close to being the fountain of youth in that it helps people control their weight, they seem to have more energy, they are less depressed, and many people find their skin looks better.

REVISION: Many health professionals call exercise the fountain of youth; it helps control weight, it gives people more energy, it combats depression, and it improves skin tone.

Check Sentence Rhythms

You can sharpen your editing skills by becoming sensitive to the cadences and tempo of your writing, and by learning how and why certain word choices and patterns affect the rhythm of prose. You must also develop an ear for the way your writing sounds. Is it monotonous, singsongy, clogged with passive verbs, heavy-duty nouns, strung-out phrases, and sentences that make the reader run out of breath? Or does it flow smoothly and help the reader move along easily?

Probably the best way to develop that ear and smooth out the rhythms of late drafts is to read them aloud to yourself. If they sound plodding or draggy or choppy, try some of the suggestions in Chapter 7. Give special attention to using more action verbs and to putting people in your sentences.

Review Word Choice

Long words—four, five, or six syllables—also slow down your writing and affect its tone. Of course, a long word isn't necessarily a difficult word, and you shouldn't hesitate to use one when it meets your needs. But if you have a choice between a long word and a short one that means almost the same thing, make your choice partly on the basis of the pace and tone you want to set for your writing. Compare these phrases and notice that the longer version is subtly different:

buy a car	purchase an automobile
a hard choice	a difficult decision
put out the light	extinguish the illumination
end the talks	terminate the discussions

Check also to see if you've used a word or forms of it too often; if so find synonyms. For example:

REPETITIVE SENTENCE: Medieval historians *know* that their *knowledge* about women in medieval times depends too heavily on church records.

REVISION: Medieval historians realize that their knowledge about women in medieval times depends too heavily on church records.

Note: When she reached the editing stage for the model paper, "Needed: Stories for Girls to Live By" (pp. 78–81), the author made these changes:

1. She rewrote the title to make it more specific.

2. She made several minor word changes, selecting stronger verbs, putting people in as sentence subjects, and trimming sentences and phrases to make them more concise.

3. She added a subtitle before the section on proposed solutions.

Improve the Body Language of Your Document

After you've finished revising your report, article, or document, lay the pages out on a table and consider how the whole package looks. Do you have an attractive document with ample margins and white space? Does it need to be broken into sections? Would graphs, illustrations, or pictures improve it? Are the paragraphs too long?

Now review Chapter 12 on document design. What strategies can you use to improve your paper's body language?

Following are the principal strategies for improving the way a document looks:

- Adding white space
- Dividing and chunking
- Highlighting

Adding white space

Remember that you never want your writing to look crowded and dense—that puts readers off. So check your margins. They should be at least one inch on both sides and one and one-half inches at top and bottom. Also leave at least two spaces after your title—often it helps to break up the title into two centered lines.

Double-space any manuscript or paper you're handing in to a professor. For other kinds of documents, experiment. Sometimes you can use one and a half spaces between lines; or, if the format calls for single spacing, always leave two lines between paragraphs.

Leave good margins around any charts, illustrations, or pictures you use and don't jam the caption too close to the bottom of the illustration.

Dividing and chunking

First, look at your paragraphs. Do some of them stretch on for half a page or more? If so, find places to break them. (See Chapter 9 for suggestions about breaking your paragraphs.)

If you spot a paragraph that's overstuffed with information, try arranging the information into a list. For example, here is an overloaded paragraph:

> The following individuals will be honored at Harvard Commencement this year: J. P. Jones, president of the Foundation for Human Potential; Mary Hardin Coulthard, winner of the Howson Economics Fellowship; Daniel Moorhead, professor of biology at Oxford University; and Maxwell Cannon, director of the Harvard Fund for Excellence.

It's much easier to follow when you break it up like this:

> The following individuals will be honored at Harvard Commencement this year:
>
> J. P. Jones, president of the Foundation for Human Potential;
> Mary Hardin Coulthard, winner of the Howson Economics Fellowship;
> Daniel Moorhead, professor of biology at Oxford University; and
> Maxwell Cannon, director of the Harvard Fund for Excellence.

Second, use headings and subheadings to break up long passages of text. Find the natural divisions in your report or article and mark them off with headings that tell the reader what is coming. Often you can accentuate these headings by putting them in different fonts, usually a sans serif font that contrasts with the serif font used for the body of your paper or report. (See pp. 195–200 in Chapter 12.) Notice that's the pattern in this book.

Third, break up long passages of text with graphs or illustrations when they can be used effectively. Putting units of information into boxes (see the next section) also helps to break up long stretches of text.

Fourth, in brochures or newsletters, break up columns of print with rows of dingbats (see Chapter 12, p. 196) or just by inserting a heavy line between units.

Highlighting

While editing, you may decide that you want to draw attention to specific points or set off particular units so that they will catch the readers' attention. Here are some ways you can emphasize specific items in your paper.

First, indent and use what printers call "bullets." You can use a variety of symbols for such bullets. In most word processing programs, you'll find several symbols under the Key Caps option. You'll find others under font choices like Wingding or Monotype Sorts. Or, if you're limited to a typewriter, choose one of the signs that come over the number keys at the top. Here's an example of a bulleted list:

Hourly wages for high-technology temporary workers

- Computer systems analysts $28.75
- Engineers $28.54
- Computer programmers $25.40
- Technical writers $22.71
- Graphic artists $17.63

Second, set off items you want to emphasize by drawing boxes around them or highlighting them with a screen: that is, a block of color or shading. Screens work particularly well when you want to highlight an item in a newsletter or a bulletin of some kind. For example, you might set off a newsletter item like this one with a screen:

Tip: Use bullets to set off items in a list that don't come in a specific order; use numbers when you want to indicate that the items are steps of a process or are in chronological order.

The grand opening of the John Henry Faulk library will be held at 3:00 PM on Sunday, April 29, in the patio in front of the library. Speakers will include the columnist Molly Ivins, humorist Cactus Pryor, Chairman of the University of Texas Board of Regents Bernard Rapoport, and Faulk's widow, Liz Faulk. The Texas Banjos will play before the event, and the library will open to the public after the ceremony.

Third, you can highlight information by putting it into a chart or graph. (See Chapter 12, pp. 208–09.) This strategy is particularly useful when you're giving figures or comparisons.

Fourth, you can set off words and phrases by boldfacing or italicizing them. In some kinds of documents, you can also increase the size of the type or even use different fonts. (See Chapter 12, pp. 198–201.)

If you're using a computer with an up-to-date word processing program, you should be able to use any of these strategies with only a little practice.

CHECK FOR ERRORS IN USAGE

This textbook makes no attempt to be a handbook of usage or a catalog of rules. What follows is only a quick review of ways to avoid certain usage problems that can be especially troublesome for readers.

Avoid Sentence Fragments

Today's editors and writers are more tolerant than they used to be about sentence fragments, that old bugaboo of traditional grammarians. Nevertheless, in most writing situations, writers still do well to abide by the traditional rules. My survey of professional people's response to lapses from standard usage (see pp. 160–62) revealed that more than 65 percent of them said that they would object strongly to finding these sentence fragments in writing that came across their desks:

> He went through a long battle. *A fight against unscrupulous opponents.*
>
> The small towns are dying. *One of the problems being that young people are leaving.*

Forty-four percent said they would object strongly to the following sentence fragment, and 32 percent said they would object a little:

> *Cheap labor and low costs.* These are two benefits enjoyed by Taiwan firms.

I think one must conclude from this evidence that most people in decision-making positions want the writing they see to conform to the rules for sentences that they learned in school.

Recognize minor sentences and formal fragments

But any person who notices sentence structure as he or she reads contemporary writing will recognize dozens of groups of words that are punctuated as sentences but don't fit the definition just given. They occur not only in advertising, where they are used for their eye-catching, emphatic effect, but in expository prose in mainstream magazines and newspapers. For example:

> That quality of elusiveness [about gangs] has deepened fears among New Yorkers shocked by a series of attacks that became known as wilding in the wake of the attack last year on a jogger in Central Park. A litany of incidents this year has involved youths in roving groups. *The Halloween night killing. An attack by 10 or 12 bat-wielding youths on two Canadian students visiting the city in September after the tourists stopped to help an elderly woman who had fallen. The slaying of a tourist from Utah on a subway platform as he tried to protect his mother from gang members who wanted money to go dancing.*
>
> —Felicia Lee, "Loose Knit Type of Youth Gangs Troubling Police," *New York Times*, 13 Dec. 1990: B3

Obviously the passage works well, communicates its ideas clearly, economically, and forcefully, yet uses few traditional sentences. The puzzled student writer might well ask why such writers feel free to use sentence fragments. The answer is that the so-called fragments that this writer uses are not really incomplete groups of words; rather they are what some grammarians call "minor sentences" or "formal fragments."

This definition recognizes that when we can read a group of words and make sense out of it, we mentally process it as a sentence whether or not it has all those elements that a sentence is traditionally supposed to have. Or to put it another way, readers can sometimes reach closure at the end of a group of words even if that group does not have a subject or verb; when that happens, that group can be marked off with a period and called a "minor sentence," a legitimate division of writing.

Recognize true sentence fragments

Groups of words that really are sentence fragments—that is, incomplete pieces of a coherent whole—are those that *don't* work by themselves. There may be several reasons why they leave the reader in suspense. They may begin an idea and not carry it through, they may express only part of an idea and thus confuse the reader, or they may form a phrase or clause that does not make sense by itself and yet is not attached to anything else.

Here are some typical examples:

There are few assertions in the article and little evidence to support them. *An example being, "It is unclear whether these intruders had anything to do with the crime."*

The italicized words here need to be attached to a base; although they are punctuated as a sentence, they make no sense by themselves.

Unlike doctors, lawyers are ready to practice when they get their degrees. *Although it is often necessary to take an expensive course in order to pass the bar exam.*

The italicized portion should be joined with the sentence; otherwise the "although" raises expectations that the writer does not meet.

Probably the best guideline to keep in mind about writing sentence fragments is not to use them unless you are trying for some specific effect. And when you do use word groups that are technically sentence fragments, think carefully about your audience and your purpose. Not only professionals but most professors prefer that you write straightforward, traditional sentences that will convey your meaning efficiently and not raise any distracting usage problems.

If, however, you are writing descriptive prose in which you want to communicate impressions or if you are writing an informal, breezy article for a general audience, you may find that putting in an occasional minor sentence or fragment will help to create the tone and tempo that you want. But do know what you are doing, and in a writing class, be prepared to defend your choices.

Avoid Comma Splices

If you use a comma instead of a conjunction to join two groups of words that could be read as sentences, you create a *comma splice* (sometimes also called a *comma fault* or a *comma blunder*). That is, you join independent clauses with a punctuation mark that is so weak it cannot properly indicate the strong pause that should come in such a sentence. Here is an example of a weakly punctuated sentence:

The first part of the book gave Jim no problem, it was the second part that baffled him.

The reader does not get a strong sense of separation between the two parts of the sentence. The emphasis would come through more clearly if it were written like this:

The first part of the book gave Jim no problem, but the second part baffled him.

Or this:

> Although the first part of the book gave Jim no problem, the second part baffled him.

Either revision correctly de-emphasizes the first part of the sentence and puts the stress on the second.

For two reasons you should avoid comma splices. First, independent commas that "tack" clauses together indicate that you are unsure or unconcerned about the relationship between the parts of the sentences. Second, commas that join independent clauses invite misinterpretation. A comma is such a weak interrupter that the reader is liable to slip right over it. However, if you want to join several short independent clauses with commas to increase the tempo of your writing, you can probably do so without creating any problems. For example:

> It's not smart, it's not practical, it's not legal.

Avoid Fused or Run-on Sentences

Sentences in which two independent clauses have been run together without any punctuation are confusing to readers. For example:

> The success of horror movies is not surprising some people have always enjoyed being frightened.

Without punctuation, a reader at first makes "some people" the object of "is surprising" and then has to go back and reprocess the sentence. Also, without punctuation the reader at first misses the cause and effect relationship of the clauses. This sentence could be revised:

> The success of horror movies is not surprising because some people have always enjoyed being frightened.

Avoid Dangling Modifiers

Modifying phrases that don't fit with the word or phrase that they seem to be attached to can cause problems for readers. Usually those misfit phrases, which we call *dangling modifiers*, come at the beginning of a sentence as an introductory phrase:

> *After leaving Cheyenne,* the cost of living became a problem.

The reader expects to find out who left Cheyenne but is frustrated.
Here is another example:

On coming back to college, child care isn't easy to arrange.

The reader stumbles over the junction after "college" and has to reread to get the meaning of the sentence. This kind of error is easy to fix once you have seen it. The first sentence could be rewritten:

After he left Cheyenne, Jack found the cost of living a problem.

The second could be rearranged like this:

Coming back to college, married women often have trouble arranging child care.

Notice that you increase your chances of beginning a sentence with a dangling modifier when you use impersonal sentence subjects. If the author of these two sentences had put in a personal sentence subject in the first place, the mistakes wouldn't have occurred.

Make Structures Parallel

Practiced writers use parallel structures frequently in order to unify and tighten their writing. That is, they incorporate two or more points in a sentence by using a series of phrases or clauses that have identical structure. For instance:

Country western fans love Willie Nelson, jazz fans love Oscar Peterson, and ballad fans love Judy Collins.
Stein hit Hollywood determined to live high, hang loose, stay single, and make money.

Sentences like these work by establishing a pattern that helps the reader to anticipate what is coming. It is like seeing groups of similar figures on a test sheet: circles together, triangles together, squares together, and so on. But when people see a figure that doesn't fit—a circle among the triangles, for instance—the exception jars their sense of unity. The same thing happens when readers find phrases or clauses that don't fit the pattern of the rest of the sentence. Here is an example of faulty parallelism:

My purpose was to show what services are available, how many people use them, and *having the audience feel the services are significant.*

The reader does a double take after the second comma because the third point is not handled in the same way as the first two.

Avoid Faulty Predication

Every complete sentence must have at least two parts: a subject and verb. The verb, along with all of the parts that go with the verb to make a statement, is called the *predicate* of the sentence. Thus the portion of the sentence that completes the assertion that began with the subject of the sentence is called the *predication of a sentence*. Sometimes, however, people write sentences that pair up subjects and verbs, or objects and verbs, that just don't work well together. We call the problem caused by such mismatched combinations *faulty predication*. Most cases of faulty predication seem to fall into one of three categories:

1. *Mismatched subject + active verb:*

    The rape center will accompany the victim to court.

    Research grants want to get the best qualified applicants.

In each of these sentences the writer has predicated an action that the subject could not carry out; a "rape center" cannot "accompany" someone, and a "research grant" cannot "want." Notice that if the writers had used personal subjects instead of abstract ones for these sentences, they would have avoided the mistake. If you start your main clause with a person as the subject, you are much less apt to join that subject with a mismatched verb.

2. *Subject + linking verb + mismatched complement:*

    The main trait a person needs is success.

    The activities available for young people are swimming pools and tennis courts.

    Energy and transportation are problems for our generation.

When people write sentences like these, they seem to have forgotten that the verb *to be* and other linking verbs act as a kind of equal sign (=) in sentences in which the word finishing the sentence is a noun. Thus when they use a linking verb after a subject, they should be sure that the noun complement they put after it can logically be equated with the subject. In none of the sentences above could the reader make that equation. "Success" is not a "trait," "activity" cannot be a "swimming pool," and "energy" cannot be equated with "problem."

Again, if the writers of these sentences had started out with personal subjects, they probably would not have gotten into these tangles. These sentences could be rewritten:

> A person needs to be successful.
>
> Young people can use the swimming pools and tennis courts.
>
> Our generation faces problems with energy and transportation.

Writers who use the construction "[Something] is when . . ." get tangled in the same kind of mistake:

> The worst problem is when motorists ignore these signals.
>
> Community property is when husband and wife share all earnings.

Although a reader is not likely to misunderstand these sentences, they are substandard usage. The writers are actually saying "problem = when" and "property = when." The best way to avoid this difficulty is simply to make it a rule not to use the construction *is when.*

> 3.   *Subject + verb + mismatched object:*
>
> These theories intimidate the efforts of amateur players.
>
> The company fired positions which had been there only six months.

In these sentences, the writers have not thought about the limitations they put on themselves when they used the verbs "intimidate" and "fired." Both verbs have to apply to people (or at least creatures). You cannot "intimidate" an "effort" or "fire" a "position." Again, notice that if they had used concrete instead of abstract words as objects, they probably would not have gotten into the problem.

One of your concerns when you read your first draft should be to check your verbs to see that you have matched them with logical subjects and complements. And although there are no rules that will keep you from getting tangled in predication knots, I can suggest one guideline for avoiding problems: Use personal and concrete subjects whenever you can, and connect your verbs to specific and concrete terms. If you do this and write actor/action sentences (see p. 110) you will eliminate most predication errors.

CHECK FOR SPELLING ERRORS

As I pointed out in Chapter 2, if you have come this far in your education and are still a poor speller, it's unlikely you're going to get much better at this stage by memorizing rules. Only a couple of rules seem helpful, and even they have many exceptions. If you are a poor speller, however, there are two things you can do:

1. Recognize that you're a poor speller and decide to do something about it.
2. Develop a set of habits to overcome your handicap.

For that is what it is—a handicap, and in many writing situations, a fairly serious one. Some readers react so negatively to bad spelling that they decide the writer is incompetent before they have read more than a page or two. Many businesspeople are almost fanatics about correct spelling because they worry, with reason, that customers and clients will react badly to poor spelling in a document that bears their company's name.

In spite of these dire warnings, don't shy away from using a word because you're not sure how to spell it. If you do, your style will suffer and your ideas might too. Hang on to your fresh ideas and stylish sentences— you can find ways to correct your spelling. Here are some suggestions:

- When you read through your third draft, circle any words about which you're in doubt or that you know are tricky: for instance, *villain, harass,* and *rhythm*. If you know you frequently confuse *except* and *accept,* mark those. Then when you proofread, look up any word you've marked. If you typically have trouble with those cussed words that end with *-ible* or *-able* but sound exactly alike, mark those too.

- Buy a dictionary and use it. No excuses. Anyone who wants to write well should keep a dictionary close at hand and cultivate the habit of consulting it often. As well as verifying spelling, it offers a wealth of information about the nuances of words and about their appropriate use.

- Buy a word list as well as a dictionary. It is an inexpensive, pocket-size book that lists words most commonly misspelled and is much easier to carry with you and consult than a dictionary would be.

- Use ingenuity to locate words you're not certain about. The yellow pages of the telephone book can show you how to spell *psychiatrist* or *prosthesis* or *business* or *stationery*. The index of a textbook will give spellings of special terms like *fiduciary* or *eleemosynary*. A thesaurus can give you the spelling of *impresario* if you know it means a director or manager.

- Keep a notebook or card file of words you consistently have trouble with. In time you'll have a collection of the words that you typically misspell and be able to look them up quickly. Develop some memory tricks that help. For instance, "remember the *gum* in argument"; "stationary" as an *a*djective has an *a* in the ending; "villains are v*ain*"; or "*Emma* is in a dilemma."

- Memorize the spelling of keywords or names you're going to use in a paper. If you're using tricky terms like *syllogism, bourgeoisie,* and *liaison* or names like *Shakespeare* or *Kuhn,* put them on a Post-It note and stick it up over your desk while you're writing.

- Watch especially for contractions that sound like other words. Common ones are *we're, they're,* and *you're.* For me, the last is particularly troublesome. I couldn't begin to count the times I've written *your* instead of *you're* in a first draft.

- Watch for other homonyms—words that sound alike but have different meanings. It's all too easy to write *site* instead of *cite, past* instead of *passed,* or *no* instead of *know.* And if you sometimes confuse *their, there,* and *they're,* circle those words to check.

- DON'T count on a computerized spellchecker to catch your errors. A spellchecker doesn't recognize the difference between *except* and *accept;* in its dictionary both are perfectly good words. Nor can it tell when you're confusing *their, they're,* and *there.* All three words are in its dictionary of correct words. Do run your spellchecker to catch typographical errors, but don't count on it to do your proofreading. It won't.

- If possible, get a second reader. Find a friend who is a good speller and ask him or her to read your paper and mark problem words. Ask your instructor to underline any problem words in your second draft. If you are working in revision groups in your class, ask your fellow students to point out misspelled words in your second draft. However, before you turn to your second reader for help, try your own resources. You can't always count on having someone else around in those final proofreading stages, and you need to develop survival strategies. Gradually you really will become a better speller, or at least you will develop an acute sense for when you need to look things up.

PROOFREAD

Proofreading is a pain, but it's absolutely necessary. Once you go public with your writing, it represents you. Thus the final checkup is crucial.

Writers go about proofreading in different ways—some recommend reading what you've written backward so you can check word by word for typographical errors or misspellings, on the theory that you're reading for technical correctness, not for meaning. I disagree. I believe an author who proofreads his or her work must read for both meaning and mechanics. Whole sentences can get lost, particularly now that computers do wipe things out occasionally. Some recommend reading and touching each word with a pencil as you go; others recommend reading aloud slowly.

My own method is to start at the top of the computer screen or of the printed page and force myself to read slowly, line by line, and pay attention to each word and sentence as I go. Try any of these methods that seems practical for you. Do keep in mind these specifics:

- *Check punctuation.* Have you put apostrophes in possessives and contractions? Do you have semicolons to separate independent clauses joined by *however* or *nevertheless*? Are all proper nouns capitalized, especially *English*?
- *Check for omissions.* Have you left out words? Or do you have words left in that you intended to delete? If you revise on a computer, sometimes you'll find leftover words that you thought you had eliminated. Look for them.
- *Check those pesky details.* Are all parentheses and quotation marks closed? Are all titles of books, plays, or movies underlined or italicized? Are long quotations indented? Are notes, if any, written in good documentation form?

Review Specifications

Review the specifications for your assignment. Does your cover sheet meet all the requirements, with title, date, and so on in the right place? Do you have a running head and the page number on each page? Are notes and a bibliography attached when specified? Check last minute details.

SET PRIORITIES ABOUT ERRORS

I believe that in matters of grammar and usage, not all errors are created equal. Some lapses are so serious that they set off bells in readers' heads, signaling "This writer is careless and/or poorly educated." For example, anyone who writes, "I seen him when I was in New York," has, with most readers, damaged his or her persona rather badly. Other lapses are so minor that they pass almost unnoticed except by the most meticulous readers. For example, the person who writes, "We have a truly unique opportunity," or "The data is confusing in places," has done virtually no damage with 99.5 percent of his or her readers.

I have felt this distinction intuitively, as I'm sure many others have, but we have had no documentation for it. I also felt that student writers would benefit if I could get some proof that indeed some errors are more damaging than others and thus it was worth their while to take pains to avoid those errors.

What Businesspeople Think about Grammar and Usage

In September 1979, I sent a questionnaire to 101 professional people, asking them how they would respond to lapses from standard English usage and mechanics in each of sixty-three sentences if those sentences appeared in a business document that came across their desks. The eighty-four people who responded to the questionnaire represented a broad range of professionals: engineers, judges, bankers, attorneys, architects, public relations executives, corporation and college presidents, tax analysts, investment counselors, and a U.S. congressional representative, to name just a few. They ranged in age from thirty to seventy, but most were in their late forties and early fifties. Twenty-two were women, and sixty-two were men. No English teachers were included in the survey.

Each of the sixty-three sentences on the questionnaire contained one error in usage or mechanics, and the respondents were asked to mark one of these responses for every sentence: Does Not Bother Me, Bothers Me a Little, Bothers Me a Lot. The last question asked for an open-ended comment about the most annoying feature they encountered in writing they had to read.

After tabulating all the responses to the sentences and reading all the comments, I came to these general conclusions about how professional people react to writing that they encounter in the course of their work:

> *First*, women take a more conservative attitude about standard English usage than men do. On every item, the percentage of women marking "Bothers Me a Lot" was much higher than the percentage of men.
>
> *Second*, the defects in writing that professional people complained of most were lack of clarity, wordiness, and failure to get to the point. They also complained strongly about poor grammar, faulty punctuation, and bad spelling.
>
> *Third*, the middle-aged, educated, and successful men and women who occupy positions of responsibility in the business and professional world care about how people write. Even allowing for the strong

possibility that they were more than normally conservative in responding to a questionnaire from an English teacher, most professionals believe that writers should know and observe the conventions of standard English usage.

Fourth, professional people clearly consider some lapses in usage and mechanics much more serious than others.

Here is the way they ranked items on the questionnaire:

- *Extremely serious lapses from the standard:*
  Incorrect verb forms ("he brung," "we was," "he don't")
  Double negatives
  Sentence fragments
  Subjects in the objective case ("Him and Jones are going")
  Fused sentences ("He loved his job he never took holidays")
  Failure to capitalize proper names, especially those referring to people and places
  A comma between the verb and complement of the sentence ("Cox cannot predict, that street crime will diminish")

- *Serious lapses from the standard:*
  Faulty parallelism
  Subject-verb disagreement
  Adjectives used to modify verbs ("He treats his men bad")
  Not marking interrupters such as *however* with commas
  Subjective pronouns used for objects ("The army sent my husband and I to Japan")
  Confusion of the verbs *sit* and *set*

- *Moderately serious lapses:*
  Tense shifting
  Dangling modifiers
  Failure to use quotation marks around quoted material
  Plural modifier with a singular noun ("*These* kind")
  Omitting commas in a series
  Faulty predication ("The policy intimidates applications")
  Ambiguous use of *which*
  Objective form of a pronoun used as a subjective complement ("That is her across the street")
  Confusion of the verbs *affect* and *effect*

- *Lapses that seem to matter very little:*
  Failure to distinguish between *who* and *whom* or *whoever* and *whomever*
  Omitting commas to set off interrupting phrases such as appositives

Joining independent clauses with a comma: that is, a comma splice

Confusion of *its* and *it's*

Failure to use the possessive form before a gerund ("The company objects to *us* hiring new salespeople")

Failure to distinguish between *among* and *between*

■ *Lapses that do not seem to matter:*

A qualifying word used before *unique* ("That is the *most* unique plan we have seen")

They used to refer to a singular pronoun ("Everyone knows *they* will have to go")

Omitting a comma after an introductory clause

Singular verb form used with *data* ("The data *is* significant")

Linking verb followed by *when* ("The problem is when patients refuse to cooperate")

Using the pronoun *that* to refer to people

Using a colon after a linking verb ("The causes of the decline are: inflation, apathy, and unemployment")

Warning: Many of your teachers may well object to grammatical mistakes that businesspeople consider rather minor, so it's well to edit your writing as carefully as you can.

11

WRITING RESEARCH PAPERS

 Learning something new can be one of life's great pleasures.

Research isn't what it used to be. In the 1990s if you have access to electronic encyclopedias, to the Internet, and to programs like Proquest and Lexis/Nexis through your college library, you have a world of information at your command through channels that didn't exist ten years ago. Today research is easier, more exciting, and more rewarding. It's also easier to communicate with others about your research and to tap into the expertise that has become available through chat groups and listservs.

But with these riches come complications. Researchers on the Internet can quickly find themselves overwhelmed by information, some of it of dubious value. In order to use these new resources productively, you have to learn more efficient search strategies than you may have used before. Perhaps even more important, you need to learn how to sift and evaluate the material you find. I'll talk more about both of these concerns later in this chapter in connection with using electronic resources.

There is a general approach for doing research papers, whether they are for a course, a magazine, a company, an agency, or an organization. This approach entails the following steps:

- *Selecting a topic*
  Defining your purpose
  Identifying your audience
  Formulating a research question

■ *Researching*
Setting up search strategies
Reading, collecting material, taking notes
Evaluating sources

■ *Writing*
Organizing your material
Writing a draft
Mastering the conventions of format and documentation

SELECTING A TOPIC

When you write a research paper, you're going to invest a lot of time and effort; so if you have a choice of topics, be good to yourself right from the start. Choose a topic that truly interests you, a question or problem that will take you on a journey of discovery that will help you learn more about something that's important to you. If your topic truly engages you, you'll write with a sense of purpose.

When you have a range of choices, pick an area you already know something about and would enjoy exploring further. For example, you might want to learn more about the Mayan civilization because last summer you went on an archaeological dig at the Tikal ruins in Guatamala. If you're interested in recent history in South Africa, you might want to write a paper on Nelson Mandela, the civil rights leader who became president of South Africa after spending more than twenty-five years as a political prisoner in that country. If you enjoy reading about that remarkable medieval queen, Eleanor of Aquitaine, some aspect of her life might make a good topic for you. Try to go where your interests lead you.

Defining Your Purpose

Whatever your topic, you should have a purpose behind your research. Perhaps your instructor has specified that purpose in the assignment by using a term such as *analyze, explain, investigate, compare, prove,* or *discuss.* He or she may also have combined terms, suggesting that you "analyze and discuss" or "investigate and compare." As you work on your draft, you should keep checking to see that you're doing what the assignment specifies.

Then think about your own purposes. Of course, a primary one is to produce a carefully researched and well-written and well-documented paper that will earn you a good grade. But beyond that, you should write your paper to demonstrate something, to convince your readers of some proposition. In a paper on Nelson Mandela, you might argue that the friendships he made in prison and his experience in negotiating with the prison authorities played an important part in developing his political skills. In a paper on Eleanor of Aquitaine, you might want to learn more about the role she played in the Second Crusade.

In this early stage of planning your paper, it's useful to get down a tentative thesis sentence that sums up the main points you plan to make. For example,

> The twenty-five years that he spent as a political prisoner for opposing apartheid in South Africa did not weaken or diminish Nelson Mandela; rather he used that time to cultivate friendships with fellow apartheid fighters and to develop the skills of diplomacy and negotiation that led him to the presidency of South Africa in 1992.

Any such thesis is only a working statement; almost certainly you would want to revise and refine it for the final version of your paper.

Identifying the Audience: Your Instructor and Beyond

Whether you are writing a research paper on an assigned topic or on a topic you've chosen, you need to begin by considering who your readers are and what they want to get from your paper. First is your professor. Professors always hope to learn something new from their students—that's one of the bonuses of teaching. But in addition to reading for content—new information and interesting ways of looking at familiar information—professors read your research papers with several other concerns in mind. They want to do the following:

- evaluate your knowledge of your subject matter
- determine your ability to make a valid claim, find information that will support it, and present your case in a clear and organized fashion
- assess your mastery of the formal conventions of research writing in a given academic field; for example, the format recommended by the Modern Language Association (MLA) for an English paper or the format recommended by the American Psychological Association (APA) for a paper in sociology or psychology

But it's useful to identify another audience besides your professor, another group of readers you would like to influence or inform. You could choose a publication that might publish something about the topic you're writing on. For example, a travel magazine might be interested in an article you would do on your visit to Tikal, the Mayan site in Guatemala. At the very least, assume that you are writing for other students in the class for which you're writing the paper and ask yourself the following:

What do they already know about my topic?

What would they like to know?

What kind of details are likely to interest them?

If you are writing your paper in a class in which students collaborate in responding to drafts of each other's papers, these questions will be particularly helpful.

Formulating a Research Question

Regardless of the conditions placed on your research assignment, your first step must be to formulate a question (or questions) that you hope to be able to answer with the help of the outside sources you consult. You may, for instance, want to find out the answers to questions such as "What can the average citizen do on a daily basis to help protect the natural environment?" or "What means of financial assistance are available to college graduates wishing to continue an education in hotel management" or "Why is California the site of so many earthquakes?" or "How does the film version of *Sense and Sensibility* compare with the novel?" If you were writing a paper on Nelson Mandela, you might phrase your question like this: "What personal and political experiences shaped Nelson Mandela into the South African leader who was instrumental in bringing about the end of apartheid?"

Regardless of the particular discipline for which you are writing, you must avoid the temptation to begin your research with questions that are based on unproved assumptions or that lead to obvious or foregone conclusions. The question, "Why is it imperative for the United States to remain involved in Latin American political affairs?" is *not* an appropriate topic for academic research because it presupposes the validity of an arguable assumption—that it *is* imperative for the United States to remain involved in Latin American affairs. Similarly, the question "How has commercialism corrupted professional sports?" would be inappropriate if the underlying assumption—commercialism *has* corrupted professional sports—cannot be convincingly established. When you are researching and writing about topics that are controversial or surrounded by debate, your first task may be to show that you're arguing from valid assumptions.

RESEARCHING

Setting Up a Search Strategy

Only when you have defined your purpose and audience and formulated your research question are you ready to begin your research. Once you reach this point, keep several important principles in mind as you plan your research strategy:

1. Make a plan for budgeting your time, working *backward* from your due date. For example, if you receive your assignment on March 15 for a paper due on April 20, you might plan your time like this:

    April 20: Submit revised final paper to instructor.
    April 16: Receive annotated draft from instructor.
    April 12: Give draft to instructor.
    April 8–10: Revise and rewrite draft.
    April 1–7: Write first draft. Confer with classmates or a second reader for feedback.
    March 24–31: Refine and focus topic, do additional research on-line and in library. Make notes and rough out an outline.
    March 16–23: Select topic; do preliminary research on the Internet, Proquest, and in Lexis/Nexis.

Believe me, it helps to set deadlines for yourself and post due dates in some prominent place where you'll see them every day.

2. Remember that everything will take longer than you anticipate. Electronic sources are wonderful, but browsing the Web or Lexis/Nexis and following up on links you may find can be extremely time-consuming. Taking careful, thorough notes on index cards, downloading articles from magazines, or making photocopies also takes a great deal of time. Inevitably you'll run into snags—copy machines don't work, you encounter a traffic jam on the Internet, or you can't locate a source. All are good reasons for delay, but your instructor doesn't want to hear excuses when the paper is due.

3. Make some sort of research outline that tells you what sources you need to consult and the order in which you need to work through those sources. If you need to send away for information or set up interviews or conduct surveys, take care of these time-consuming research tasks first so that you will have time to think about your information before you begin to write your paper. Then if your research takes longer than you anticipated, you won't find yourself having to begin writing your paper without having consulted your most valuable sources.

4. Set a deadline when you must stop researching and begin drafting your paper. Sometimes it's tempting to keep looking for more information, especially when you discover new leads to sources you did not know about when you started. However tantalizing these leads are, you may not be able to follow up on them, simply because you are running out of time. If this is the case, you might mention in your conclusion or in an informational note the potential value of these sources for further study.

Using Primary and Secondary Sources

After planning your research strategy, begin collecting data that will help you answer your research question or that will prove or disprove your hypothesis. You will be concerned with two types of information sources—*primary* and *secondary* sources. In general, the difference between these types of sources is the difference between firsthand and secondhand information. Primary sources are those that deal most directly with your topic—reports of a person's contemporaries, letters, reports, and so on. Secondary sources generally comment on and help you to interpret your primary sources.

In a research paper for a history course, for instance, your primary sources might be newspaper articles or government documents, letters or diary entries written or published during the historical period you are writing about. Your secondary sources might be books or articles written by historians who have also consulted those same primary sources in their analyses of the same historical period or event. But remember that you need to bring a fresh perspective to those secondary sources.

In a research paper for a literature course, your primary sources would be the literary texts that you are interpreting or criticizing, or the letters or journals of the author whose work you are investigating. Secondary sources would include books, articles, lectures, and reviews by literary critics on the subject of your paper. In a scientific research paper, your own observations and experiments might be your primary sources, whereas reports of other scientific investigators on the same or a closely related topic would constitute your secondary sources.

Doing original research

It's important to remember that if you are asked to do original research, you must work almost entirely from primary sources. For example, suppose you were asked to do original research on student protests against the Vietnam War in the 1960s. First, you would probably have to go to an encyclopedia to find out when and where such protests took place; then you would need to pick a period and place on which to focus your attention—perhaps the protests at Kent State when four students were killed or protests at the Democratic national convention in 1968. You would then go to newspaper indexes for papers like the *New York Times* and the *Los Angeles Times* to find news stories from those dates that would tell you what happened at such protests, writing your paper from the information you found in those papers or in magazines such as *Time* or *U.S. News and World Report*. You should not use articles or books that reflected on the protests or tried to interpret them, usually at a later time, although you might want to read such articles for your own enlightenment.

If you were asked to write a paper based on original research in an American literature course, you might pick a topic such as the role of women in Willa Cather's novels. You could then select four novels—perhaps *My Ántonia, The Professor's House, The Song of the Lark*, and *A Lost Lady*—read them carefully, analyze the way Cather portrays her women characters, and write a paper identifying and reflecting on her handling of the women characters. In such an assignment, resist the temptation to see what other writers have said—the professor who asks for original research wants to know your response, not that of the critics.

Searching outside the library

Although a great deal of academic research takes place in the library, it is by no means the only place where you can collect data for college research papers. Indeed, the dividing line between library and nonlibrary research is becoming blurred as computer access to the Internet makes it possible for you to search through some library materials and indexes from your own desk without making an actual trip to the library. A separate section in this chapter addresses some of the new research possibilities and problems introduced by modern information technology. Although you may turn first to the Internet, there are times when other nonlibrary sources can provide more direct, specific, and up-to-date information than you can find in your library's holdings.

Suppose, for instance, that you wanted to find out how your own community was responding to a water shortage brought about by the summer's drought. Because your question refers to a local situation, it is unlikely that you would turn up much useful information in the sorts of national and international publications that make up the bulk of a university library's holdings. Instead, you would want to gather information locally—looking for materials such as announcements published by city officials, perhaps, or arranging interviews with city council members, employees at the local water works plant, or members of local citizens action groups. You might even want to interview or survey private citizens to get a sense of how the local population is responding to suggestions made by city or state officials.

Local news broadcasts on radio or television and locally published newspapers are other potential sources of information that could help you answer your research question.

Keep in mind that nonlibrary research can be used in combination with library research. On a college or university campus, for instance, you may well have access to knowledgeable experts in the subject of your research. Suppose you are investigating the question "What is feminism?" The question is extremely broad—so broad that it defies a single, definitive answer, since feminism, like any political philosophy, is ultimately defined in the practices and beliefs of many and various individuals and groups over time.

Your objective may be to gain a sense of the range of ways feminism has been defined and to discover how these definitions diverge from one another or how they converge on common ground. Or you might want to trace the historical development of feminism as a political force in a particular context—in U.S. legal codes, for example, or in college curricula. Because the question is so broad and so complex, you may find it useful to begin your research by consulting local experts—faculty in the political science or women's studies departments, for instance, or staff members at the campus women's resource center. Such individuals may be able to streamline your research process by giving you suggestions about where to begin your search of library sources, and they may be able to offer you some of their own insights on your research topic. Experts whom you consult in person can sometimes provide you with brochures or in-house publications on your topic that are not readily available in libraries.

Other potentially helpful nonlibrary sources include television and radio broadcasts, documentary films, and informational pamphlets published by professional organizations or special interest groups. You may even have a research question that calls for you to perform your own empirical research, either by conducting polls and surveys or by scientific experimentation.

If you feel that collecting data through empirical research is in order for your research paper, you should be aware that there are certain ground rules to follow in designing questionnaires and conducting surveys. Your professor may be able to give you some guidelines on these and related matters or to direct you to other people or printed sources that can give you the information you need.

Using the Library

Another type of research—one that is important in all disciplines from the sciences to the fine arts—is library research. Library research involves printed or taped or otherwise published sources of information that you can locate by consulting various indexes, bibliographies, and catalogs in the library. Your topic, and your research question, will determine what kinds of library resources are most helpful to you. For topics that are very timely—for instance, legislation currently being discussed or enacted by Congress, or the latest developments in computer technology—newspapers, periodicals, government documents, and government sites on the Internet, such as *Thomas: Legislative Information on the Internet,* are more likely sources of information than books or reference works such as encyclopedias, which require considerable time for the publication process.

While libraries today include an ever-widening range of types of materials in their holdings, including maps, pamphlets, and videotapes, the sources that are most frequently used in college research fall into several broad categories:

- Periodicals
- Newspapers
- Government documents
- Books
- Electronic sources

Periodicals

Periodicals are printed materials such as magazines, newsletters, and professional journals that are published *periodically*—monthly, seasonally, annually, etc. Because of their publication schedules they often contain more up-to-date material than you can find in books, and so they are an extremely important source of information for college researchers. Usually the most recent issues of periodicals are shelved unbound, while older issues are bound into individually indexed volumes. Some heavily used periodicals, such as newsmagazines, are often stored on microfiche instead of or in addition to bound volumes.

Finding articles in these sources requires that you consult special guides or indexes to periodical literature. The most general of these, and one that is apt to be found in even very small libraries, is the *Readers' Guide to Periodical Literature.* If you didn't learn to use this reference work in high school or in an introductory college writing course, you can easily teach yourself how to use it now, or you can ask your reference librarian for assistance. Other, more specialized guides and indexes to periodicals are likely to be more useful to you as a college-level researcher who will be consulting specialized academic journals. Some of the major indexes of this sort are the following:

- *Applied Science and Technology Index*
- *Art Index*
- *Biography Index*
- *Book Review Digest*
- *Business Index*
- *The Education Index*
- *Engineering Index*
- *General Science Index*
- *Humanities Index*
- *Index Medicus*
- *MLA International Bibliography*
- *Public Affairs Information Service (PAIS)*
- *Social Sciences and Humanities Index*

If your library is fairly large, it probably has many more specialized indexes and bibliographies, which can be located by consulting the subject entries in a special catalog for reference works. Many libraries today have computerized card catalogs that allow you to search from a computer terminal for articles in the library's periodical holdings. Usually, guides to using on-line indexes are provided at terminals in the library. They will tell you what indexes are available to you on-line and will give you instructions for accessing the available indexes and for conducting various types of searches. Sometimes libraries give short courses to help you learn to use on-line search tools; you should consider signing up for such a course. It could save you lots of time in the long run.

When you find a citation in an index or bibliography for an article that sounds helpful to you, copy down the full citation. This will not only help you locate the article itself but will also save you time later on, when you need to compile a bibliography for your paper. The same is true, of course, for citations of materials from other sources as well—newspapers, documents, books, pamphlets, TV and radio broadcasts, documentary films, the Internet, interviews, and so forth.

While using bibliographies and indexes is an efficient way to locate periodical articles, you will find that current issues of most periodicals are often not indexed. If up-to-date information is essential to your investigation, check the most recent issues on the periodicals display shelves. You can also ask a librarian if Proquest is available; it contains a wide variety of fairly current articles on CD-ROM disks that you can read on screeen. Often you can print out an article from Proquest on a library printer. Usually you'll have to pay (generally by the page).

Newspapers

The procedure for locating newspaper articles is similar to that for finding information in periodicals. The major indexes for newspaper articles on national and international topics include the following:

- *The New York Times Index*
- *National Newspaper Index*
  Lists articles from the *New York Times*, the *Christian Science Monitor*, and the *Wall Street Journal*
- *The Newspaper Index*
  Lists articles from the *Chicago Tribune*, the *Los Angeles Times*, the *New Orleans Times-Picayune* and the *Washington Post*. These four papers also give regional news for their areas.

Printed versions of these indexes often do not arrive in libraries until some time after their publication, so computerized indexes are your best bet if you are researching current news stories. You'll find some of the most useful computerized search tools in Newsbank, which indexes a microfiche collection of stories from over 400 U.S. newspapers. Yet another source of national and international news stories is the World Wide Web, which allows on-line access to current articles in most major newspapers published in this and other countries. Look for such access with search engines such as Yahoo or AltaVista.

Government documents

Most large libraries contain a special section for U.S. government publications, a type of source that can be especially useful to you if you are writing a research paper for history, political science, law, or social science courses. Some government publications are indexed in the public catalog and are shelved according to Library of Congress or Dewey Decimal numbers. Other, uncataloged documents are kept in the government documents section of the library, arranged according to Superintendent of Documents numbers. Still others are kept on microform in collections called microform sets. These too are filed according to Superintendent of Documents numbers.

Below are listed a few of the major indexes you can use to locate government documents publications. In many libraries you will find a number of other indexes as well, and you should ask a librarian for assistance if you have difficulty using them.

- *Monthly Catalog of United States Government Publications*

- *The Federal Index*
- *Index to U.S. Government Periodicals*
- *C.I.S.U.S. Serial Set Index*
- *Washington Information Directory*

Books

Books or sections of books can also be extremely valuable sources of information for research papers on a wide range of topics. Sometimes you will find entire books listed in the specialized indexes and bibliographies that you consult, but you can compile a more extensive list of potentially helpful books by consulting the card catalog or on-line search terminal in your library. Books are indexed according to subject, title, and author, but generally speaking, the subject category will be the most useful to you. To find out how your topic is likely to be indexed in the catalog, you may want to consult the two-volume *Library of Congress: Subject Headings*, which lists all the subject headings and their subdivisions that appear in the catalog. When you have identified the subject headings under which you are most likely to find useful information, begin searching for book titles first under the headings that most specifically describe your subject.

Computer searches

Many college libraries now have computerized indexes and databases that will let you do computer searches as part of your research. Ask your reference librarian about what facilities are available and how you get started. Fortunately, computer indexes in libraries are almost always accompanied by detailed instructions and user's guides. Usually you can learn the rudiments very quickly. Do ask about costs, though. Some libraries charge for searches, and you'll want to know ahead of time how much you may have to invest.

Like printed indexes, computerized databases are arranged by author, title, and subject, but a computer index has additional advantages:

- It can be continually updated.
- It can be searched quickly.
- It can give you a printed copy of what you find.

Computer databases work by key words, or *descriptors*, as librarians call them. So if you were doing research about prenatal care among teenage mothers, the descriptors to punch in for your search would be *prenatal care* and *teenage mothers*. If you were particularly interested in the correlation between adequate prenatal care for teenage mothers and the high school attendance record of these mothers, you could add a third descriptor: *high school attendance*. The computer then does a three-way search, narrowing its search to articles that address all three issues. Sometimes you have to be imaginative about your descriptors. For instance, if adding the term *high school attendance* doesn't seem to work, try *high school dropouts*.

Listed below are some useful computerized indexes. If none of these meets your needs, ask the librarian if others have been added recently. More indexes are becoming available all the time.

Topic	*Computer Index*
astronomy	INSPEC
business	ABI/INFORM; Info Trac
contemporary events	Newsbank
contemporary periodicals	Academic Index; Info Trac; PAIS (Public Affairs Information Service)
economics	PAIS
education	ERIC
general information	Wilsondisc (covers same material as *Reader's Guide*)
humanities	Info Trac
literature	MLA Bibliography
mathematics	MATHFILE
psychology	Psyclit
public affairs	PAIS
social science	Info Trac

When you have the information you want on the screen, you can print a copy, and you're in business.

Electronic sources

Many university libraries now have integrated systems that make use of the World Wide Web to direct users to information that is available on the Internet, an ever-expanding worldwide network of several million computers that facilitates information exchange among institutions and individuals. The advent of the Internet has transformed the nature of research by rapidly expanding its scope and increasing the speed with which information can be accessed.

With these expanded possibilities, however, come new problems and challenges for the researcher. The first of these, of course, is mastering the technology that allows access to the Internet. Fortunately, extensive user-friendly documentation and instructional programs are widely available, and in the past year several books have been published specifically to help students learn to use the Internet for their academic tasks. Following is a list of four such books:

> *The Online Student: Making the Grade on the Internet* by Randy Reddick and Elliot King (Harcourt, 1996)
>
> *A Student's Guide to the Internet* by Carol Lea Clark (Prentice Hall, 1996)
>
> *English on the Internet: A Student's Guide* (designed specifically for students in college English classes) by Andrew T. Stull (Prentice Hall, 1997)
>
> *Web Works: A Norton Pocket Guide* by Martin Irvine (Norton, 1997)

A trip to the bookstore may reveal even more recently published guides of this sort.

If you are not already experienced at "surfing" the Internet, you may want to check with your institution's computer center or the library itself to see if you can sign up for a short introductory course that can get you started on the Net. You will need to familiarize yourself with software options called "clients" or "Web browsers," such as Netscape or Microsoft Explorer, that allow you to communicate with "servers" by accessing information in the form of Web pages.

Narrowing your search.   I find that a major problem with using the Internet is narrowing a search so that it will yield a manageable number of items to consider. Using a search engine such as Lycos or AltaVista, you may type in what seems like a fairly specific term only to find it will bring a staggering number of citations. The terms "Lewis and Clark," for example, brought up over 20,000 entries! Now researchers are worse off than before, because they can't begin to examine or assess the value of those entries. So it's important to find very specific terms that will give highly focused and limited results; but sometimes the effort of doing that through trial and error doesn't seem worth the trouble. You might be better off just to go to the library and dig out some books.

Trying to narrow the search and sift through the results can also be frustrating. For instance, in trying to narrow down the Lewis and Clark topic, I typed in the term *Sacajawea,* the name of the Indian woman who acted as guide and translator for the Lewis and Clark expedition. That

entry brought up over 400 citations, supposedly listed in order of useful-
ness. Well, not exactly! Among the first ten entries was a play about Sacajawea written and presented by fourth graders in a small city in Washington. Several others were the Web pages for various schools named after
Sacajawea. So sometimes the cruising the Web can be a great waste of time.
You'll have to decide how much time you want to invest in your search
before you give up and go to less convenient but perhaps more useful
sources.

Evaluating electronic sources.   The Internet opens up a staggering amount of
information to the researcher, but now you have to sort and evaluate the
information you're getting. Remember that no one is in charge on the Internet; there are no editors, instructors, or censors who have approved what's
"published" on it. Anyone can contribute to the store of information available on-line, and as a result, the Internet is full of trash, flames (insults),
lies, and trivia in addition to legitimate factual information, scholarly conversations, and valid, well-considered ideas. Confronted with this staggering array of unmonitored sources and unedited information, individual
researchers must assume increased responsibility for reading critically and
evaluating the sources they find on the Net.

Some of the traditional means of evaluating printed sources—considering the reputation of the author, the reputation of the publishing house and
the date of publication—simply do not hold for Internet sources. There are,
however, some general principles that you can employ to help you evaluate
on-line sources.

All Web pages have *addresses*, called Universal Resource Locators
(URLs for short). There are three main components to every URL: a protocol, a server, and a pathway. Consider the following example, the URL for
a source that provides information about documentation formats for information obtained on the Internet:

http://www.pitsco.com/wel.html

http:// is the *protocol* portion of the address, designating how the
information is stored.

www.pitsco.com/ identifies the *server*, the person or agency responsible
for putting the information on the Internet.

wel.html identifies the *path*, the location of the Web page on the
server. (This designation is omitted on many electronic addresses.)

Particularly important to the task of evaluating the source is the three-
letter code at the end of the server portion of the address. This code desig-
nates the *domain* to which the server belongs. In this case, the domain is
"com," meaning that the server is a *commercial* entity.

MOST COMMON DOMAINS

com—commercial entities   mil—military agencies

edu—educational institutions   org—special interest organizations

gov—government agencies

Knowing the domain of your source will helps you figure out why that site is on the Net. "Com" identifies a for-profit organization that is selling something. "Edu" represents an educational institution serving academic interests, but many thousands of students have put their personal Web site on the Net or have "published" papers they have written—and not necessarily A papers, either. Thus you shouldn't assume that "edu" in an address necessarily legitimizes a source. The suffix "gov" signals a government agency that represents an official government information source; it communicates information similar to that found in printed government documents. "Mil" signals military agencies that represent branches and subgroups of the army services. The suffix "org" represents a wide variety of groups, everything from political parties and lobbying groups—Emily's List or the Heritage Foundation, for example—to nonprofit educational organizations such as the Aspen Institute.

The first portion of the server address may also be useful in helping you decide how to evaluate the source. Sometimes you can tell from this part of the entry if the Web page is the product of an individual, a university, or some other institution. Learning as much as possible about the identity of the source of information on the Internet is the best way to begin knowing how to judge the reliability of the information itself. Some Web pages also tell you when they were last updated. This information is analogous to the publication date on printed materials and is useful in determining how up-to-date the material contained on the page is at the time you access it.

Most of all you'll have to use common sense and your critical faculties to judge the value of information you find. Look for details that show the credentials of the person who put out the information. Does she have an academic title or is he a member of some reputable organization like the Smithsonian Institution or the American Museum of Natural History? Does he or she work for a well-known foundation? Can you find the author in a bibliography related to his or her discipline? Is the information presented in reasonable terms, not highly connotative or exaggerated? Are claims supported? Be skeptical of overstatements or unsupported allegations.

Documenting electronic sources.   Documenting Internet sources poses another challenge for on-line researchers. Information from the Internet or other electronic sources must be documented just as carefully as material obtained from more traditional sources. You have to let readers know where you found the material and how they can duplicate or follow up on-line portions of your research. When the sources to be cited are simply on-line versions of printed materials such as newspapers and journals, the documentation forms are similar to those for printed sources, but some of the nontraditional source materials available on the Internet require innovations in documentation format.

At the time of this writing, the major style manuals have not yet published print versions of their preferred formats for documenting on-line sources, and there is as yet no universally accepted standardized set of on-line documentation guidelines. An even more serious challenge arises because the Internet is not a static entity—it is always changing, and there is no guarantee that the same information will be in the same place the next time you look. Sometimes users will be forwarded to the new location of information that has been transferred from one site to another on the Net, but this is not always the case.

Nevertheless, if you conduct research on the Internet, you must do your best to cite sources as accurately as possible. Probably the best place to find out how to document information you find on the Internet is the Internet itself. The sample URL above is the address of the Pitsco home page, a site that includes information about documentation formats, illustrated with sample entries, for Internet sources in the styles most commonly used for academic and work-related research. From the Pitsco home page, you can get to "Pitsco's Launch to Citing WWW Addresses." It will allow you to access further pages such as the following:

"APA Publication Manual Crib Sheet"

"Bibliographic Formats for Citing Electronic Information"

"Citing Internet Addresses"

"MLA-Style Citations of Electronic Resources"

"MLA Guidelines to Evaluating Computer Related Work"

The documentation information you can access through the Pitsco home page is thorough and continually updated.

There are a number of other Internet sites that provide guidelines for Internet citations. Among them are the following:

- http://www.cas.usf.edu/english/walker/mla.html
  Janice Walker, Department of English, University of South Florida
  (MLA style)

- http://www.uvm.edu/~xli/reference/estyles.html
  Xia Li and Nancy Crane, University of Vermont (APA and MLA styles)

- http://www.nmmc.com/libweb/employee/citguide.html
  Melvin E. Page, Humanities-on-Line and History Department, East Tennessee State University (citation style based on Kate Turabian's style manual)

In print form, a widely used manual for citing on-line sources is *Electronic Style: A Guide to Citing Electronic Information* by Xia Li and Nancy B. Crane (Westport, CT: Meckler, 1995). The citation format offered in this manual is modeled after the APA documentation style currently used by researchers in the sciences and social sciences.

The essential elements of on-line citation forms are the author's name, the title of the document, the date the document was entered onto the Internet, the date the document was retrieved by the researcher, and the address or URL where the document was found. For example:

Sampson, Cornelia. "The Care and Feeding of Budgies" (Online), (Sept. 7, 1995, Retr. August 1, 1996), Available: http://www.uiowa.edu/birds/domestic/internet.html

This citation format is *not* a universally accepted, standardized form, but it is useful because it provides a basic form and informs readers when the cited information could be located at the given location, even though it might no longer be found at the same place.

Any information you get by e-mail should be documented with the e-mail address of the person who sent it to you, and, if it is especially important, with direct quotes from the e-mail. Remember that because e-mail can be impossible to trace or verify once it has been read and deleted, you should use it only sparingly in research.

Serendipity

However you conduct your search, remember to cultivate serendipity (see Chapter 3). Because experienced researchers know the value of such lucky accidents, they stay alert for them, glancing at the titles of books shelved next to the ones they are seeking or running their eyes over the table of contents in a periodical that contains the article on their prepared list. Similarly, on-line "surfing"—exploring Internet hyperlinks without a specific purpose in mind—is a popular pastime for many scholars because it can lead to unexpected, yet valuable, discoveries. Often they find that unplanned breakthroughs in research investigations are prompted by conversations, by media broadcasts or news stories, or by the casual perusals of materials in a library or bookstore. The key is keeping your mind open to the unexpected source; your best piece of information may be the one you stumble onto while you are looking for something else.

You should also try joining electronic conversations on your topic, particularly if you can find a group that's highly focused—for instance, a group that is conversing about a new kind of insulin pump for diabetics might contribute valuable, up-to-date information. Such groups can give you useful names and references. But the interchange on Usenet groups can also be discursive and trivial, not worth your precious research time.

Taking Notes

Sometimes the chore of taking notes for a research paper looms so large that you are tempted to photocopy everything you find, then worry about making sense of it after you leave the library. That's not a good idea, however, unless for some reason you have only limited access to the library. Not only is it expensive to do extensive photocopying, but it also delays the selective skimming you need to do in order to decide which material is usable.

Moreover, if you use photocopies, you will very likely be tempted to simply underline or highlight rather than take notes on what you have read. This practice encourages you to rely too heavily on the original words of your sources before you have digested their ideas and can articulate them in your own words. Photocopying, then, is often a shortcut that actually defeats the whole purpose of research, and in addition can lead to inadvertent plagiarism.

Many people prefer to take notes on index cards because cards are easier to sort and reorganize than sheets of notebook or typing paper. Others, however, prefer to keep all their notes in a notebook because in this form they are easier to carry around and are less likely to get lost. Still others take notes at the computer and organize them in files; an advantage to this method is that you can make back-up files to guard against lost notes and outlines. Whatever method you choose, be sure that you always include full details about the source along with the information. And *always* write down the page numbers for *all* the information you record, whether you directly quote that information or simply refer to it in a summary or paraphrase. If you don't keep track of page numbers at this stage, you will waste time going back to your sources to hunt for those numbers.

Managing Sources and Quotations

Informal citations

Those who write books, magazine articles, or newspaper columns usually cite their sources informally. For example, the columnist William Raspberry might mention a government report he read recently and name the agency that published it but not bother to give the date or location of the report. In a magazine article on gambling, an author might cite the statistic that between 1988 and 1994, casino revenues in the United States grew from $8 billion to $15 billion but not give the source of that statistic. He assumes his readers will accept it. In an academic paper, however, you don't have that luxury. Your instructor wants all the facts connected with a claim, and part of your responsibility is to learn how to present those facts.

In an academic research paper you're obligated to leave a careful and accurate trail that will let readers follow the path of evidence you're presenting and verify that evidence if they wish. You need also to name your sources so readers can judge for themselves what interests those sources might represent. For instance, knowledgeable readers might know that Emily's List is a political organization committed to electing pro-choice, Democratic, women candidates or recognize that the Heritage Foundation is a conservative, Washington-based think tank whose goal is to influence public policy. If they didn't have such information, they should be able to find it from your reference or by looking it up in an encyclopedia or on the World Wide Web.

If you were citing the statistic about the increase in casino gambling in an academic paper, you would need to present the information like this: "In an article in the Autumn 1995 issue of the *Wilson Quarterly*, Professor Robert Goodman says that between 1988 and 1994, casino revenues in the United States nearly doubled—from $8 billion to about $15 billion annually." Then you would give a full citation for the article in the Works Cited portion of your paper so the reader could easily find the article if he or she chose to do so.

When you are attributing opinions or theories to an organization or movement, you need to specify the group that has expressed those opinions or theories. For example, you might write, "The communitarian movement, as described by its founder Amitai Etzioni in his forthcoming book, *The Golden Rule: Community and Morality in a Democratic Society*, holds that there are four basic principles of social justice: equality, mutuality, stewardship, and inclusion." You would then include full information about Etzioni's book in your Works Cited page.

Direct quotations

Give the exact source of every direct quotation. You can do this with footnotes, endnotes, or parenthetical notes within your paper. (See pp. 185–90 for more information about and examples of these conventions.) Integrate quotations of three to four lines or less into the body of your paper, using terms of attribution such *asserts*, *claims*, *argues*, *writes*, and so on, and enclosing them in quotation marks.

Longer quotations should be indented and typed without quotation marks. For example:

In *Great Books*, David Denby says,

> Accepting death in battle as inevitable, the Greek and Trojan aristocrats of the *Iliad* experience the world not as pleasant or unpleasant, nor as good or evil, but as glorious or shameful. We might say that Homer offers a conception of life that is noble rather than ethical—except that such an opposition is finally misleading. For the Greeks, nobility has an ethical quality. You are not good or bad in the Christian sense. You are strong or weak; beautiful or ugly; conquering or vanquished; living or dead; favored by gods or cursed. (39)

In student papers, of course, quotations like these should be double-spaced so they're easy for an instructor to read.

If you omit something from a quotation, you must insert ellipsis marks (. . .) to indicate that something has been left out. For instance:

> After all, Western literature begins with a quarrel between two arrogant pirates over booty. At the beginning of the poem, the various tribes of the Greeks . . . assembled before the walls of Troy are on the verge of disaster. Agamemnon, their leader, the most powerful of the kings, has kidnapped and taken as a mistress from a nearby city a young woman, the daughter of one of Apollo's priests; Apollo has angrily retaliated by bringing down a plague on the Greeks. (Denby 34)

Of course, your omission should never alter the sense of a quotation.

Finally, give additional information in brackets for any term within the quotation that needs further explanation:

> The crux of the poem [*The Iliad*] comes in Book IX, well before Achilles reenters the war. As the Trojans await at their night fires, ready to attack at dawn, the Greeks, now in serious trouble, send three ambassadors to Achilles with promises of gifts. The three warriors . . . beg Achilles to give up his anger. This is what they offer: tripods, cauldrons, horses, gold, slave women, . . . and even the return of Achilles' slave mistress, whom Agamemnon swears he has never touched. What more can Achilles ask for? (Denby 48)

Use quotations sparingly

Don't overload your paper with quotations. You don't want your paper to look as if you patched it together from other people's ideas instead of giving your own opinions and interpretation. Each one should be used for a definite reason:

- To support an important point you are making
- To illustrate a writer's particular point of view
- To cite examples of experts' contrasting opinions

- To illustrate the flavor or force of an author's work
- To give an example of the author's style

Usually you'll do better to summarize an opinion or point of view rather than illustrate it with a quotation, particularly if the quotation would be long. I find that I tend to skim over long quotations because I want to get on to find out what an author herself is saying. I prefer a succinct summary of a point of idea, always assuming it does the original justice.

WRITING THE PAPER

Getting Started

If you have been taking notes in your own words and playing with systems for organizing your notes, you have already begun the process of writing your paper. If you find you are having trouble getting past the hurdle of that first paragraph, you may want to take some time to return to your original research question and do some informal writing about what you have learned since you began looking for answers. How do you understand your topic differently now than you did when you started out? What seem to be the most important things you've learned, and why do you believe they're important? What are the most interesting things you've learned, and why do you find them interesting? Doing such freewriting may help you focus your thoughts and could produce some chunks of text that you will want to incorporate into your draft. Other forms of preparatory writing may include outlining or brainstorming on paper (see Chapter 3).

Choosing a Plan of Organization

Probably the best way to get all of your material under control is to make a rough outline based on the categories you have set up for your notes. Doing so will establish the broad classifications that you are going to cover in your paper and show a logical way to order them within your paper. Write those classifications down and make notes about subpoints you want to cover in each category. As you work, develop a series of general assertions that can serve as the framework for your paper. And as you outline, jot down subheadings you might use to keep your reader on the track.

You can also write an abstract for your paper (see an example of an abstract in Chapter 12). If carefully done, an abstract or summary can give you substantial guidance for organizing your paper and for beginning to articulate some of the points you want to make. Supplemented by a list of secondary or supporting points, a comprehensive abstract will serve you just about as well as an outline.

Whatever plan of organization you choose, have something written down that will serve as an anchor as you work and give you something to check your draft against to be sure you've covered your main points. Then it's a good idea to do the following:

- Check to see if you have a focused thesis sentence in the first paragraph or two.

- Underline the first or second sentence of each paragraph and review them to see if they act as a kind of skeleton for the paper. If you see that you're leaving out an important point, insert it.

- Check for strong transitions from one paragraph to the next and from each section to the next.

- Review your opening paragraph and your conclusion. Do they work together to frame the paper? They should.

- Insert headings and subheadings to divide the paper into digestible parts. If your instructor likes the idea, you might even incorporate a pull-quote or two (see p. 203). But ask before doing so.

- Insert any charts or illustrations you're going to use, being sure to give credit for each one.

- Check your documentation to see that it conforms to the standards appropriate to the field in which the paper is written.

- Remember to include a Works Cited or References list at the end that gives full information on all the works you have cited in the paper.

MASTERING THE CONVENTIONS OF DOCUMENTATION

If you have used the bibliographies or endnotes provided in books and articles to expand your own search for information, you already know how helpful clear documentation can be to a fellow researcher. Remember you're documenting for two reasons:

1. To let readers know where you found the material that you include in your paper.

2. To make it possible for readers to locate and use that material themselves if they choose to follow up on your research.

Uses of Documentation

Documentation is not just a matter of using the correct form of footnotes and bibliography entries. When you do research, you gather *ideas* from your sources as well as direct quotations and statistical and factual information, and your readers should always be able to tell exactly which contributions are your own comments, evaluations, and interpretations, and which are reports of someone else's words and ideas. The text of your paper should enable a reader to make these distinctions easily.

In the case of direct quotations, when you are using someone else's exact words, you supply this information *partly* by using quotation marks (for quoted material that is four lines or fewer) or block indentation (for quoted material that is five lines or longer). But you also need to supply an introduction to material gathered from outside sources, whether you are paraphrasing or summarizing that material or quoting it directly. Introductory comments should precede the cited material, even though the material itself may be enclosed in quotation marks or indented, and even though you provide a footnote or parenthetical citation. Such introductory comments not only make it clear exactly which information is being documented, they also help integrate quotations smoothly and gracefully into the text of your paper.

The following example is flawed by a number of documentation errors:

> Until very recently it was thought that penguins were unique among the members of the animal kingdom, being the only birds to exhibit altruistic behavior. "In order to test the icy waters for the presence of seals, the penguin's deadliest enemy, one penguin risks her own life by plunging off the ice floe into the water where her predators possibly wait."[1] If this penguin survived and the area thus appeared to be free of seals, the rest of the flock would follow her into the water. Later on, however, ornithologists came to believe that they had misinterpreted this particular aspect of penguin behavior.[2] "It appears now that the lead penguin is not willing to sacrifice herself for the survival of her group. Quite the contrary, our observations have led us to believe that she does not even jump into the water of her own accord, but rather that she is actually *pushed* into the water by the other members of her flock."[3]

In the paragraph above, the writer has used direct quotation where simple paraphrase or summary would easily suffice. In fact there are points at which the original wording is awkward when combined with the text of the paper. In addition, a reader cannot tell where the information in the paragraph comes from. If more than one source is involved, how are they related, and why is the writer of the paper presenting them together in this paragraph? Who are the "we" referred to in the last sentence? The reader might be able to find the answers to these questions by studying the footnotes at the bottom of the page or the endnotes that follow the paper, but such an interruption in the reading of the text is annoying, confusing, and unnecessary.

The following revision of the paragraph eliminates the unnecessary use of direct quotation and incorporates the missing information smoothly into the text. Full citations are still needed, of course, because the writer of the paper is presenting information that originally appeared in other sources, and because readers need full citations in order to conduct follow-up research.

> Until recently it was thought that penguins were unique among the members of the animal kingdom, being the only birds to exhibit altruistic behavior. Arctic explorers Nichole and Sam Thigpen reported in the log of their 1951 expedition that the lead penguin from a flock would apparently risk her own life for the survival of the flock by jumping off the ice floe into the water where arctic seals, mortal enemies of the penguin, were possibly lurking. If this penguin survived, the other birds in the flock would follow her into the water, assured that no predators were in ther area (Thigpen and Thigpen, 1951). Fifteen years later, however, when the Thigpens, accompanied by ornithologist Jordan Jones, made a second arctic voyage, they revised their earlier assessment of penguin behavior, claiming that the lead penguin was not at all willing to sacrifice herself, but rather that the flock seemed willing to sacrifice *her* to ensure their own survival. This conclusion derived from the explorers' observation that the lead penguin apparently did not jump into the potentially seal-infested water, but instead was actually pushed by her followers (Jones, Thigpen, and Thigpen, 1966).

Styles of Documentation

Styles of documentation vary considerably across disciplines, so you will need to find out which style is preferred in the field for which you are writing. Your professor will probably indicate which type of documentation he or she wants you to use and which style manual you should consult if you have questions. Another way to find out this kind of information, particularly if you do not have a professor's guidance, is to check the form of notes and bibliography entries in articles published in scholarly journals in the field you are researching. You will find examples of APA style and MLA style in the section below.

The most common styles of documentation currently used in academic writing are those endorsed by the MLA (Modern Language Association), the APA (American Psychological Association), and the CBE (Council of Biology Editors), as well as those published by the University of Chicago

Press. Each of these organizations publishes its own style manual, which explains the basic principles of each documentation style and illustrates note and bibliography entries for a wide variety of sources. Here are the titles:

> *MLA Handbook for Writers of Research Papers*, Joseph Gibaldi (4th edition, 1995)
> *Publication Manual of the American Psychological Association* (4th edition, 1994)
> *Chicago Manual of Style* (14th edition, 1993)
> *Scientific Style and Format: The CBE Manual for Authors, Editors and Publishers* (6th edition, 1994)

Most college libraries have copies of all four of these style manuals and many more besides.

At the end of this chapter you will find sample footnote and bibliography entries in MLA style for commonly cited types of sources. APA and MLA are the most widely used documentation styles for research writing in the social sciences and humanities. Both MLA and APA advocate the use of *internal documentation* with an accompanying bibliography. This means that brief citations appear in parentheses in the text immediately after the cited material (see the citations that appear in the second example of the penguin text, above). These parenthetical citations contain enough information to enable the reader to identify the cited sources from the Works Cited or References list, where full bibliographic information is given for all of the sources the writer has consulted in order to write the paper. Thus footnotes or endnotes are used only to give explanatory material that is somehow tangential to the text.

The major differences between APA and MLA styles are matters of punctuation, capitalization, and arrangement of information in notes and bibliographic entries. The following examples demonstrate how the same source would be cited in a paper using APA style and one using MLA style:

APA	*MLA*
This approach corresponds to the frequently cited theory that scientific revolutions come about through paradigm shifts (Kuhn, 1970, p. 79).	This approach corresponds to the frequently cited theory that scientific revolutions come about through paradigm shifts (Kuhn 79).

Notice that the APA system uses the date of publication in the parenthetical citation, whereas MLA usually does not. Regardless of the system you were using, you would need to provide a full citation to Kuhn's text in the bibliography at the end of the paper.

Bibliographic Entries in APA and MLA Styles

A bibliography is a list of all the sources that helped you formulate the content of your paper, whether or not you have cited them specifically in your text. Bibliography entries for both MLA and APA systems are arranged alphabetically according to the first word of the entry, usually but not necessarily the last name of the author. The following bibliography entries for Kuhn's book illustrate the major difference between MLA and APA styles:

APA	*MLA*
Kuhn, T. (1970). *The structure of scientific revolutions.* Chicago: University of Chicago Press.	Kuhn, Thomas S. *The Structure of Scientific Revolutions.* Chicago: U of Chicago P, 1970.

Notice that in APA style only the first letter of a book title is capitalized and the date comes immediately after the author's name. For detailed information on compiling these Works Cited and Bibliography pages for your research paper, see the appropriate manual.

The sample bibliography entries listed below illustrate the current MLA-endorsed form. For more unusual types of entries, you should consult the most recent editions of the appropriate manual. For citations of electronic research, check pages 178–80.

A BOOK WITH A SINGLE AUTHOR

King, Martin Luther. *The Trumpet of Conscience.* New York: Harper, 1968.

A BOOK WITH TWO AUTHORS

Nasta, Marie, and Abildskov, Marilyn. *Stranger Than Fiction: The Literary Development of the Nonfiction Essay.* New York: Simmons, 1996.

A SIGNED PERIODICAL ARTICLE

Walters, Samuel K. "Survival Tips for Third World Travelers." *Journal of the American Travel Association* 12 (1995): 32–40.

AN UNSIGNED MAGAZINE ARTICLE

"Reporter." *Texas Monthly* Feb. 1997: 20.

AN ARTICLE IN AN ANTHOLOGY

Adorno, Theodor. "On the Concept of Ugliness." *Contemporary Critical Theory*. Ed. Dan R. Latimer. New York: Harcourt, 1989. 350–54.

A TRANSLATION

Lueth, Elmar. *Niemandsland*. Trans. Rebecca Soglin and Ellen Fagg. Lincoln: U of Nebraska P, 1995.

A PAMPHLET

Subterranean Termite Control Proposal. Key no. 33020. [Memphis, TN]: Terminix International, 1995.

GOVERNMENT DOCUMENT

United States. Joint Committee on the Investigation of Alternative Energy Resources. *Hearings*. 104th Cong., 1st sess. 11 vols. Washington: GPO, 1983.

MATERIAL FROM AN ELECTRONIC INFORMATION SOURCE SUCH AS ERIC

Hartono, Triyanto, ed. *Academic and Cultural Exchange Programs Between the U.S. and Asian Countries*. International Education Conference Proceedings, 1994. ERIC ED 247 6855.

LETTER TO THE EDITOR

Taylor, Annette. *Mount Vernon Sun* 57 (1996): 11–12.

TELEVISION PROGRAM

"Ludwig von Beethoven: A Musical Biography and a Salute to Genius." Narr. Nancy Ratner and Charlotte Bonavia. Writ. and prod. Patricia Vivian. *Famous Figures in the Arts*. NBC. KCRG, Portland, OR. 27 May 1995.

AN INTERVIEW

Brayton, Abigail. Telephone interview. 2 Oct. 1996.

12

DOCUMENT DESIGN

 Effective design favorably predisposes people to accept your product, service, or point of view.
—Roger Parker, *Looking Good in Print*

WHAT IS DOCUMENT DESIGN?

Over 2,000 years ago in the Greece of Plato and Aristotle, everyone valued 19the ability to speak well because people got their information and formed their opinions from listening to speeches in the public forums, in the academies, or in the courts. The speech teachers of the time—men like Plato, Isocrates, and the Sophists—knew that a speaker's body language played an important part in the way his listeners responded to what he said. (The speakers were always men.) Thus, in addition to coaching their pupils in how to create, organize, and word their messages, teachers taught *delivery*, the art of enhancing oral messages by striking a confident stance, using effective gestures, making eye contact, and using good timing. They taught speakers how to make their body language work for them.

Document design is a modern delivery system that does for printed material what the orators' body language did for speech. It shows writers how to present their messages in visual form that will appeal to readers even before they begin to read. These days readers appreciate such user-friendly attention. Television, video, and the Internet have made most of us so visually oriented that we're impatient with long stretches of plain print that are not artfully presented. Thus it's in the best interest of all writers to learn the basics of document design. They're not that difficult, and they can serve you well.

You don't need an elaborate desktop publishing program to turn out good looking documents. As the desktop publishing expert Roger Parker says, "The power is in the user, not the software." If you have an up-to-date computer and a reasonably powerful word processing program, you have the capacity to do handsome work that a few years ago could have come only from a print shop. This entire chapter was done by a less-than-expert computer user using only a word processing program and inexpensive clip art.

The Uses of Document Design

Academic papers

You can incorporate design into your academic papers in a number of ways:

- If your instructor doesn't require that you follow exactly the style and format prescribed by the guidelines of the Modern Language Association, the American Psychological Association, or the *CBE Manual*, you can create your own format and produce an attractive, easy-to-read paper by combining different fonts and type styles and by breaking your paper up with headings and subheadings.

- You can add interest to papers for courses in such disciplines as literature, history, or American studies by introducing pictures or drawings from another source. See model 1 on page 206.

- You can use charts or graphs to present statistical information or comparisons that you want to incorporate into your papers. See model 2 on page 208.

- For a class project, you can create handsome slides to augments or reinforce an oral presentation and show them on a computer screen or an overhead projector. See model 3 on page 210.

On-the-job writing

You can use document design effectively when you apply for a job or in work-related writing projects:

- Office newsletters combining news stories, announcements, and pictures in an attractive publication that will catch people's attention and keep them informed. See model 4 on page 212.

- Brochures using graphics and text to educate readers or to promote a product or service. See model 5 on page 214.

- Presentations displaying information on a computer screen or on an overhead projector. See model 3 on page 208.
- Announcements, news releases, and a variety of other documents. See models 8 and 14 on pages 220 and 232.
- Application letters. See model 12 on page 228.
- Résumés. See model 11 on page 226.
- Agendas for meetings. See model 10 on page 224.
- Simple proposals. See model 15 on page 234.

Extracurricular projects

If you're active in your church or a community organization or if you volunteer at an agency like a children's shelter, you can use document design for a variety of publications:

- Brochures similar to those produced for a business. Organizations often use informational brochures to educate their clients and sponsors or as part of their fund-raising campaigns. These can be simple, done in black and white, or they can use colorful graphics and pictures. See model 5 on page 214.
- Newsletters, also similar to those produced in a business. In a nonprofit organization, newsletters keep clients and donors up to date on performance and financial needs. See model 4 on page 212.
- Posters and flyers to announce events. See models 6 and 8 on pages 216 and 220.
- Programs. See model 7 on page 218.

Planning

You need to start any design project with a plan. Since you'll be incorporating several elements into a publication, you have to think ahead about how each part will fit into the whole.

1. Start with a preliminary analysis that asks these questions:
   - Who is my audience? Are they likely to have conservative expectations about how this document should look? Will they welcome something different?
   - What is my purpose? What is the effect I want to create?
   - How would I describe the tone I want to convey? What impact do I want this document to have?

- What components will I be working with? A variety of type, illustrations, charts, photographs, or what?
- What constraints am I working under? How much time do I have? How much can I spend? What are the limits of my expertise?

If your project were a fund-raising brochure for a children's museum, a working plan based on this analysis might look like this:

Audience: Civic leaders whom I want to support the children's museum and interested citizens who might become donors.

Purpose: To show that the museum is an educational and cultural asset for our community and thus worthy of both public and private support.

Tone: Informal and friendly—I want them to like the museum. Use a light-hearted type and open layout with borders.

Components: Information about what the museum offers. Some graphics and, if possible, pictures of children enjoying the museum.

Constraints: Two weeks to do the brochure. As a nonprofit, we shouldn't be spending much money so design must be kept simple.

2.   Using pencil and paper, sketch out a design for items such as brochures, newsletters, posters, announcements, and so on. This will help you decide where to put headlines, drawings, pictures, and so on. For example, a sketch of one possible layout for your sample brochure might look like this:

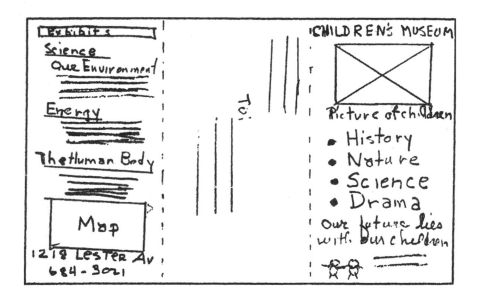

3. Think about costs. Once you've decided on size, illustrations, two-color, four-color, or black and white, get an estimate of costs. That estimate will affect your final decisions.

LEARNING ABOUT TYPE

As an amateur designer of documents, you don't need to know all the fine points of working with type that would concern a book or magazine designer or graphic artist. For your purposes you need only an introduction to three elements of type: *fonts*, *styles*, and *sizes*. Modern word processing programs make it easy to work with all three.

Fonts: Various typefaces such as Times, Helvetica, and **Chicago**

Styles: Styles such as *italic*, **boldface**, outline, **shadow**, CAPS, or SMALL CAPS. You can also expand or reduce spacing between letters. For example, CHRISTMAS or C H R I S T M A S.

Sizes: Type sizes range from very small (8 point) to large (16 point)

and larger (24 point), up to 72 point for posters.

Fonts (Typefaces)

If you're using an up-to-date word processing program, you have a wonderful variety of fonts available to you, ranging from routine, serviceable fonts to dramatic display fonts and graceful or playful decorative fonts. You can also buy inexpensive supplemental font packages that will provide you with dozens more.

Fonts divide into four categories:

Serif fonts: These are the fonts that have little feet or serifs attached to the ends of letters. The most common are

Times
Courier
Palatino
New Century Schoolbook
Bookman

These fonts work well for extended passages of print because the serifs help move the reader's eye along from one word to the next. They also look traditional and comfortable because we're used to seeing them in newspaper and magazine articles.

Sans serif fonts: These are cleaner, more modern-looking fonts. Some of the more popular ones are

Helvetica
Futura
Korinna
Chicago

These, and others like them, work well for display type—headlines, headings, announcements, posters, and such—because they have an assertive, no-nonsense quality. They don't work as well for long blocks of print because they're not quite as easy to read as serif fonts.

Decorative fonts: These come in a dazzling variety, ranging from ultra-old-fashioned to flowing to jazzy to brash. Just a few are

𝕱ette 𝕱raktur
ARIANNA
Avant Garde
Swing Bold
Mistral
Gill Sans
Belwe Medium
Regency Script

These decorative fonts—and there are many, many more—are special effect fonts, lots of fun to play with. They should be used sparingly, however, because they're attention getters and often don't combine well with their less flashy fellow fonts.

Symbol fonts: Sometimes called "dingbats," these fonts provide you with a broad range of icons, ornamental signs, and geometric symbols. Look under Zapf Dingbats, Monotype Sorts, and Windings in your font menu. Here are just a few of the decorative symbols you'll find:

You'll also find useful icons such as these:

There is also an assortment of arrows, geometric figures, and mathematical symbols.

You can use dingbats for borders, bullets, decoration, identifying pictures, or to separate chunks of text.

Choosing your fonts

Fonts have distinctive personalities and, perhaps more than any other print element, help to set the tone of your document. Thus it's important that you choose carefully, keeping in mind your audience, your purpose, and the effect you want to convey. When you're thinking about which ones you want to select, it may be useful to think of font categories.

It's also a good idea to print out a sample of all your fonts and keep it close by for easy reference. If you don't, you'll spend too much time checking to see what you have available.

Workhorse fonts: Usually serif fonts, they do most of the routine work in documents and hold up well for the long pull. They're unobtrusive and easy to work with. For example,

Courier
Palatino
New Century Schoolbook
Times
Century Expanded
Futura

Authority fonts: These display fonts command attention and point the way in headlines and announcements. Typical ones are

Chicago
Gill Sans
Century Old Style
Helvetica Black
Poster Bodoni

Show-off fonts: These are the cut-ups that make a point of being different. They're fun but a little goes a long way. Here are just a few of them.

Missive
FUNKY FROSH
Lambada
EAST BLOCK OPEN
Dolmen

Elegant fonts: These are lighter, more delicate, fonts that give a touch of class. For instance,

Arianna
AUGUSTEA
CASTELLAR
Centaur
Belwe Medium

Script fonts: These are graceful, flowing fonts, useful for quotations, invitations, or programs. For example,

Regency Script
Nadianne Book
Mistral
Zapf Chancery
Freestyle Script

Caution: Type sizes aren't uniform among fonts. For example, 10-point type in Courier, **Helvetica**, and Bookman is quite readable, but 10-point type in *Mistral*, Futura, or *Vivaldi* looks tiny. You'll need to adjust type sizes as you see how your fonts appear on the page.

Combining fonts

Typography experts recommend that you use only two fonts, or at the most three, in any document. More can look jumbled and confusing. In straightforward news announcements, usually you'll see a traditional serif font for the body of a report or article and a sans serif font for the display type—headlines or headings and subheadings. Here is an example with a headline in the sans serif font Helvetica, and the body in the worker-bee serif font Bookman:

Emotional Intelligence Author to Speak

On Tuesday, December 5, at 7:30 p.m. Daniel Goleman, author of the best-selling book Emotional Intelligence, will speak at the City Center auditorium. Dr. Goleman, who is a social science writer for the New York Times, will outline the principles of his book and explain why parents should be more concerned about helping their children develop emotional intelligence than about trying to get them enrolled in prestigious colleges.

Here is a less formal combination of fonts for an announcement about an upcoming event. It combines Missive for the headline with Palatino for the text.

Edgar Winner to Talk about Writing Mysteries

On Sunday, May 17, at 2:00 p.m., Mary Willis Walker will read from her novel of suspense, *Under the Beetle's Cellar*, on the third-floor atrium of Book People. Ms. Walker, who won the coveted Edgar award for her 1994 mystery, *The Red Scream*, will also talk about her experience of working with other writers in critique groups, a practice she considers essential to her own writing process.

Here's an example of too many fonts combined in one document:

On April 9 you'll have the privilege of hearing
Ronald E. Dickson
of
Harvard University
author of the autobiography It Ain't Necessarily So
The title of Dr. Dickson's talk will be
"Trying to Tell the Truth—It's Not Easy"
BASSET HALL   THIRD FLOOR   7:30 P.M.

The Missive font of the first line and the title of the speech clashes with the commonplace Schoolbook font of the fifth and sixth lines, and the heavy-handed Chicago font used for the speaker's name and institution doesn't go well with the elegant Peignot font of the last line. The total impression is that of overkill.

There are no actual rules about using specific fonts or for combining fonts—just guidelines. For good examples of how professionals combine different fonts to achieve contrast and readability, look over the front page of a major newspaper such as the *New York Times* or the *Los Angeles Times* or the introductory pages of a magazine like *Time* or *Newsweek*. For your own documents, play around and experiment. You have a wealth of possibilities open to you that no one would have dreamed of a few years ago—get creative when you have an opportunity.

Type Styles and Sizes

Boldface

Boldface type adds emphasis to a headline, heading, or subheading and singles out a particular word or phrase for attention. For brochures, newsletters, or posters you can boldface borders or dividing lines. But remember three cautions about boldface type:

- Using too much boldface, like using too many exclamation points, reduces its impact.
- Large amounts of boldface type in a document make it look dark.
- Type expands when you boldface it, so a sentence that fits on one line in regular type may spill over onto the next line when you boldface words in it.

Italics

Italic type is conventional for several uses—the titles of books, plays, magazines and papers, and for foreign words and phrases. You can also use it sparingly to emphasize special words or phrases—usually it's preferable to setting off something in quotation marks. For example:

Julio's *manners* are lovely. It's his intentions I question.

In many cases, italics or even small caps replaces underlining in a report or paper. For instance, if you are writing a paper for an instructor who doesn't insist on strict MLA or APA style (see Chapter 11) you might put a book or play title in small caps: GONE WITH THE WIND or ALL'S WELL THAT ENDS WELL. Extensive underlining makes a passage of print hard to read. As a rule, confine underlining to a paper that must conform strictly to a style manual that requires it or when you are writing a paper for publication. In the latter case, inquire from the editor to whom you're submitting the paper.

Specialty type styles

For the heading of a newsletter or an announcement or for special contrast, you might want to use either of these styles:

Shadow type: **A YOUNG PERSON'S GUIDE TO THE FAIR**
Outline type: THE TROY HOMEOWNER'S NEWSLETTER

Such specialty types work well for items you want to stand out in an informal document of some kind, but they're out of place in most academic writing.

Type size

Type size correlates with importance—if you want your readers to notice a phrase or word, then make it bigger. Headings and subheadings in reports and academic papers should be only slightly larger than the print in the body of the paper—perhaps two points larger. (See models 1 and 2.)

For academic papers and any manuscripts you may be submitting to editors, use either 10- or 12-point type in a readable font.

Headlines

Pay special attention to headlines in documents such as announcements, newsletters, and brochures. If you don't catch your readers' attention with a headline, they won't read the rest of the item. Following are some useful guidelines:

- Make headlines from three to four times as large as the type in the body of the article. Notice the models on pp. 212 and 214.
- Limit headlines in all capitals to just a few words. Think of headlines as sentences to be read quickly. Use no more than three lines—one or two is better.
- For longer headlines, capitalize the first letter in words but use lowercase letters for the rest.
- For most headlines, choose a sans serif font such as **Helvetica, Avant Garde** or **Monaco**. You can use a more light-hearted font for the display type in posters or announcements—perhaps FUNKY FRESH or PEIGNOT.

ORGANIZING YOUR DESIGN

Pay attention to the body language of your documents by planning layouts that will engage your reader. Fortunately, you don't have to be a graphic designer to do so; amateur designers can put together good looking documents by keeping four fairly simple organizational principles in mind:

- Create a layout that moves the reader in the right direction.

- Use white space effectively.
- "Chunk" or separate information.
- Position graphics and artwork carefully.

Direction

Readers from Western cultures are used to reading documents from left to right and top to bottom. Thus you should arrange the elements of your document to lead them in that direction. Put your most important information at the top. If you use two or three columns, lead the eye from top to bottom down the first column, then up, and down again. If you're using a photograph, you can put it at the top of the second or third column or in the middle of the first column. See models 4 and 5 on pages 212 and 214. Put supplementary information such as phone numbers or addresses in smaller print in the lower corners.

If you are going to incorporate several elements—for instance, a title, a photograph, two or three short pieces, and borders or boxes—sketch out model of how it might look before you start. It's also useful to use the page setup or view command that lets you see a page in miniature as you work. Doing so will show how it's going to look from a distance.

When you're creating a document like a brochure or booklet that involves several pages, plan two or more pages at a time so you can see how they will fit together.

White Space

White space—sometimes called "negative space"—includes margins, the vertical space between columns and the horizontal space between paragraphs or lines of type, open areas around headlines or graphics, and the bands of space at top and bottom of a document. How you arrange this white space strongly affects the look of your document.

For most documents, start by telling yourself: *Keep it open, spacious, and uncrowded.* Keep this in mind especially for brochures, newsletters, posters, announcements, or anything else that you want your audience to like immediately. But it's also an important guideline when you're writing things like academic papers, reports, or grant proposals. You want them to look readable too. So remember:

- Leave plenty of white space around titles and headings.
- For reports or papers, make side margins at least one inch.
- Leave three-eighths to one-half inch between vertical columns.

- Double-space between paragraphs when possible.
- Leave a margin around graphs, photographs, or artwork.
- For presentations, double- or triple-space between lines.
- If necessary, cut text to avoid crowding.

Chunking or Separating Information

People absorb information better when you arrange it into units and blocks. You can create such units in several ways. Here are just a few:

- Make lists. (Number the items if their order is important; bullet them if it is not.)
- Put boxes around summaries or information you want to highlight, such as a tip.
- Use a screen to highlight a unit.
- Set off items with borders or lines.

Notice that this book uses all these strategies. It also opens the chapters with a feature called "pull quotes." A pull quote is a sentence set off in some way to call special attention to it. Magazine and newspaper editors frequently insert a pull quote, set in larger type and a different font, into the middle of a page or column to catch the reader's eye and entice him or her into reading. They also work well in newsletters, pamphlets, or any informal publication.

Currently pull quotes aren't much used in academic papers or reports, but if you find them effective in the magazines or newspapers you read, you might ask your instructor if he or she would accept one or two in an academic paper. I think they work well to catch and focus readers' attention.

Positioning Graphics and Artwork

While there are no actual rules about where you should put graphics and illustrations, these guidelines may be helpful:

- Put photographs toward the top of the document, especially for newsletters or posters.
- You can put charts and graphs anywhere in a document but keep them close to the data they illustrate; the reader shouldn't have to look around to connect a graph with text.

- Avoid putting several illustrations on one page; one or two illustrations on a page have more impact than several.

- If your document has several pages, try to put at least one of your illustrations on the first page.

- When you can do so conveniently, place illustrations so that the text flows around them. They will look more integrated into the document.

- Leave plenty of white space around illustrations.

- Be sure every illustration connects directly to the information in the document; never use graphics primarily for decoration.

MODEL DOCUMENTS

The second part of this chapter gives you models of several kinds of documents along with checklists that identify the main features of each kind of document.

The documents are as follows:

Model 1   Academic Paper

Joachim Gonzalez
English 316
Professor N. Wang
October 18, 1996

ROSA PARKS: NO ORDINARY WOMAN

Rosa Louise Parks was a middle-aged African American woman working as a seamstress and a domestic when, in 1955, she served as the spark that ignited the celebrated bus boycott in Montgomery, Alabama. That boycott of the Montgomery bus system by black workers, and the federal lawsuit that followed in 1956, brought about the end of historically segregated transportation in the southern United States. As a result, one woman's firm refusal to go to the back of a segregated bus has become one of the landmarks in the post World War II Civil Rights movement in the United States.

Rosa Parks's role in that Civil Rights movement did not begin with the

Rosa Louise Parks, 1988

Montgomery bus incident in 1955. Contrary to the legend that has grown up around her, she was not just a simple housekeeper who one evening decided she was too weary to obey the bus driver's order to give up her seat to a white rider. Parks had been active in the Montgomery Voters League and the NAACP Youth Council for years before she challenged the bus ordinances of Montgomery. In 1943 she was even elected secretary of the local NAACP.

So her rebellion was no casual decision. Rather there is good reason to think that Rosa Parks knew what she was doing and perhaps intended to

Comment: This model represents only the first page of a simple academic paper that the author has enhanced with a photograph imported from the electronic encyclopedia *Encarta*. Since the paper is not intended to represent a major research assignment, the form does not strictly follow MLA guidelines in the font of the title. Rather it uses boldface Helvetica, a non-traditional sans serif—a crisp display font frequently used for titles and headings in newspapers and magazines. If there were additional headings later in the paper, those would also be in Helvetica font. Otherwise the form of the paper is quite traditional; the font used in the body of the paper is Courier, a common serif font. The caption under the picture is Courier, but in italic style.

The author has left ample one-inch margins all around the paper and has double-spaced the lines for easy reading. The author's name, the name of the course, the professor, and the date are single-spaced in the upper left-hand corner. (You can invade this upper margin to type in such information by choosing the headings window from your screen menu.)

When you're planning your paper, you should consider whether you want to use pictures or graphics in it and then plan where you want to place them. It works much better to insert them as you work and have the type flow around the box than it does to try to reformat the type to accommodate them later.

Be sure to ask your instructor ahead of time whether he or she will accept this less formal style of paper that takes advantage of the capacities of your computer. If not, check out the conventions of the form your instructor prefers and conform to them.

Checklist:

1. Find out what format and documentation style your instructor prefers for each academic paper and follow those instructions.

2. If an informal style is acceptable, think about how you can use pictures, graphics, charts, and so on to reinforce and enrich your academic papers.

3. Write your name and other pertinent information at the top of the paper according to your instructor's instructions.

4. Choose a traditional serif font—Courier, Times, Bookman, for example—for the body of your paper. If permitted, put the title and headings in a sans serif display font such as Helvetica or Lucida Sans.

5. Double-space the paper. Leave one-inch margins on all sides.

6. Edit carefully for repetition, omissions, and grammatical lapses.

7. Proofread carefully. DON'T depend on a spell checker to catch your spelling mistakes

Model 2   Academic Paper with Graphs

Elaine Coles
Communications 314
Professor Marilyn Hennessy
October 6, 1996

WHO'S USING THE INTERNET?

In its 1995 year end issue, *Newsweek* magazine proclaimed 1995 as "The Year of the Internet," saying it "could be the greatest medium ever for linking the world together." That sounds rather like media hype, but certainly new users joined the Net at record rates last year. Two demographic firms estimate there were between 20 and 24 million users by the end of 1995.

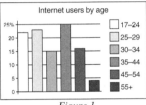

Figure 1

One firm, O'Reilly Associates, breaks down the age range of those users like this. Predictably, they're young but perhaps not as young as one might have expected. This chart shows that almost half, or 44 percent, are over 35.

So some people in the executive suites must be learning about computers although perhaps they're using the Net only for e-mail. Increasingly, e-mail dominates interoffice communication at many companies.

Here is how users break down by income. Most of them—almost two-thirds—cluster in the 25 to 75 thousand dollar range. But among the very affluent—over 150 thousand dollars—few are using the Net. Many believe that number will soon grow, however, as top executives realize that

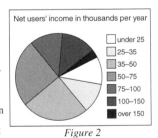

Figure 2

Comment: Our culture has become so visually oriented that charts and graphs now seem like an essential element of communication. For me, learning to create charts and graphs was pretty tough going at times, and I'm still not entirely comfortable with the process. But anyone who wants to be visually literate these days needs to master the skill. As the desktop publishing expert Roger Parker says, "Charts and graphs communicate with more impact and fewer words than paragraphs of text containing the same information."

While you may not find many occasions to use charts or graphs in papers you write for your English classes, such graphic supplements can significantly enhance papers you write for other courses or presentations you may do at work. The model paper, for example, uses charts to dramatize statistics about how many people are using the Internet and show what categories they fall into. Without such visual reinforcements, statistical information often makes little impact on readers.

Charts are also useful for making comparisons and showing trends. For example, in a political science paper you might use charts to compare voter turnout in 1992 and 1996; in an educational history course you might use graphs to show the rising number of Hispanic students expected to enroll in public schools by the year 2000.

You can do simple charts and graphs with many of today's word processing programs—Microsoft Word 7, for example—although I wouldn't call such programs easy, by any means. If you know how to work with presentation programs such as PowerPoint or ClarisImpact, your job becomes easier—feed the numbers in properly and the graphs magically appear. If you're taking a statistics or economics course, you can definitely improve your papers by mastering these programs. They're also invaluable for making presentation slides for a computer presentation or slides shown on an overhead projector.

Checklist:

1. Keep the charts and graphs simple; too many details or too much information in one chart can be confusing.

2. Choose pie charts to show parts/whole relationships; use bar charts to show comparisons.

3. Provide a caption for each chart so the reader can identify each figure quickly.

4. Use color if you can.

5. Use only one or two charts per page.

Model 3   Simple Presentation Slide

ARE YOU AN ADDICTED SHOPPER?

1. When you're depressed, do you shop to feel better?

2. Does your shopping cause family conflicts?

3. After you shop, do you feel anxious?

4. Are many of your purchases never used?

5. Do you lie about what you spend?

6. Do you have trouble paying off your credit cards?

Comment: The most crucial element in any presentation slide is *visibility.* Few things are as annoying as sitting in a dark room when someone is showing slides and not being able to read what's on the screen. If viewers in the last row can't read what a slide says, you're going to lose them before you get started. So use large, easy-to-read type, use only a few lines per slide, and leave plenty of space between lines. And test out your slides ahead of time so if they're hard to read, you'll have time to revise them.

Remember that the information on a slide should serve several purposes. The title forecasts the content of the whole presentation. Then the subpoints below it give the audience members an overview of the speaker's topic and focus their attention. Second, the sentences or phrases act as headings that mark off the parts of the presentation. Third, the phrases act as prompts for the speaker. In the model slide, created for a presentation on addictive behavior, the speaker would expand on and give examples to illustrate each point. The words on the slide are there as reinforcement for what the speaker is saying, not as a text that the speaker will walk the audience through.

Good presentation slides require careful planning. Know the content you want to present well ahead of time and make an outline that organizes it into connected parts that develop your thesis. Decide what examples you will use to develop each point and have notes to remind you of what those are. Practice your presentation so you can talk confidently, looking at the audience and moving around as you speak. Be sure to have a pointer to work with and stand to the side as you indicate points. Don't get in front of your slides.

When you make slides and do presentations in your college classes, you're getting excellent preparation for speaking in front of groups, something you may do frequently when you become a professional.

Checklist:
1. Organize your presentation to have a clear progression of ideas.
2. Use large, highly legible type and be sure your slides are easy to see.
3. Put only a few points on a slide.
4. Keep sentences to six or eight words, all on one line if possible.
5. Leave plenty of white space around the print and between lines.
6. Be sure your slides are clearly numbered in sequence and organized in the order that you will use them.
7. Use information on slides only as cues and as reinforcement. Don't walk your audience through the text.
8. Test all your slides ahead of time so you can revise if necessary.
9. Make notes to help you remember the examples you'll use to illustrate your points.
10. You might use a graphic that's in keeping with the content of the slide, but don't decorate the slide with extra pictures or graphics

Model 4   Newsletter

The Hyde Park Volunteer

Volume 6 Issue 4   **October, 1996**

RECYCLING

Hyde Park Leads the City Again

Last month Hyde Park's citizens showed their commitment to the enviroment by recycling more newspapers and plastic containers than any other area in the city. July figures showed an increase of 14% over the same period for 1995. Members of the neighborhood Task Force for Recycling continue their push to have glass bottles and styrofoam added to the categories that can be salvaged. We urge you to attend the City Council meeting on November 1 at 7:30 to add your voice to this effort.

❖❖❖❖❖❖❖❖❖❖❖❖❖❖❖

CAN YOU BE A HOST?
JoEllen Cates, director of the HOSTS program at Pierce Elementary School, is calling for volunteers who can work one-on-one with students to improve their reading skills. HOSTS— Help One Student To Succeed—has been proven to work, but it depends on volunteers—lots of them. If you can spare one hour a week, call Mrs. Cates at 472-6000.

Champion Rosita Lopez

Texas All-Star tennis player Rosita Lopez will play an exhibition match under the lights on the River City Courts on October 15 at 7:30 pm. A graduate of Hyde Park schools, Lopez turned professional three years ago and has since become one of the state's top women players. She won the Lone Star tournament in El Paso last year.

Look for your neighbors at this benefit performance that Lopez is dedicating to her sister. Tickets for the match will be $10 at the gate. All proceeds will go to the Muscular Dystrophy Association of Texas.

❖❖❖❖❖❖❖❖❖❖❖❖❖❖❖❖

VOTER DRIVE

Take a Friend to Vote

The Hyde Park branch of the League of Women Voters is starting its campaign to turn out 90% of our neighborhood at the polls on November 5. Holly Johns, chair of the local branch, says the League, which has traditionally been nonpartisan, is particularly concerned this year with getting women to the polls. Chair Johns points to several national issues that she believes especially concern women.

Clean air standards
Early child care
Health care
Educational funding
Family planning bills

If you can help with the phone bank, distributing voter guides, or by driving voters to the polls, call

Carrie Jordan 346-1210
or
Richard Mann 478-2020

❖❖❖❖❖❖❖❖❖❖❖❖❖❖❖❖

DATES TO REMEMBER
October 30
    Halloween Party
November 5
    Election Day!

Comment: Now that desktop publishing has become relatively easy and inexpensive, a variety of organizations publish their own newsletters. Such newsletters, whether they are simple two-column affairs of one or two pages or more elaborate productions with several pages and color graphics, provide an excellent means of internal communication for a group or agency. The simpler ones are not difficult to create, but they do require planning.

When you're planning a newsletter, consider what elements you want to include and how they will work together for the final product. Do you want to use a picture? If so, where will you get it and where should it go in the layout? What stories do you want on the front page? Which is the most important and where should it go? How much space do you need to allot to the story? What headlines will you use? Once you've made notes of all your components, do a pencil sketch and experiment with different layouts. You may need to tinker around with several sketches before you get the best layout.

As a rule, start the most important story in the upper right-hand corner and put any accompanying picture close by. Set off separate items within the newsletter by borders, boxes, or with a screen (a wash of light color or gray) but don't use so many that the page looks chopped up. Leave plenty of white space so that the page doesn't look crowded. Graphics—either a picture or an appropriate icon or figure from clip art—liven up a newsletter and help catch the reader's interest, but use restraint. Too many decorations on a newsletter are distracting and make it look cluttered.

Choose a distinctive font for the title banner across the top and use the same banner for every issue of the letter. Put the headlines in contrasting, sans serif display type and use a serif font for the body.

Checklist:

1. Make a tentative decision about the content of the newsletter and estimate how much space it will take up.

2. Decide on whether the content will work best in a two- or three-column format, and decide on which you will use. Remember that articles will need to be shorter for a three-column format.

3. Do preliminary pencil sketches to figure out how to arrange the elements of the newsletter.

4. If the newsletter will run more than one page, plan all the pages ahead.

5. Create a distinctive heading that runs all across the top of the page, using a type font and style that harmonizes with the spirit and purpose of the newsletter.

6. Use borders, boxes, or screens to separate and set off items.

7. Write short paragraphs to avoid long unbroken stretches of print.

8. Position graphics and photographs near the top of the page.

9. Leave plenty of white space around elements; avoid a crowded look.

10. Use some complementary symbols or graphics if you wish, but avoid decorative clutter.

Model 5   Simple Brochure

Wizardspace

Student run ~ student owned

Whether you've just arrived on campus with your new computer or you've recently upgraded to a super machine and it's intimidating you, we can help. At Wizardspace, everyone speaks plain English, not cybertalk. All our consultants are computer teachers, not programmers. We'll get you started, then be on call when you need us.

CLASSES FOR MAC AND WINDOWS

Introductory: Sept. 2 to Oct. 3
 Introduction to Macintosh
 Introduction to Windows 95
 Microsoft Word 6.0.1
 ClarisWorks 4.0

DESKTOP PUBLISHING

Classes begin October 10
 QuarkXPress
 PageMaker
 Adobe Illustrator
 Photoshop
 PowerPoint
Call Horace McNally, our document design consultant, for more information on advanced classes.

FOR SMALL BUSINESSES

Classes begin September 14
 FileMaker Pro
 Quicken
 Adobe PageMill
 Claris Organizer

☎ For additional information, schedules and fees, call
 Carrie   473-3367
 Mark   343-6859

SPECIAL SERVICES

Introduction to the Internet
 Research Online
 Choosing a Search Engine
 Designing a Home Page

Advice on Selecting Software
 Analysis of your needs
 Comparative pricing
 Program demonstration

On-Site Troubleshooting
 House Calls
 Information Retrieval

Partners in Wizardspace
 Mayling Tso
 Raymondo Garcia
 Roosevelt Curtis
 Horace McNally

Visit us at
 1505 College Drive
 Boulder, Colorado
 303-477-6868
or at
 http://www.wizardspace.com

Comment: In our society, brochures have become one of the most popular ways of packaging information for easy distribution. Like newsletters, they can be simple or elaborate, on glossy or plain paper, in full color or black and white. With a little practice, you can do simple, informational brochures with an up-to-date word processing package; for the more elaborate ones with complex color graphics you really need a desktop publishing program such as PageMaker or QuarkXPress. This discussion covers only the simple variety.

The cover of a brochure should be simple but attractive with a title and cover design that makes a potential reader want to pick it up. Don't try to cover too much information inside—a brochure should give just an overview of an agency's main function or tell the theme of a museum exhibit, then let readers know where they can get more information if they need it.

Brochures require careful planning, particularly if you plan to mail them. Start by folding a piece of paper of the size you propose to use—let's assume it will be 8 1/2 by 11 inches—into three equal sections and decide what content is going to go on the inside and what on the outside. Looking at the panels will also help you see how much information you can get on each one—it's not much. Decide what your main headings will be and whether you will use a photograph or some clip art. Then make some sketches similar to that shown on page 194 to try out possible arrangements—figure out what will work best.

When you start working on the computer, divide your screen into three columns and use the horizontal page setup. Put in open boxes where you want to put pictures or clip art and run your copy around them. Decide how you're going break the information up into units and how you will separate them. Then you're ready to compose your copy and fit it in. You'll probably find that you'll have to do a lot of editing, tinkering, and rearranging before you get all the elements to work together satisfactorily. Brochures are tricky but fun to do.

Checklist:

1. Plan your layout carefully ahead of time, keeping in mind how the brochure will fold.

2. Decide what information goes on each panel and do pencil sketches of possible layouts.

3. Keep it simple. Readers expect only basic information but want to know how to learn more if they wish.

4. Break the information into chunks with lines, boxes, and white space.

5. Make each panel a self-contained unit.

6. Use simple graphics or symbols to catch the reader's eye.

7. Leave plenty of white space at the edges and between elements.

8. Use type, graphics, and layout that suit the tone and subject of the brochure.

9. Use sans serif display type for headings.

The Austin Sierra Club
presents

Dr. Joan Gardner Lewis

speaking on

SUFFER THE CHILDREN
The environmental disaster in Eastern Europe
and its effects on children's health

Dr. Gardner, a pediatrician at Northwestern Clinic in Seattle, recently returned from spending six months in the industrial regions of Albania and Hungary. She will talk about her work there with children suffering from asthma and other respiratory diseases.

7:30 pm, Tuesday, October 15
Jessen Auditorium
University of Texas at Austin

Comment: Your first goal with any poster is to get your readers' attention. Often your poster will be only one of many on a bulletin board or tacked up on a wall or a utility pole at a busy crossroads, so yours should be eye-catching and easy to read. Often posters on colored paper stand out more easily.

Give all the information your readers need, but no more. Usually that means giving answers to the basic questions: Who? What? When? Where? Why? This model tells you that an environmental advocacy group is sponsoring a qualified medical expert who will speak about the effects of pollution on children's health and gives you the time, date, and location. The most important information—the speaker and the title—is in large print and close to the top. Leave plenty of blank space around the elements of the poster so the message stands out, unobscured by any unnecessary clutter.

For a strictly informational poster like this one, use a simple display font, usually a sans serif font with clean but distinctive lines. Use a decorative border or frame to set off information. If the budget allows, include a picture or appropriate graphic to catch the reader's eye. And be conscious of the tone you're creating. Do the fonts and images you're using convey a mood and image that meshes with the topic it's announcing? The subject in this model poster calls for a serious, conservative tone; a jazzy font and bright colors wouldn't work here.

Checklist:

1. Put the most important information in the largest print.
2. Put the most important information close to the top of the poster.
3. Use a font that conveys a mood and tone appropriate for the subject.
4. Be sure the poster answers these questions directly or by implication: Who? What? Why? When? Where?
5. Separate information into chunks that are easily understood.
6. Leave plenty of white space around the print and graphics.
7. Make sure graphics or other decorative elements are appropriate to the topic.

Model 7   Program

The Hayden-Mozart Ensemble
presents
An Evening of Baroque Music

Marilyn Szcyki   First Violin
Joanna Stiles   Second Violin
Hai-li Nguyen   Cello
Claude Childs   Viola
Ida Kashikurian   Guest Violist

🎵 🎵 🎵 🎵 🎵 🎵 🎵

Wolfgang Amadeus Mozart (1756–1791)

Quintet in C, K. 515
  Allegro
  Andante
  Menuetto: Allegretto: Trio
  Allegro

Wolfgang Amadeus Mozart (1756–1791)

Sonata for Violin and Viola, K. 423
  Allegro
  Adagio
  Rondeau: Allegro

Intermission

Luigi Boccherini (1743–1805)

Quartet in B Minor, Op. 58, No. 4
  Allegro Molto
  Andantino lento
  Rondo

Johann Sebastian Bach (1685–1750)

Suite No. 6 for Cello in D Major, BWV 1012
  Prelude
  Allemande
  Courante
  Sarabande
  Gavottes 1 & 2
  Gigue

🎵 🎵 🎵 🎵 🎵 🎵 🎵

The Haydn-Mozart Ensemble thanks Christopher
Brothers Music Company and the Anastasia Pottery
Shop for their generous support of this concert.

Comment: You can do simple, inexpensive programs for most organizations using only a word processing program that includes several fonts and type sizes. Such programs may include the order of service for a church, the playbill for a theater production, or the program for a recital or concert. When you create such a program, your main concern should be to organize the information on the page in an attractive and accessible format so the reader can see immediately what to anticipate and can easily follow the program as it proceeds. You accomplish that goal by chunking your information in various ways—with borders, with lists, and with information put into blocks.

As always, choose fonts that help to set the mood you want to create. For a jazz concert, you would choose fonts quite different from the ones you would choose for a concert of classical music or for the program for a children's Christmas play. The font used for the title in the model is Harrington, an elegant, rather formal font that meshes with the eighteenth century classical music featured in the concert. The most important information is in the largest print, and each element in the program is set off by abundant white space.

Although programs follow certain conventions, you can experiment with arrangement and type to produce a program that reflects the mood and flavor of the entertainment it announces. For instance, you could choose bells (△ △ △) and snowflakes (✳ ✳ ✳) from your dingbat menus as decorations on a Christmas program, or you could use the symbol of a cross (✝) on a church program or a Star of David (✡) on a program for a synagogue. If you have access to a clip art program, you will find a wealth of symbols and graphics for almost any occasion. But use them sparingly—you don't want them to overwhelm the content of the program. You will also find a number of dingbat symbols, such as the curved bows shown in the model program, from which you can make lines to mark off sections of the program.

Checklist:

1. Organize the information in the program into separate, easy-to-follow elements.

2. Leave plenty of white space around the sections of the program.

3. Put the most important information in the largest type.

4. Lay the information out on facing pages so the complete program can be grasped at a glance.

5. Choose type fonts that complement the subject matter of the program and create a mood that's in keeping with the content.

6. Create borders from clip art or dingbat symbols that reflect the mood of the program.

7. Give credits or acknowledgments at the bottom of the program.

You are invited to the Grand Opening of

The Family Place

A NEW COMMUNITY CENTER FOR CENTERVILLE

opening on
October 18

FEATURING
- An activity center for young adults
- Parenting classes for new families
- A well-child clinic
- Programs on healthy eating and shopping
- Flu shots and immunizations for everyone
- Adult literacy courses

PLACE: SOUTHWESTERN VILLAGE PLAZA

SOUTHWESTERN BLVD. AT 19TH STREET   ☎ PHONE 346-7733

Comment: Flyers are much like posters but usually simpler and less expensive because you'll be printing many more of them—or running them off on a copy machine. You can also include more information because the readers will pick them up and read them rather than view them from a distance. Still, many of the same principles apply. Keep them simple but be sure you answer the important questions: Who? What? Where? When? Why? (or for what purpose?).

Use a crisp display font for the most important information and put the most important points at the top of the page. Leave plenty of white space—don't crowd the page.

Checklist:

1. Put the most important information in the largest print.

2. Put the main announcement close to the top of the page.

3. Use a simple display font for the most important lines.

4. Be sure to tell who, what, where, why, and when.

5. Separate information into chunks or lists.

6. Leave plenty of white space around the individual items.

Model 9   Summary or Abstract

Needed: Stories for Girls to Live By

Eleanor Hennessy

The myths and legends that young people grow up with interpret their cultures and give youngsters a sense of their possibilities. Unfortunately the tales of heroism and courage that most young people encounter in our Western culture are male-centered and offer almost no role models that encourage girls to excel or become leaders. Handsome books recounting the adventures of Odysseus, Jason, Hercules, Theseus, and William Tell crowd the shelves of school and public libraries, but the images of women in these same tales are patronizing and negative. None show strong women performing feats of courage and winning prizes.

Models of powerful and heroic women can be found in both myth and history, yet because of conventional wisdom about girl and boy readers, few stories about such women have been written for girls. It's time to challenge that conventional wisdom if we want today's young girls to have stories that allow them to see themselves as leaders and achievers. Elementary school librarians and teachers must bring books about courageous women into the early grades before girls begin to take their role models from the dominant culture. Educators must also take the lead in convincing publishers to seek out and publish attractive books about women heroes, and they must enlist parents in the push to give their daughters literary role models of strong women. By changing the stories we tell young girls, we can begin to change their view of the women they can become.

Comment: In this era of information overload, you need more than ever to know how to write a good summary. If you're skillful at previewing your ideas for your readers in capsule form, you may catch their interest and lead them on to read the full article rather than skipping it in the first place because it's too long. Even if they don't read the full report immediately, they may file it for a later time if they like the summary.

A good summary captures the essence of a paper, report, or article in a brief, informative statement that can be read and digested quickly. It's hard to generalize about how long a summary should be because it does have to contain the substance of the original. One page is the best; one paragraph is even better, although often such brevity isn't possible. The summary should state the main assertion or idea of the original, give the key supporting points and the principal conclusions, and be able to stand alone as a self-contained message. Its tone and style should reflect that of the original.

You may be able to create the skeleton of your summary by writing down the key sentence of your opening paragraph and following it with the topic sentences from subsequent paragraphs. Then make an outline from the material you've selected. Identify which examples are essential to the understanding the original and use only those. Write a draft, being sure to state the conclusion forcefully. Finally, rewrite the draft into a lucid and coherent whole. As the technical writing expert John Lannon points out in his book *Technical Writing*, "Although the summary is written last by the writer, it is read *first* by the reader." That's why it's worth taking the time to do a good job.

Checklist:
1. Read the original carefully and underline key points.
2. Make an outline incorporating the main ideas and crucial supporting evidence.
3. Write a full draft, including everything that seems important.
4. Reread the draft and condense it where you can.
5. Check to be sure you have stated the main idea clearly, supported it with the most important examples, and finished with a strong conclusion.
6. Reread the original and compare the summary to be sure it contains all necessary points.
7. Revise the draft into a summary that can stand alone.
8. Polish the last draft to be sure it reflects the style and tone of the original.

First Unitarian Church of Austin
Austin, TX 78751

Executive Committee Meeting

Wednesday, April 9, 1997
7:00 p.m.
Emerson Room

AGENDA

1. Call to Order

2. Approval of Agenda *

2. Approval of Minutes *
   March 11, 1997, meeting

3. Report from Finance Committee on proposed budget
   Matt Barnes, Finance Chair

4. Report from canvass committee; pledge total to date
   Mary Ann Lewis, Canvass Chair

5 . Report of Search Committee for new religious education director
   Louise Tanaka and John DuPuy, Co-chairs

6. Items for discussion
   Possible relocation of minister's office
   Secretary's request for new copy machine
   Tentative date for annual meeting

7. Old business

8. New business

9. Adjournment

* Action item

Comment: An agenda can be an important document, particularly at a meeting where there may be controversy or a great deal of discussion. The agenda, which should be distributed ahead of time, lets participants who plan to attend the meeting know what business is going to be discussed and in what order. It often indicates who will be at the meeting, and shows which items require action. An agenda stands as an official record for an organization, and any discussion of an item can be challenged if it was not included on the agenda. Thus it's important that the agenda be complete and specific. If you write the agenda for a meeting of an organization you belong to, confer with the person who is going to be running the meeting to be sure you include the important items and in the right order. He or she may even want you to include a suggested time limit for discussing each item.

Checklist:

1. In the heading, include the official name of the organization and the day, date, and time of the meeting. (Notice that in the model the heading from the organization's official stationery is used.)

2. Center items in the heading.

3. Set forth the order of business, starting with the call to order, approval of the agenda, and approval of minutes from the previous meeting. Number the items.

4. Ordinarily list committee reports next, followed by items for discussion. This order is flexible, however, depending on participants' schedules and needs.

5. Conclude with call for follow-up of old business, any new business, and finish with adjournment.

6. Put items in the list in parallel form. Indent subtopics.

7. Leave plenty of space between items; keep the format readable.

Model 11   Résumé

Eleanor Hennessy
1622 Exposition Blvd., Apt. 29D
Austin, TX 78703
512-472-8832

OBJECTIVE	Beginning position as editorial assistant for college publishing firm. Special interest in working on textbooks for electronic media.
EDUCATION	M.A. in Rhetorical Studies, Texas Christian University, 1996 B.A., magna cum laude, double major in English and Rhetoric, University of Texas at Austin, 1994. Writers' workshop at University of Iowa, summer, 1994 Yale seminar in rhetorical studies, summer, 1993
AWARDS	Best Master's Thesis in Rhetoric, Texas Christian University, 1996 Member, Sigma Delta Rho, honorary liberal arts fraternity, 1995-96 Regents' prize for Outstanding Woman Graduate, University of Texas at Austin, 1994 Presidential Scholar, University of Texas at Austin, 1994 Second prize, *Alcalde* essay competition, 1994 Richard Weaver Scholarship in rhetorical studies, 1993-94
EXPERIENCE	Part-time aide, TCU Computer Facility, 1995-96 Graduate student resident hall manager, Texas Christian University, 1994-95 Summer intern, HarperCollins College Division, Summer, 1995 Research assistant to editor of *Rhetorical Studies*, 1993-94 Assistant editor, *Daily Texan*, University of Texas at Austin, 1992-93
EXTRACURRICULAR	President, College Youth Group, First Unitarian Church of Austin, Texas, 1993 Big Brothers and Big Sisters, Austin, Texas, 1990-92

References available on request

Comment: Your résumé is such an important document that you should invest the time to get it exactly right. Do your research. Go to your college's placement service office, and look at various models of résumés and ask about which ones would best serve your purposes.

Check in the library too. Consult business or technical writing books and look at models there. You can also get help on the Internet. Look for résumé services, or try typing in the key words "student resumes" and see what comes up. Many universities let students post their résumés through the university server, so you can see actual models.

You'll find standard advice about résumés in every book or service that you consult and in the checklist that follows. Be aware also of two important additions to the conventional wisdom about résumés.

First, many companies are consulting web sites when they look for job candidates. If you want to post a version of your résumé on the World Wide Web, look at models of online résumés to see how they differ from printed résumés. Also, try to find out if the companies or agencies to which you'll be applying are likely to be using the Internet to look for job candidates.

Second, some companies now use computerized scanners to review résumés for key words that might show if a job candidate has specific qualifications or skills. If the scan picks up the appropriate terms, that résumé will be set aside for a person to read. Examples of terms that a personnel director might look for are "technical writer," "merit scholar," or "Java script." Though such terms vary according to the company and job, be sure to include key terms that describe your special skills or achievements.

Finally, find out as much as you can about any organization to which you are sending a résumé. The more you know about your audience, the more likely you are to create a résumé that will get favorable attention.

Checklist:

1. Keep your printed résumé to one page. If you're putting it online, however, you may have to use more than one screen.

2. Include information about education, achievements, awards, and related extracurricular activities, but be sure every item makes an important point about you.

3. List employment history in reverse chronological order, and account for all significant periods of time.

4. Include only relevant personal information. You do not need to mention age, sex, race, or marital status, and you should not send a photograph.

5. Focus each résumé for a specific job, and emphasize the qualifications related to that job.

6. If you're creating a résumé to post on the Web, avoid using flashing symbols or moving print. Such decorations are irrelevant and distracting.

7. Indicate how the readers can get references or additional information.

8. Make the résumé easy to read. For printed résumés, use a traditional typeface such as Bookman or Schoolbook; use a sans serif font such as Helvetica for online résumés.

9. Proofread meticulously and get others to proofread for you.

10. Send an application letter with the résumé.

Model 12   Letter of Application

1622 Exposition Blvd., Apt. 29D
Austin, TX 78703
512-472-8832

May 16, 1996

Ms. Susanna Griffith, Senior Editor
Houghton Mifflin College Division
222 Berkeley St., Fl. 7
Boston, MA 02116-0764

Dear Ms. Griffith,

I would like to be considered for the position of editorial assistant in your college
publishing division that was advertised in last week's Sunday edition of the *New
York Times.* Specifically, I would like to work in the area of college publishing
that is developing software for writing programs and working in visual literacy.

I have degrees in English and rhetorical studies from the University of Texas at
Austin and from Texas Christian University. I worked as an editor on the college
newspaper, the *Daily Texan,* while I attended the university in Austin. As editor
at the *Texan,* I oversaw the work of columnists and contributors and acted as
liaison person with the faculty sponsor. In my senior year at the University of
Texas, I was a research assistant for the editor of the journal *Rhetorical Studies.*

I spent the summer of 1995 as an intern in the college publishing division of
HarperCollins in New York. In that job, I assisted Senior Editors Bruce Boxer
and Martha Esquivel as they worked on manuscript development, and I did
general errands within the college division.

In my two years as a graduate student at Texas Christian University, I worked in
the English Department's lab designated for research in computers and writing
and became proficient in navigating electronic sources. I trained instructors to
teach writing in the university's networked computer classrooms, and I helped
publish the newsletter put out by the Computers and Writing Lab.

Because of my experience in editorial work and my competence in computer-
related studies I believe I would be a useful entry-level employee in the college
division at Houghton Mifflin. If you believe I might fit into your company, I will
be available for an interview any time after June 1.

I look forward to hearing from you.

Sincerely,

Eleanor Hennessy
Eleanor Hennessy

Comment: Writing a good letter of application can be a tricky rhetorical
exercise. You want to sound confident and positive without seeming to
exaggerate your accomplishments. Probably the best way to achieve that

balance is to focus strictly on facts, selecting the facts most favorable to your situation and presenting them positively but without using adjectives that might be seen as boastful.

If possible, learn the name of the person to whom you're applying and address the letter to him or her, giving the correct name and title or position. If you're writing to a woman, use Ms. in the inside address and salutation. In the first paragraph, get to the point immediately by specifying the job for which you are applying, then go directly to the education and experiences that qualify you for that job. Use your letter to expand on items in your résumé that pertain most closely to the job for which you're applying.

Maintain a formal tone and avoid contractions, first names, or any language that is overly informal or colloquial. Be polite but avoid overpraising the company or its accomplishments.

Keep the letter to one page, leaving one-inch margins all around and double-spacing between paragraphs. Close with a formal "Sincerely" or "Yours truly" and sign your letter with your full name written over your typed name. And, as with your résumé, proofread the letter several times and get someone else to check it for you. A perfectly done application letter may not get you an interview but a sloppy one will almost certainly keep you from getting one.

Checklist:

1. Choose a standard block format and use it consistently throughout the letter, double-spacing between paragraphs.

2. Include a return address and date at the top of the letter and begin with a full salutation giving the addressee's name and title if possible and the name and address of the company or organization.

3. Get to the point immediately in the first paragraph, specifying the job for which you are applying.

4. Maintain a polite and respectful but confident tone.

5. Check your letter over carefully to be sure it's completely accurate and you have not mispresented yourself in any way. Remember that the letter will become part of your permanent record if you go to work for the company.

6. Close with an appropriate, formal closing and your full named signed over your typed name.

7. Proofread with great care and get a second person to read the letter. DON'T count on a spell checker to catch errors.

8. Enclose your résumé with the letter.

Model 13   Business Letter

ELEANOR HENNESSY
1622 EXPOSITION BLVD., APT. 29D
AUSTIN, TX 78703
512-472-8832

January 10, 1997

Customer Service Manager
AT&T Universal Visa Card
P.O.Box 44167
Jacksonville, FL 32231

Dear Service Manager,

My name is Eleanor Hennessy; until very recently I held AT&T Universal Visa card #5108-4453-0277-6171.

While I was visiting in New York City on December 17, 1996, I had my purse stolen in a subway station and accordingly lost my AT&T Visa card. Within an hour after I lost the card, I reported the theft and was assured by your representative that I would not be liable for any charges made on my card after that time. Your customer service department issued me a new card in 48 hours.

Yesterday I received my January bill from AT&T Visa and found that it has three invalid charges on it. They are as follows:

December 20, 1996 $456 at The Gap, 2280 Broadway, New York
December 21, 1996 $723 at Empire Camera, 416 Mott, New York
December 23, 1996 $386 at Bloomingdales, Elmira, New York

I am puzzled that they should appear on my statement at all since I was assured on December 17 that the card to which they were charged had been canceled.

I will appreciate it very much if your fraud department will investigate these charges and call me immediately with an explanation. If I do not hear from you before January 15, I will deduct the $1565 in invalid charges when I pay the bill in full.

I look forward to hearing from your department. Thank you.

Yours truly,

Eleanor Hennessy

Eleanor Hennessy

Comment: Like all communications, business letters differ according to circumstances, but they do tend to have certain characteristics in common. First, they tend to have a rather formal tone since often the correspondents don't know each other. Second, most business letters are direct, get to the point quickly, and cover only information that is pertinent to the subject. Third, they are usually very specific; they state their purpose precisely, giving all the facts necessary for their request to be processed or their complaint responded to. Finally, they are usually respectful but firm.

When you're writing a business letter, remember that it will probably become part of a file that will be kept on your request or complaint. For that reason it needs to be as complete and accurate as possible. When you can, give dates and full information when you're making a complaint. When you're making a request, give all the information that the receiver will need to fill it. And when possible, write to the person directly responsible in the appropriate area. When you have a serious complaint, go to the highest authority you can locate.

Over the years, I have written dozens of business letters, many of them complaints or requests for compensation or reimbursement, and I've had almost uniformly good results from them. I think that's because I've worked at writing straightforward, fully detailed, and firm but civil letters. It's amazing what a well-done letter to the right person can accomplish.

Be almost as careful about editing and proofreading a business letter as you are with a letter of application. The letter does represent you, and the better impression you make, the more likely you are to get what you want. Notice that with a computer you can create a handsome letterhead for yourself any time—you don't have to buy personalized stationery anymore.

Checklist:

1. Give your complete address and the date within the letter.
2. Include a complete salutation with the name and title of the person whom you're addressing and the full name and address of the company. Sign the letter with your full name written over your typed name.
3. State the problem or request in the first paragraph.
4. Give all the facts pertaining to your problem or request, including dates and names when possible.
5. Use a consistent block form, double spacing between paragraphs.
6. Keep the letter to one page if possible.
7. Remember that the letter will become part of a permanent record about your request or complaint.
8. Maintain a firm and confident but civil tone.
9. Edit and proofread the letter carefully; you want to make a good impression.
10. Keep a record of your letter on file for future reference.

Model 14   Press Release

CHILDREN'S ORTHOPEDIC CENTER OF DALLAS
1123 Harry Hines Boulevard
Dallas, TX 75321

FOR IMMEDIATE RELEASE   Contact: Melinda Nguyen

Public Relations

214-655-7200

CHILDREN'S ORTHOPEDIC CENTER SELECTS NEW HEAD

The trustees of Children's Orthopedic Center of Dallas announced yesterday, October 3, that Dr. Lucy Brigham Johnstone will become its Chief Executive Officer on January 1, 1998. Dr. Johnstone comes to Dallas from Memphis, Tennessee, where she has served as Executive Director of Shriner's Children's Hospital since 1991.

Dr. Johnstone received her M.D. from the University of Texas Southwestern Medical Center at Dallas in 1980 and did her residency in orthopedic medicine at Parkland Hospital in Dallas. She was on the faculty of Fisk Medical College in Nashville, Tennessee, from 1984 to 1991, and supervised the residency program in pediatric orthopedics there from 1989 to 1991. She held the Christine Holt Endowed Chair of Pediatric Medicine at Fisk during those two years.

Dr. Johnstone's specialty is pediatric hip and knee malformations; she received an award for her work in this area while she was at Fisk Medical School and hopes to continue her research at the Children's Center. She says she was especially drawn to Children's Orthopedic because of its outstanding staff of physicians working on children's hip problems.

Dr. Johnstone is married to Dr. Claude DuBois, who will also move to Dallas and join the surgical staff of Baylor Medical Center. Drs. Johnstone and DuBois have two sons, ages 12 and 14.

--30--

Comment: When you write a press release, you're looking for free advertising. You are putting out information about an organization or program to which you want to draw favorable attention, hoping that the newspaper, radio and television stations, or professional newsletters to which you send it will publish it as it is or write a news story based on the information you're giving them. Thus press releases usually follow the typical format of a news story: they answer the questions "Who? What? Where? When? and Why?" and they put the most important information at the beginning. The heading for the press release serves the same purpose as a newspaper headline.

Remember that with a press release, you're writing to an editor who will decide how to use the information you're giving him or her. Ask yourself, "How can I best serve that editor's needs? What does she want from me?" The answer is that she wants your release to be accurate, clear, and succinct so she can use the information you're giving her as efficiently as possible to produce a story that will catch people's attention. Thus give her the key facts quickly and let her know where she can get more information if she needs it.   For example, with the model press release on page 232, an editor might send a reporter to interview Dr. Johnstone for a feature story on the city's medical facilities. The editor of a small business journal might print the press release just as it is, pleased to have a well-written, informative piece.

Be sure your press release supports the image you want to project of the organization you're representing. The formal, neutral tone of the model release, for example, reflects the dignified image you want a local prestigious hospital to project. A press release for a different occasion—for example, the opening of a children's room in the local library—would call for a more informal, friendlier tone.

Checklist:

1. Print the press release on the organization's letterhead stationery or put the organization's name and address at the top of the sheet.

2. Give your press release a clear, informative heading that announces the topic at once. Think of it as a headline.

3. At the top of the page put the name and phone number of the person to contact for more information.

4. Put the most important information in the first paragraph.

5. Arrange the subsequent paragraphs in descending order of importance so the least significant information is lost if the release is cut from the bottom.

6. Focus on facts and avoid adjectives or adverbs that might be viewed as self-promoting.

7. Double-space the press release so it can be easily edited if necessary.

8. Close the release with the traditional "30," preceded and followed by dashes. If a release runs more than one page, write "--more--" at the end of a page that is to be followed by another, then put the "--30--" at the end of the last page.

Model 15   E-mail

Date: Wed., March 5 1997 14:20:00
To: lagarcia@mail.utexas.edu
From: anna.smith@commonground.org
Subject: grant proposal

Lucia,

Sorry to be late in getting back to you about clarification of Common Ground's guidelines for the grant proposals due next Wednesday, but I've been out of the office and received your e-mail only today. Here's more info on the points you asked about.

1. Yes, we need a detailed estimate of expenses you expect to incur for any travel connected with your visits to the six communities participating in your study. If you're going to drive, estimate mileage costs; if you're flying, give approximate airfares based on current economy class fares. Base estimates about meals and lodging on the per diem rate allowed by your university.

2. You'll need an additional recommendation from someone who knows your previous work with community housing projects—a faculty member from the School of Social Work there would be good. Know it's late to be asking for a recommendation, but I think it's essential.

3. What do I think the people reading the grant proposals looking for? Hard to say exactly but it's pretty safe to assume they want to hear about OUTCOMES. That's the big buzz word these day—what specific results do you expect to get from your study? Who'll benefit and when?

Hope this helps—DO get the proposal in ON TIME.

Anna

Comment: For many people, e-mail is now an important medium for conducting business or academic correspondence, yet the form is so new that few conventions have evolved to govern it. Thus you have only your common sense to guide you when you're writing e-mail messages. That common sense should take you back to that old maxim: THINK ABOUT YOUR AUDIENCE. How will they respond to your e-mail message when they see it on the screen?

First, think about how the message looks. All the detail at the top of an e-mail message makes it look cluttered before someone even starts to read it, so you need to use special care to put in enough white space to keep the screen from looking crowded. Space down and use a brief salutation and then skip a line before you start your message. Then chunk that message into blocks with short paragraphs and double spaces between paragraphs. If you want to present quite a bit of information in a single paragraph, make a bulleted list by indenting each item and putting an asterisk before it. Keep the items short.

Second, keep the entire message brief. College faculty and business people sometimes find themselves inundated with e-mail messages, and they want to be able to read them quickly and efficiently. Don't try your reader's patience with a message that goes on for two or three screens.

Since you can't underline or italicize words on e-mail, use all capitals to emphasize points. You might even want to put an exclamation point before and after some point if you want to give it particular emphasis—but again, think about your audience first. Might they find that too jarring?

As the model illustrates, even in business correspondence e-mail style tends to be less formal than that used in printed letters and the conventions seem less important. Perhaps that's because the necessary routine information is automatically taken care of at the start, and we plunge into e-mail as we would a conversation, using contractions and colloquialisms. Nevertheless, I believe when you're using e-mail for business or to communicate with your professors, you should remember that it represents you just as a letter does; your tone may be casual but don't be sloppy about spelling and punctuation. You can't assume the reader won't notice.

Remember that e-mail is, by its nature, temporary, well suited for sending memos, reminders, and quick messages. It's not well suited for writing about important matters when you need to have a record of your correspondence. Then you're better off writing a letter. When you do want to keep copies of e-mail you're sending, you need to set up a system within your e-mail server for doing so. Otherwise, they'll get lost. One way to make a copy would be to list yourself after the cc line in the address.

Checklist:
1. Be sure you get every e-mail address exactly right. The slightest error will abort the transmission.
2. Think about how your message looks on the screen; leave plenty of white space.
3. Keep your messages brief.
4. Write short paragraphs and double-space between them.
5. Adapt your style to your audience. Although e-mail is less formal than regular business correspondence, keep a respectful tone in professional and business communication.
6. For professional and business communications, edit and proofread just as you would printed letters.
7. When it's important that you keep track of e-mail that you're sending or receiving, figure out how to store it. Even better, print it out and file it.

Model 16   Simple proposal

Whole Hearted Breads
AUSTIN'S FINEST BAKERY

June 2, 1997

Ms. Judy Conover, Owner
Whole Hearted Breads Corporation
1616 Red River
Austin, TX 78705

Dear Judy,

As manager of your midtown bakery and coffee shop for the past two years, I believe I understand what your goals are for your company. You have often spoken of your desire to expand our business if we could find additional space and if we could be sure of getting good people to staff a larger operation. We may now have the opportunity you've been wanting.

The owners of the Good Morning, Texas! cafe that adjoins our building on the south have told me they're going to retire in August, leaving their place empty after September 1. As far as I know, no one else is looking at that property.

I believe Whole Hearted Breads could take over the space of 1,100 square feet and add a delicatessen that would feature a lunch menu featuring sandwiches, salads, and oversized cookies. We have done very well with our specialty breads—Viennese rye, 9 grain health bread, bran-barley loaf, and oatmeal walnut. With a selection of such sandwiches and some simple salads to accompany them, I think we could attract substantial lunch crowds, especially from the staff of nearby St. David's hospital and from the students on the University of Texas campus. We could also attract take-out business.

I believe we could hire Esther Chang, who now runs the deli counter at the Texas Union, as manager for the deli. She has told me she's less than happy with the new management at the Union and is ready to move on.

We'd have to get estimates about cost, but my brother-in-law, who is a subcontractor for Calcasieu Lumber, thinks it could be done for around $200,000. Does that sound reasonable?

If you like this proposal, let me know and I'll be glad to get more information, especially details about costs. Thanks for your attention.

Sincerely,

Marc Tijerino

Comment: Writing grant proposals has become so complex and specialized that if you are seeking a grant from a foundation or organization, you need to consult an expert or a study one of the many books available on the subject. In most cases, the competition for grants is so keen that you'll need help.

You should, however, be able to write a effective internal proposal for a small office or organization and stand a good chance of getting what you want. The key is to state your proposal clearly and succinctly, support the plan with evidence and figures, show how it could be put into effect, and explain how it would benefit those to whom it is addressed.

With an internal proposal you know some or all of the people you want to persuade so you can state your ideas informally. Be aware, however, that if your proposal involves spending money or making a major change—and most proposals do—you should also think about the outsiders who may read what you write. Thus you need to include pertinent facts they will need in order to make a judgment.

The proposal should be well organized so it can be easily read and should contain specific details that show you have done your homework and can speak with authority. Your tone should be positive and confident.

Checklist:
1. Give a brief overview of your plan.
2. Indicate why you are qualified to make the proposal.
3. Identify the specific problem or need.
4. Explain how your proposal would address the problem or need.
5. Identify personnel who would be needed and where to get them.
6. Estimate costs involved.
7. Offer to provide additional information.
8. Check proposal for appropriate tone and style.
9. Proofread carefully for mistakes or omissions

INDEX